# THE CHILDREN'S PARTY HANDBOOK

Fantasy, Food, and Fun

By Alison Boteler

**BARRON'S**

New York • London • Toronto • Sydney

All inquiries should be addressed to:
Barron's Educational Series, Inc.
250 Wireless Boulevard
Hauppauge, New York 11788

Library of Congress Catalog Card No. 85-15113
International Standard Book No. 0-8120-5636-1

**Library of Congress Cataloging-in-Publication Data**

Boteler, Alison Molinare.
   The children's party handbook.

   Includes index.
   1. Entertaining.   2. Cookery.   3. Children's parties.
I. Title.
TX731.B63   1985   642'.4    85-15113
ISBN 0-8120-5636-1

PRINTED IN THE UNITED STATES OF AMERICA

   8   977   9 8 7 6

Credits
Book and cover design by Milton Glaser, Inc.
Color photography by Matthew Klein
Food styling by Andrea Swenson
Photo styling by Linda Cheverton

# CONTENTS

This book is dedicated to three special people:

✦ Lucile Connett Boteler—my grandmother, interior designer, and "Renaissance woman," who could turn "trash" into art treasures and cottages into castles. Her Midas touch leafed everything with gold. She left me with the valuable lesson of how to combine ingenuity and imagination.

♥ Charla Molinare Boteler—my loving "Supermom," who taught me how to entertain myself with anything, anywhere. Creativity banishes the word *boredom* from the vocabulary.

☾ Mary Beth Mueller—my childhood friend who spent many afternoons with me, mixing rocket fuel to return to Mars, playing pioneers on a "real" stagecoach, and giving tea parties for trolls.

Many thanks to my editor, Carole Berglie, who made this book possible, and to Jackee Mason, for helping me put it all together.

# INTRODUCTION

A party is, perhaps, one of the most precious gifts that a parent can give to a child. Toys may wear out, but memories last a lifetime. As soon as a toddler is old enough to feed himself and put on a hat, he's ready to discover the magic world of crêpe paper, cake, and ice cream.

This book is designed for the parent who wants to create an afternoon of original fantasy-fun, the kind that can never be bought from a bakery or a card and party shop. It's a complete guide for helping even the busiest working parent plan a successful party from start to finish.

## TYPE OF PARTY?

The two deciding factors in choosing the type of party to give for your child are *age* and *interest*. What entertains a child of four will change dramatically by the time he or she is eight years old. Not only do interests vary among age groups, but among individual children as well. It's quite common for kids to become "fixated" on a certain subject, to the exclusion of everything else. An almost universal example of this is the childhood fascination with dinosaurs. "Pterodactyl" and "triceratops" roll off the tongues of tots, when adults stumble to pronounce them. As a parent, you are probably the best expert on your child's interests. Keeping up with each phase, however, will challenge even the most observant eyes and astute ears. A typical example of this is the child who pleaded for a train set at Christmas. When he was presented with it later, on his birthday, the confused parent discovered that he was now "into" outer space.

Children will change, but times change as well. Fads come and go. What's "hot" one year will be forgotten the next. Movies, heroes, books, cartoons, and toys have their influence on every generation; your child's peer group is no exception. There are also those timeless themes that will always be good, and many that even transcend age differences. For all practical purposes, this book focuses on these classic children's parties.

## DISCOVERY

A children's party can be educational as well as entertaining. By exposing them to new experiences in food, games, costumes, and decorations, you frequently arouse a curiosity and awareness of history, geography, science, and literature. Younger children will discover the world of Beatrix Potter or Winnie the Pooh. Older children can become knights of King Arthur's court. Holidays take on new excitement, when kids join the Queen of Hearts for a game of crazy croquet on St. Valentine's Day or hold a séance in a haunted house on Halloween.

## HOW MANY, WHERE, AND WHEN?

Size is another important consideration. As the guest list increases, so do food and material costs. At the same time, your ability to control the situation on your own diminishes with each additional child. In fact, never attempt to throw a children's party alone. It's one of you against an army of busy little bodies. Always recruit the aid of friends, neighbors, or relatives. For young toddlers, it's often a standard practice to include each child's parent as a guest. The benefits to this arrangement are quite obvious. When children reach a more "self-sufficient" age, a good rule of thumb is to allow one adult for every eight to twelve children present (with a minimum of at least two adults).

Never invite more children than you have space for. Although the logical solution is to hold a large party outdoors, this is impossible during certain months, in most parts of the country. Even in midsummer, there's one major risk in planning an outdoor party . . . *rain!* If you don't have an emergency alternate plan (one in which you can transfer all of the kids and the activities indoors), then you'd better plan on having a rain-check date. This can be indicated on your invitation. Remember that some of the most successful parties, particularly for younger children, are no larger than twelve. However, the older a child gets, the more difficult this size restriction becomes. They may have a list of party "pay-back" obligations, just like adults. It often proves to be one of the first difficult lessons in etiquette, when a parent struggles to explain why a child should invite a "friend" he doesn't like. It's also awkward to exclude any children from a class or a close-knit neighborhood. If over half of the children in your child's class at school are invited, then you'd better invite the rest of the class.

## SHORTCUTS

Time is precious—some of us never seem to have enough. Most of the food prepared in this book is based on "from scratch" recipes. However, don't let this stand in your way of trying one. Cake and frosting mixes (practically any flavor your child likes) can be used in place of the recipe. Simply follow the same assembling directions. Frozen bread dough can be used as a substitute for yeast dough recipes. Biscuit mixes or canned refrigerated biscuits work equally well in recipes made with biscuit dough. Refrigerated cookie dough, even prepared cookies, comes in handy with many projects. Bottled sauces, dips, and salad dressing can also be used. Invitations and decorations are simply to stimulate ideas and get you started. You don't have to attempt everything. Remember, when it comes to saving time, anything goes!

## OPENING PRESENTS

Opening presents is one of the time-honored rituals at a birthday party. Children almost instinctively know how it's done, and relish the attention of being "king" or "queen" for a day. But every parent is already aware of the great great lows that accompany the highs of this experience.

It's normal for children to anticipate the party and presents for weeks in advance. This can sometimes result in unrealistic expectations of what their friends or family may actually give them. If the gifts are disappointing, or there are many duplicates (It always seems to happen—I once got four "Beenie Copters"), your child may become frustrated or angry. Even the most "glorious" birthdays are usually followed by a period of mild depression. So much excitement has built up for so long that there's a big let-down when it's all over. The mood, which sometimes sets in halfway through the party, comes from the realization that all things must end. If the party hasn't lived up to the child's expectations, he or she may break into tears, or become rowdy or uncontrollable in an effort to "live it up" while there's still some time left.

For this reason, many parents prefer to save present opening for the climax of the party. There are advantages to this. It prolongs the mystery while postponing disappointment and broken toys. Remember, too, that the child who comes as a guest is frequently reluctant to relinquish his or her gift. A sufficient amount of party "loot" (hats, goodies, favors, and prizes) helps to even the exchange.

# WHAT TO EXPECT FROM EACH AGE

## ONE

A birthday party at this age is really not a celebration with the child as much as for the child. Most parents acknowledge this milestone by a small, simple gathering of grandparents, relatives, or adult friends. However, in some communities it's a growing custom to recognize first birthdays more elaborately. These parties usually include adults and a wide age range of children. Although the one-year-old is the honored host, the party and its theme are actually to entertain the guests.

## TWO

Children of two are actively discovering themselves and the world around them. The concept of a birthday party is both exciting and awesome. There is much they already understand and much that yet needs to be explained. They enjoy the presence of other toddlers but have difficulty in relating and interacting in play. Two-year-olds tire and cry easily and frequently panic when not in the company of "Mommy." For this reason a two-year-old party usually includes the mothers (or fathers), and much of the preparation is really for their enjoyment.

## THREE

Unless the child is extremely shy or somewhat wild, three-year-olds are usually ready to attend a birthday party on their own. In fact, they're frequently on their best behavior when not accompanied by a parent. Still, there should be several adults present at a party for this age. Much of their social precociousness depends on the amount of previous exposure they've had in preschool situations. Discipline or object lessons are not in place at parties. When squabbles arise, simply separate children from each other or the source.

## FOUR

This is the age when the complete realization of *birthday* sinks in. The four-year-old is an enthusiastic audience for just about anything you present. They tend to be cooperative with games and accepting of foods—they may not eat it, but they don't complain or cry. They relate and react well with other children, until they wear each other out. Avoid too many activities that overstimulate and overtire.

## FIVE

Five-year-olds are less interactive with each other than four-year-olds. Self-conscious-ness sets in with some children, while others single out and latch onto one friend. It usually takes a little more effort to draw this age group into group activities—don't depend on harmony. Keeping track of newly acquired property (hats, favors, prizes) is of great importance and difficulty for five-year-olds. You can help avoid any unpleasant scenes by giving each child a shopping bag, with name, to tote his or her party treasures home.

## SIX

The six-year-old wants to become more actively involved in the preparation and planning of his or her birthday party. Holiday themes also start taking on important significance. This age is much more aggressive and destructive than the year before, so make allowances for expending energy. The six-year-old sense of competition surfaces, and multiple prizes for multiple winners are necessary to appease egos.

## SEVEN

By seven, children become more cooperative again about taking turns and understanding of rules. In fact, they frequently have a tendency to become "stuck" in a game or situation that has lost its spontaneity, and need to be guided into a new activity before behavior starts to deteriorate. Seven-year-olds tend to follow the group, with one leader emerging. Depending on the child who surfaces as "leader," order can become chaos. Adult direction is needed to keep such energy from getting out of hand.

## EIGHT

The eight-year-old is becoming more skeptical and sophisticated. Coed parties are extremely difficult by this age. The children tend to run through games and activities very quickly. Many parents find eight-year-olds easier to entertain by combining the party with an outing (the zoo, a park, or a movie) and returning to home base for food and opening presents. Prizes and favors become less important than the party experience itself.

## NINE

Nine-year-olds need to be "impressed." When it comes to parties they feel very grown up, as if they've "seen it all." Novel food, games, and decor win respect and reduce the "boredom" that too easily sets in. This age group enjoys showing off, and feels a need to demonstrate physical or mental skills. Competition and will to win is strong. Contestants in relay-type games should constantly be regrouped, or one child may take the blame for a losing team.

## TEN

Many parents and teachers consider this a wonderful age to work with. Ten-year-olds are, on the whole, more enthusiastic and responsive and less critical. They are receptive to new experiences and willing to contribute to the party's success. This age is eager to help out, and appreciative of the adult's efforts and preparations. Birthday parties in themselves, however, become less important, and ten-year-olds are often anxious to combine birthdays with holidays and seasonal themes.

## ELEVEN

Planning parties at this age becomes difficult with the growing stress between the sexes. Many eleven-year-old girls are interested in including boys, while boys are uncomfortable in their presence and become insulting or unruly. Rebellion also begins to emerge at this age, and children want to take control of their own parties. Tight cliques and bitter enemies frequently strain relations between girls. Adults are reaching the stage where they should be "seen but not heard."

## TWELVE

This age is really the "last hurrah" for structured parties. Even by twelve, most birthday celebrations have evolved into slumber parties, skating parties, or large musical jam sessions with pizza and records. Boy-girl parties are attempting to get off the ground. Holiday parties are perhaps the last remnant of childhood that twelve-year-olds cling to.

## THE INVITATION

Invitations should be mailed or hand delivered in time to reach every child two weeks before the date of the party. The general rule is to "R.S.V.P." for smaller parties and "Regrets Only" for larger ones (otherwise, you may lose access to your telephone). If the party is planned for a weekend, as many are, be prepared for the "conflict factor." This occurred throughout my own childhood. There always seems to be two children born during the same week, and they both want to celebrate their birthdays on the same Saturday. This situation must be dealt with the moment that it comes to your attention. If left to fester, it can turn into a full-scale war, and many children's feelings will be unnecessarily wounded. There is nothing more cruel than to let rival parties develop into a popularity contest. The best thing to do is simply call the other parent and try to work out some sort of compromise. One of you will have to reschedule, preferably for another day. As a last resort, it is possible for one child to attend two parties in the same day. It has been done by planning one party in the morning and one in the afternoon. If all of the same children have been invited, you can even suggest arranging for transportation (car pools) from one party to the other. The most logical solution, however, would be to organize a double birthday party.

Invitations need not be commercially produced cards from a stationery or party shop. A creative party deserves a creative invitation. For a Circus Party, why not mail guests "tickets" to "The Greatest Show on Earth"? Invitations don't even have to be mailed. Hand-delivered invitations allow for imagination and variety in size and shape (not to mention the savings on postage). A note in a small bottle, with a treasure map to your house, is the perfect invitation to a Pirate's Party. Most school teachers are very cooperative in letting your child distribute invitations in class, provided that every child is included.

## INSTANT INVOLVEMENT

The key to a successful children's party is to involve each child the minute he or she walks through the door. For a very young child, this almost has to be done on an individual basis. Until age four, children have a tendency to just play around one another; the interaction isn't always there. It's often easier to interest them in a hat than the child next to them. Food, favors, costumes, decorations, and centerpieces should tie the whole theme together and unify the children into one common fantasy.

Dressing the part is essential to acting the part. Children love to assume the character of someone or something else. Even shy children will find it easier to shed their inhibitions and participate with the group. A costume can be as simple as a pair of Peter Rabbit ears, passed out at the door, or a Teddy Bear hat marking each place at the table. Suggestions for more comprehensive dress may be included in the invitations. However, a costume should *never*

become too complicated, too expensive, or mandatory. A quick pattern for a pillowcase tunic, or a caveman suit from an old bathrug requires little skill from a parent or a child. "Spacesuits," for a Space Station Party, are very easy to construct out of silver plastic trash bags and colored plastic tape. They are so simple and inexpensive that you can pass one out to every "alien" that arrives. Whether dressing the head, or head to toe, costumes set the tone for the event.

Just as the decor creates a certain ambience in your favorite restaurant, decorations create the atmosphere of your child's party. If nothing else, a centerpiece motivates a child to sit still long enough to eat. It seems to send out a signal: Something fun is going on. The excitement really grows when the ornaments are edible. Younger mouths munch anything that isn't on the plate. Whether you decide to give a complete luncheon, or stick to strictly cake and ice cream, remember that children delight in food that takes on new forms. A child who balks at Mom's meatloaf will eagerly devour a slice from a giant Brontosaurus Burger. Kids are known to have more adventurous appetites at other people's houses. Think about it—most of your "acquired" tastes were probably acquired away from "home plate," where you weren't constantly being urged to "try it, you'll like it." Children's parties are excellent opportunities to sneak in new experiences.

## HELPING HANDS

In younger age groups (two to four), it's difficult to expect much of a contribution toward party preparation. Your child's enthusiasm and best intentions may seem more destructive than constructive. But it's important to remember whose party it is. A child, or younger brothers and sisters, should never feel left out. There's always something someone can do—even the smallest of tasks. Balloons, for example, can be blown up at almost any age. Some will get broken, but that's part of the fun. Tying up streamers and ribbons is another activity small children enjoy, along with cutting out cookies and helping to decorate the table.

By five and six, children become more creatively opinionated and skilled. They can now help out with assembling hats and putting together costumes. Children who print well can also help write out invitations. At age seven and up, children start becoming very involved in details. They may want to help with the cooking or frosting the cake. They may be ready to take over the invitations and hat making altogether. The older the children get, the less work you have to do. You can sit down and plan out an entire project schedule, so they'll know what day to make decorations and what day to bake desserts. Helping hands are happy hands!

## GAMES

Most successful games relate to the theme of the party. Searching for a chocolate treasure chest at a Pirate Party, for example, stimulates a child's imagination and involvement with other children. Many of the principles are based on familiar games like Pin the Tail on Eeyore (Pin the Tail on the Donkey), The Roly-Poly Pudding (Hide and Seek), or Dizzy Dinosaurs (Upset the Fruit Basket). With new characters, props, and appropriate prizes, old favorites take on an entirely new meaning and sense of excitement.

Age is the major factor in planning any activities. Toddlers are still too young for much organized social interaction. Games with structured rules or teamwork can be confusing and frustrating. This group must be entertained. It's a discovery time in their lives, and visual stimulation is important. Reading and telling stories, simple dramatizations, puppet shows, movies, and filmstrips (available from your public children's library) are usually the most effective. Once children enter preschool and kindergarten, they are eager to participate in simple games. As they mature, rules can become more sophisticated and challenging. Older children, eight to nine years, appreciate scientific and historical references the most. Nine is an awkward time, particularly with all-boy parties.

By this age they start to become skeptical and uncooperative when it comes to anything that might seem "babyish." Since they have now become "grown up," it's important to let them feel in charge of the party—without letting them take control.

## IT'S NOT WHETHER YOU WIN OR LOSE, IT'S HOW YOU PLAY THE GAME

Anyone who gives children's parties eventually gets their share of poor winners and poor losers. Much of this reaction is related to the age group. But certain personality types are prone to antisocial behavior, which becomes magnified in this setting. The child who insists on winning every game may feel insecure and seeks recognition and status from his or her peer group. The best way to handle this situation is to acknowledge the child, without embarrassing or setting the child on a pedestal in front of others. Example: Take the child by the hand and say, "Tommy, since you're our official champion, I'd like to have you judge the next race (or referee the next game)." This gives the child a sense of confidence and importance, while giving other children a chance to win. Your job is not to change Tommy, but adapt him to the party experience as harmoniously as possible.

A similar psychology works on the child who is traumatized by not being able to win anything. Make him or her feel "special" in some way. Find something they can do, even if it's helping you or other children at the party. Reward them in some way for a "job well done." This helps boost a fragile ego by leaps and bounds, and even improves children's attitudes toward themselves and their peers.

## FOOD AND PREPARATION

Most children are finicky eaters, but you can give into their tastes without compromising nutrition or imagination. There are, of course, universally accepted foods that a child will eat: hamburgers, hot dogs, pizza, pasta, peanut butter, and sometimes even meatloaf. However, you don't have to serve these in their traditional state. You can even incorporate them with new foods to expand taste buds. Children are fascinated with finger food, oversized and undersized food, as well as anything that looks like something else (spinach by any other name is okay).

As a busy parent, you already know that budgeting your time is important in every project you undertake. Planning a children's party works the same way. There's no reason for it to involve lengthy, last-minute preparations. Cake and ice cream desserts can be baked and frozen up to several weeks in advance. Set aside a few evenings to make invitations, hats, decorations, or party favors. Most of the recipes can be made in advance, too. It's all a matter of pacing yourself. And don't overlook your child—if old enough, he or she can be your biggest helper of all.

## SOURCES AND SUPPLIES

Every party from this book is based on materials that are readily available throughout the country. It's simply a matter of knowing where to shop for what. Wide assortments of tissue and crêpe paper can be found at stationery, card, and party shops. Construction paper, poster board, and paints are usually in dime stores or art shops. The most "exotic" item you'll even encounter will be gold foil. Look in your phone book for the nearest craft store, hobby center, or cake-decorating supply place. If you can't find one, you'd be surprised at how helpful your local florist can be. They'll usually be happy to sell you several yards of colored foil, fancy ribbon, or special wire.

## CAKES AND PANS

There's no doubt about it. You can't have a party without a cake or cakelike dessert. The cake should be the climax of the entire event, not just two layers with candles on top. A whole industry has been built around making cake pans in every shape from Santa Claus to Superman. However, these really

aren't worth the investment when you consider how rarely you'll use them. This book contains a collection of creative cakes, from Chocolate Mastodon to Solar System, and you'll never need to purchase any specialty pans. Each recipe is based on standard 9-inch round and square baking pans you already have in your cabinet. The secret is in the "sculpting." By making a few slices and re-arrangements, you can turn two round layers into a Fire-Breathing Dragon, Tigger, or the Jolly Roger (complete with wind-filled sails).

## DECORATING TIPS AND TOOLS

Cake decorating does not require great skill or elaborate equipment. Yes, you will need a couple of pastry bags with a star and round writing tip. If you don't already have some around the house, pick up a set at a nearby department store or cookware shop. There are even disposable bags on the market now, which make cleanups so much easier. Whatever you do, don't be without one (even if you make a cone out of waxed paper). They are invaluable for garnishing all types of food.

There's one technique that must be developed before you can finish your first cake: crumb coating. Unfortunately, "crumble pox" is a disease that afflicts many first-time party cakes. It can be prevented. Don't make the mistake, once you've already started to pick up crumbs, of spreading layer upon layer of frosting. Instead, fill a pastry bag with the appropriate color of frosting and pipe rows of stripes for the background of the area to be covered. Then, using a metal spatula, lightly smooth the frosting rows together. (Gently tap the surface of the frosting—never dig or scrape into the cake.) Your coating should be crumb free. Now you can proceed with real artistry, giving shape, color, and definition with additional layers of frosting.

## HOW TO USE THIS BOOK

The recipes in each chapter yield twelve servings. They can be easily cut in half, or doubled to accommodate the size of your party. Most cakes also serve twelve. There's really no point in cutting a cake recipe in half for smaller parties. In most cases, that would ruin the effect. Besides, whoever has leftover cake around for very long? For large parties, you can bake two cakes, or simply cut smaller servings and increase the number of ice cream desserts.

Preparation times are based on the actual time it takes to prepare a dish; I have also included baking, chilling, freezing, and rising times to give you an idea of how you can divide up your time. Read each chapter carefully and decide what projects to do when, so you can best "dovetail" your time. Many things can be done simultaneously. It's just a matter of organizing yourself.

Remember that menus are merely suggestions. If you only want to serve dessert, then just serve dessert. If your child insists on a favorite food, then that's what you should have. Never forget whom the party is for. Adults have a tendency to get so caught up in details that they sometimes miss the whole point. *Have fun.*

Think of this book as your party manual. Refer to it for age group, themes, invitations, costumes, hats, food, favors, cakes, centerpieces, games, entertainment, helpful hints, and advice. But don't take it too literally. There's plenty of room for you and your child to insert your own special imagination.

# MOTHER GOOSE PARTY

**T**he timeless rhymes of Mother Goose are probably the first poems that children ever hear. What often sounds like nonsense today was frequently of historical and political significance. Handed down through the centuries, they are as important to a child's development as learning to tie his or her shoe.

## MENU

CANDLESTICK SALADS

HUMPTY DUMPTY DEVILED EGGS

BLACKBIRD PIES

PEASE PORRIDGE PUDDING

PECKS OF PICKLED PEPPERS

BO PEEP'S SHEEP

THERE-WAS-AN-OLD-WOMAN-WHO-LIVED-IN-A-SHOE CAKE

RUB-A-DUB TUB LEMONADE

**FEATURES:** Miss Muffet Bonnets, Spider Hats, Meringue Mother Goose, Pat-a-Cake Baking

**GAMES:** Jack Be Nimble, Three Blind Mice, London Bridge

**INVITATIONS:** Storybook Cards with Mother Goose Covers

## INVITATIONS

This handmade invitation is less time consuming than one might think, because the tedious part—writing out the date, time, and place—is simply photocopied. The card resembles a Mother Goose storybook, bound with a ribbon bookmark.

12 INVITATIONS
PREPARATION TIME: 1¼ HOURS

12 sheets (9 x 12 inches each) pink construction paper

*There-Was-an-Old-Woman-Who-Lived-in-a-Shoe Cake (recipe pages 26-27)*

*Chocolate-Chip Cookie Wreath (recipe pages 173-174), from the Christmas Cookie Factory*

 appears at the top with the Mother Goose illustration.

3 sheets (9 x 12 inches each) white construction paper for goose cutouts

1 sheet (9 x 12 inches) pale gray construction paper for hats

1 sheet (8½ x 11 inches) typing paper, for photocopies

Yellow, black, and green opaque felt-tip markers

¼-inch green ribbon, or use green curling ribbon

12 envelopes that will accommodate a 4½ x 6-inch card

Scissors, glue or paste, stapler

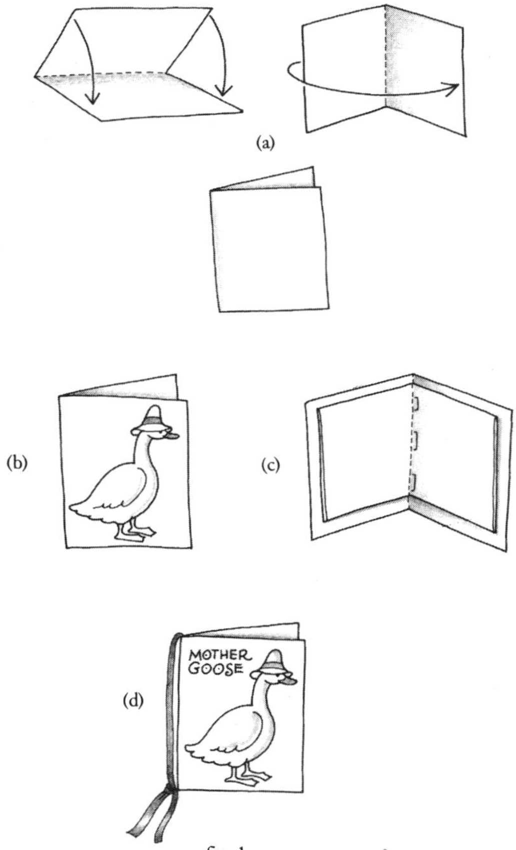

Fold sheets of pink paper in half to 9 x 6 inches. Fold again, like a book, to 4½ x 6 inches. Folds should be on the left and across the top (fig. 1a). Cut out 12 geese from white paper. Cut out 12 hats from gray paper (see fig. 1 on page 13). Paste a goose on the center front of each card. Paste a hat on top of each goose's head. Color in beaks with yellow marker. Use black marker to make a hat band and eye (fig. 1b). Use green marking pen to draw grass around the goose's feet, and write MOTHER GOOSE at the top of the card. Type or write invitation as shown on page 14. (Some pages will be upside down until they are folded. Do not draw dotted lines or else they will be photocopied; they're simply guides for folding.) Have 12 copies made of the page. Fold pages (print side out) in the same fashion as the book cover. Bind with 3 staples down the spine and center page of the book (fig. 1c). Cut ribbon into 12 16-inch lengths. Tie around binding as shown (fig. 1d). Close books and slip into envelopes. Address envelopes and mail 10 days to 2 weeks before the party.

(a)

(b)

(c)

(d)

fig. 1

## DECORATIONS/HATS

As with any children's party, the stimulation of brightly colored streamers and balloons is always essential. Work in the Mother Goose theme wherever possible. Start by setting the large meringue Mother Goose centerpiece (directions

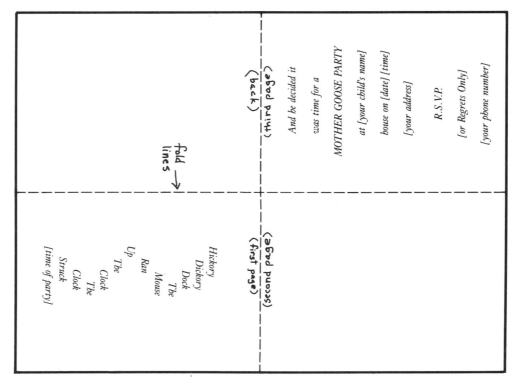

follow) in a place of honor at the table. Surround it with a nest of green crumpled tissue, crêpe paper, or streamers. Large, colored poster boards (20 x 30 inches) can be folded in half and stood on edge like storybook covers. Decorate the book jackets with titles and illustrations of famous nursery rhymes.

If the party takes place in the fall, a clever decoration can be made from a pumpkin. Hollow out the seeds and pulp, and cut windows and a door in the shell. Place a doll inside for Peter Pumpkin Eater's wife. In cold weather, you can also string up a clothesline and clip up Three Little Kittens' mittens with clothespins. Fill inexpensive yarn mittens with trinkets and candy as party favors;

let each child pick out his or her pair. In spring and summer, you can set up Mary, Mary Quite Contrary's garden. Wrap individual plastic pots of pansies with tissue or floral foil and tie with ribbons. Line them up in a planter box and let each child pick out a pansy for a party favor.

It's important to the success of this party that someone, perhaps you, assumes the character and dress of Mother Goose. The whole party comes to life when all of the adult attendants dress in some kind of "Olde English" costume (pastoral dresses, bonnets, knee britches, and "funny" felt hats). You don't have to go to a costume shop. You can get the effect you're after by experimenting with old clothes from the closet or attic.

# MERINGUE MOTHER GOOSE

A spectacular centerpiece that will delight children and fascinate adults. It looks difficult, but is actually very easy to make. A foil structure is made in the shape of a goose and covered with meringue. The "goose" sits in the oven for several hours until dry. Adorned with a bonnet, she takes center stage at the table.

PREPARATION TIME: 18 MINUTES
BAKING TIME: 3 HOURS,
   45 MINUTES
COOLING TIME: ABOUT 3 HOURS

| |
| --- |
| 8 egg whites |
| ½ teaspoon cream of tartar |
| 2½ cups superfine sugar |
| 2 chocolate chips or raisins (for eyes) |
| Heavy-duty aluminum foil (18 inches wide) |
| Mother Goose Bonnet (directions follow) |

Make a frame for the goose by crumpling 2 yards of foil into a 9 x 12-inch football shape. Take 2 more yards of foil and wrap around foil ball (fig. 2a, b), shaping neck and head with one end and tail with the other. Place on baking sheet covered with parchment or unglazed brown paper.

Preheat oven to 250°F. Using a large mixing bowl and a sturdy electric mixer, beat egg whites with cream of tartar until very foamy. Gradually beat in sugar, 1

tablespoon at a time, until all has been incorporated. Continue beating for 8 minutes, or until meringue forms stiff, unwavering peaks when beaters are lifted. Spread meringue evenly over foil frame, making sure that you cover any exposed foil. Smooth surface with a spatula and use chocolate chips or raisins for eyes. Bake goose on bottom shelf of oven (you'll have to remove upper racks) at 250°F for 45 minutes. Reduce heat to 200°F and bake 3 hours longer. Turn off oven and allow to cool in oven 3 hours or overnight.

(a)

(b)

(c)

fig. 2

## MOTHER GOOSE BONNET

An effective bonnet can be made from a paper cupcake liner and a 12 x 14-inch strip of crêpe-paper streamer. Spread cupcake liner open and invert over the top of Mother Goose's head. Secure in place by tying the streamer over the top of the hat and under her "chin" (or shall we say "beak"?) (fig. 2c).

## **PARTY HATS**

These hats are a form of entertainment in themselves. Just watch the eyes light up as you pass out frilly Miss Muffet bonnets and spider hats with long, dangling legs. It's never safe to assume that all little girls want to be Miss Muffet, or that some little boy isn't afraid of spiders.

These instructions allow for making up to 13 hats of each kind. For a party of 12, say perhaps 8 girls and 4 boys, it would be a good idea to make 9 Miss Muffet bonnets (in case one tears) and 8 spider hats (in case some tear, or some girls want to be spiders, too).

PREPARATION TIME: 1½ HOURS

## MISS MUFFET BONNETS

| 1 package (20 sheets; 20 x 30 inches each) tissue paper (white, pastel, or assorted pastel colors) |
| 1 roll pastel crêpe paper streamers in contrasting color |

| 6½- to 7-inch bowl |
| Rubber band |
| 1 roll masking tape (1 inch wide) |
| Scissors, stapler |

(a)

(b)

(c)

fig. 3

Cut tissue paper into 40 circles 15 inches in diameter. This can be done quickly by cutting through several thicknesses at once (each sheet of tissue makes 2 circles). Cut 13 strips of crêpe paper 2 yards long. Drape 3 circles together over bowl and slip a rubber band over the tissue so it gathers the paper around base of bowl (fig. 3a). Wrap a 24-inch strip of masking tape around tissue-covered bowl about 2½ inches from bottom (fig. 3b). Remove rubber band and lift hat up from bowl. Staple around masking tape band, through layers of tissue, in 4 places. Set hat back on bowl. Tie crêpe-paper streamer around hat, covering masking tape, like a ribbon band. Tie a big bow in the back. Slip hat off bowl again and staple band in place through all thicknesses (fig. 3c). Repeat same process for each hat.

## SPIDER HATS

| |
|---|
| 2 packages (40 sheets; 20 x 30 inches each) black or brown tissue paper |
| 13 rubber bands |
| 26 paper plates |
| 26 round white pressure-sensitive labels (¾ inch diameter), for eyes |
| Black felt-tip marker |
| 1 roll black or brown crêpe paper streamers |
| 13 mask bands |
| Stapler, Scotch tape, hole punch |

Wad up a sheet of tissue into a tight ball. Crisscross 2 sheets of tissue and place ball in center. Gather paper around ball and secure with rubber band to form spider head (fig. 4a). Stack 2 paper plates together; place spider head on bottom of plate. Staple edges of paper under plate, all around edges, until it is completely tucked in. Turn hat over and tape down loose edges with an X of Scotch tape. Turn hat right side up. Stick 2 eyes on each head, and make pupils with a magic marker (fig. 4b). Cut crêpe paper streamers into 4 strips, each 2 yards in length. Tie streamers around neck of spider head to make 4 long legs that hang over each side (fig. 4c). Tie knots at the end of each leg. Punch holes on each side of plate and string with mask band.

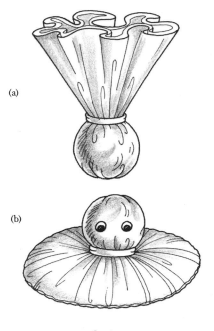

(a)

(b)

fig. 4

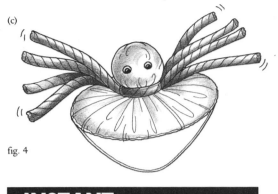

(c)

fig. 4

# INSTANT INVOLVEMENT

When very young children first arrive at a party, there's a need for an orientation period—a time to grow accustomed to the atmosphere and children surrounding them. It's difficult to plan organized activities, because many children are still coming through the door. They may not have any preconceived idea of what to expect at a Mother Goose Party. However, if they have any concept at all, they probably expect to see Mother Goose. Wouldn't it be nice if she were there to greet them? You can assume this role yourself, as long as you have helpers keeping the party under control. You can also recruit another parent, or a good story teller, to dress the part and read nursery rhymes from a Mother Goose picture book. There are some beautifully illustrated editions available from most public libraries. Be sure that the children have a chance to look at the pictures and repeat the verses. This exercise helps break the ice and makes the whole theme of the party more meaningful.

After the nursery rhyme "Little Miss Muffet" has been read, it's time to pass out the party hats. This event should be saved for when all of the children have arrived.

Another activity that immediately involves little hands is Pat-a-Cake. In fact, this can become so engrossing that some children may be reluctant to move on to something else.

Children are first introduced to each other, then to a table (or group of tables) that have been covered with foil. In the center of the table(s) are 2 or 3 "blobs" of colored shortbread dough, surrounded by dishes of M&Ms, chocolate chips, and red hots. Show each child how to take a small mound of dough, mold it and pat it into shape, and decorate it with candies. As more children come along, they can learn from watching others around them. After each child has made a couple of "pat-a-cakes," place them on a baking sheet and bring them into the kitchen. Some children may be old enough to make their initials on the cookies, but it's a good idea for you to label them with a colored toothpick or plastic straw so that their rightful owners may claim them. Bake the cookies at some time during the party, and present them to the children as they leave. They'll take great pride in saying "Mommy—look what I made!"

For easy modeling, this dough should *not* be firmly chilled. It's a pliable, nonsticky dough at room temperature. Whether you've prepared the dough ahead of time or

frozen it, be sure to give it plenty of time to soften up.

PREPARATION TIME: 15 MINUTES

| 2 cups butter, softened |
| 1 cup sugar |
| 5 cups flour |
| 2 tablespoons vanilla extract |
| Food coloring |

Beat butter and sugar until light and fluffy. Blend in flour and vanilla until dough clings together and forms a ball. Divide dough into several parts and mix in desired tints of food colors: red, green, blue, yellow, etc. Wrap dough in plastic wrap; keep refrigerated or frozen. Defrost completely and let stand at room temperature before using.

## GAMES

These are simple games based on Mother Goose rhymes that even the youngest child can participate in and enjoy. They have no definitive "end" or winners. Games of this nature simply conclude when they've worn themselves out (although it's a good idea to move on to another activity before this even happens). The attention span for these games can run anywhere from 10 to 20 minutes—it really depends on the age and the size of the group.

## JACK BE NIMBLE

In this game, children line up and take turns jumping over a small, unlighted candle in a holder. After each child has completed a turn, the candle is elevated by a book. One by one, the whole line jumps again over the now higher candle. This continues as the candle is progressively raised. If a child knocks over the candle, he or she sits out, and the candle starts over on the ground. As soon as another child knocks over the candle, he or she trades places with the child who is sitting out.

## THREE BLIND MICE

Most children know this chant, but just in case they're unfamiliar with it, be sure to teach them the verse before playing the game. Three children are selected as mice and are blindfolded. The rest of the children form a circle around the mice. The mice stand in the circle and slowly spin around (clockwise), while the ring of children join hands and circle (counterclockwise), singing:

Three blind mice! Three blind mice!
See how they run! See how they run!
They all ran after the farmer's wife,
Who cut off their tails with a carving knife.
Did you ever see such a sight in your life
As three blind mice?

When the verse stops, a parent walks around the outside of the circle and taps 3 children on the head. Each child calls out the name of a different mouse. The blindfolded mouse must come toward the circle and find the child who called his or her name. If successful, the mouse and the child trade places.

## LONDON BRIDGE

A classic example of a nursery rhyme created as a game. There were originally 9 verses, but you don't have to use all of them. Two children join hands and hold them up high to form a bridge. The rest of the children form a circle and continuously pass under the bridge, singing the "London Bridge" chant. On the refrain "My fair lady," the bridge drops and whoever is caught in the middle becomes part of the bridge. The child who is replaced joins the circle.

### LONDON BRIDGE

London Bridge is broken down,
Broken down, broken down,
London Bridge is broken down,
My fair lady.

Build it up with wood and clay,
Wood and clay, wood and clay,
Build it up with wood and clay,
My fair lady.

Wood and clay will wash away,
Wash away, wash away,
Wood and clay will wash away,
My fair lady.

Build it up with bricks and mortar,
Bricks and mortar, bricks and
  mortar,

Build it up with bricks and mortar,
My fair lady.

Bricks and mortar will not stay,
Will not stay, will not stay,
Bricks and mortar will not stay,
My fair lady.

Build it up with iron and steel,
Iron and steel, iron and steel,
Build it up with iron and steel,
My fair lady.

Iron and steel will bend and bow,
Bend and bow, bend and bow,
Iron and steel will bend and bow,
My fair lady.

Build it up with silver and gold,
Silver and gold, silver and gold,
Build it up with silver and gold,
My fair lady.

Silver and gold are stolen away,
Stolen away, stolen away,
Silver and gold are stolen away,
My fair lady.

Set a man to watch all night,
Watch all night, watch all night,
Set a man to watch all night,
My fair lady.

## RECIPES

## CANDLESTICK SALADS

Inspired by "Jack jumped over the candlestick," this fruit salad easily becomes finger food. The dressing can be prepared several days in advance, but the salad should be assembled just before serving or the bananas will turn brown.

PREPARATION TIME: 30 MINUTES
CHILLING TIME (FOR DRESSING):
  ABOUT 1 HOUR

| 2 packages (3 ounces each) cream cheese, softened |
| 1 tablespoon strawberry preserves |
| 2 tablespoons mayonnaise |
| 12 broad, decorative lettuce leaves (romaine, red leaf, or salad bowl) |
| 12 fresh or canned pineapple rings |
| 6 medium to large bananas (select fairly straight ones) |
| 12 fresh strawberries, stems removed |

Beat cream cheese until smooth and creamy. Blend in strawberry preserves and mayonnaise. Chill before using.

Arrange lettuce leaves on individual serving plates, and center a pineapple ring in the middle of each. Cut bananas in half, across the middle, and peel carefully. Stand bananas upright (cut side down) and secure in the hole of each pineapple ring. Making a level slash, cut about ¼ inch off top of each banana to provide a surface for resting the strawberry. Drizzle about 1 tablespoon of chilled dressing over top and down sides of each banana "candle," to resemble melted wax. Perch strawberries on top of bananas, resembling the flame of a candle. Serve at once, accompanied by remaining dressing.

Note: If strawberries do not balance well on top of bananas, use toothpicks or plastic straws to anchor in place.

# HUMPTY DUMPTY DEVILED EGGS

"Humpty Dumpty sat on a wall. Humpty Dumpty had a great fall" is the theme of this edible centerpiece. Most children love deviled eggs, especially when they have faces and personalities. These can be prepared a day in advance and arranged on the "brick wall" just before serving. Allow 1 egg (2 halves) per child.

PREPARATION TIME: 35 MINUTES

| 12 hard-cooked eggs |
| 1 tablespoon prepared mustard |
| 1 tablespoon sweet India relish |
| 1½ cups shredded cheddar cheese |
| 6 tablespoons mayonnaise |
| Salt (optional) |
| 6 pitted ripe olives (slice each olive into 4 circles) |
| 24 thin strips of pimiento |
| Brick Wall Centerpiece (recipe follows) |

Slice eggs in half lengthwise. Scoop out yolks and put in the bowl of a food processor along with mustard, relish, and ½ cup of the shredded cheddar cheese. Process until smooth (or mash with pastry blender in a bowl). Stir in mayonnaise. If desired, season with salt. Restuff eggs "on the half shell," mounding filling in the middle of egg whites and smoothing with a knife or spatula. This will

(a)

(b)

(c)

fig. 5

be Humpty's face. Using 2 olive circles for eyes and pimiento strips for mouths, add features to faces, giving each one a slightly different expression. Sprinkle remaining cheddar cheese across the tops for hair (fig. 5a). Cover and chill until serving time. When ready to serve, arrange on brick wall centerpiece.

## BRICK WALL CENTERPIECE

| 1 head salad bowl lettuce |
| --- |
| 1 small bunch fresh parsley |
| 3 fairly smooth red bricks |
| Sturdy platter or serving tray |

Wash bricks and dry thoroughly. Arrange leaves of lettuce attractively on tray, covering as much of it as possible. Position bricks as shown

(fig. 5b), with stems of parsley tucked underneath bricks so it resembles bushes. Arrange deviled eggs around tray. Prop a few up against the wall and set a couple on top (fig. 5c). This can be placed in the center or at one end of the main table, or on a separate table of its own.

## BLACKBIRD PIES

"Four and twenty blackbirds baked in a pie. . ." Most children would agree that it was indeed "a dainty dish to set before a king." For the sake of simple serving, these are individual "blackbird" pot pies, tailored to a tot's appetite. Each comes with its own puff-pastry blackbird, perched on top.

PREPARATION TIME: 1 HOUR
BAKING TIME: 30 TO 35 MINUTES
REHEATING TIME: 10 TO 15
   MINUTES

| |
| --- |
| ½ cup butter |
| ½ cup chopped onion |
| ½ cup chopped green pepper |
| ½ cup flour |
| 1 teaspoon onion salt |
| 1 tablespoon onion powder |
| 1 teaspoon dried sage |
| 1 teaspoon dried thyme |
| 2 cups chicken broth |
| 2 cups half-and-half |
| 1 package (10 ounces) frozen succotash (carrots, limas, and corn), cooked and drained |
| ½ cup chopped fresh parsley |
| 3 cups cooked, cubed chicken |
| 1 package frozen puff pastry, defrosted 20 minutes |
| 1 egg, lightly beaten |
| 12 ramekins, custard cups, or aluminum-foil pie tins (each of 6-ounce capacity and 3 inches in diameter) |
| Toothpicks |

Melt butter in a large, heavy saucepan. Add onion and green pepper. Sauté about 4 to 5 minutes, until tender. Blend in flour and seasonings to make a smooth, bubbling roux. Slowly whisk in chicken broth and half-and-half. Bring to a boil, stirring occasionally until sauce thickens. Stir in succotash, parsley, and chicken. (At this point, you can freeze filling or refrigerate for 2 days before assembling pies.)

Preheat oven to 400°F.

Roll one sheet of pastry into a 12 x 12-inch square. Cut into nine 4-inch circles. Unfold second sheet of pastry and trim off one third of the dough (the pastry comes folded into thirds). Roll this piece into a 12 x 4-inch rectangle, and cut out 3 more 4-inch squares. Place squares on an ungreased baking sheet, and prick with tines of a fork. Brush lightly with beaten egg and bake for 20 minutes, or until pastry is puffed and golden.

Meanwhile, roll remaining pastry into an 8 x 12-inch rectangle. Using a bird-shaped cookie cutter, cut out 12 blackbirds. Place birds on a large, ungreased baking sheet and brush lightly with beaten egg (do not prick). Bake 10 to 13 minutes, or until puffed and golden brown. (Pastry can be baked the day before, wrapped in foil and reheated in a warm oven.)

To assemble pies, reheat filling in large saucepan (and reheat pastry in a 200°F oven for 10 to 15 minutes). Spoon about ⅔ cup filling into each ramekin, custard cup, or pie tin. Cover pies with pastry rounds, and *gently* insert toothpicks into base of pastry blackbirds. Use toothpicks to stand birds upright in the center of each pastry bonnet. Assembled pies can be kept warm in a 200°F oven for up to 30 minutes before bringing to the table, but remove toothpicks before serving.

## PEASE PORRIDGE PUDDING

"**P**ease porridge hot . . . pease porridge cold," this pudding can be served either way—warm as a vegetable, or chilled, unmolded, and topped with a spoonful of mayonnaise as a salad or garnish to the pies.

PREPARATION TIME: 20 MINUTES
BAKING TIME: 30 MINUTES

| |
|---|
| 2 cups cooked peas, well drained |
| 1 cup heavy cream |
| ⅓ cup sour cream |
| 3 eggs |
| 2 slices white bread, crusts removed |
| 1 teaspoon salt |
| 1 tablespoon onion powder |
| 2 tablespoons fresh dill or 2 teaspoons dried |
| ½ cup chopped fresh parsley |
| ¼ teaspoon freshly grated nutmeg |
| 12 aluminum cupcake liners |

Preheat oven to 350°F.
Place all of the ingredients in the bowl of a food processor or blender and process until smooth. Spoon into a muffin tin lined with the aluminum cupcake liners, which have been heavily buttered.
Fill a large casserole dish or cake pan with 1 inch of hot water. Set muffin tin in hot water and bake for 30 minutes, or until knife inserted in center of puddings comes out clean.

Puddings can be served warm, right from the cups, or carefully unmolded (peel away cupcake liners) and inverted on plates alongside pies. You may also serve cold, on a leaf of lettuce, garnished with mayonnaise and tomatoes.

## PECKS OF PICKLED PEPPERS

**J**ust like "Peter Piper picked," only instead of large peck baskets, you'll need pint baskets (wooden or green plastic cartons used for cherry tomatoes and strawberries). Baskets are lined around the sides with shredded cabbage (like the grass of an Easter basket), and filled in the center with mild pickled peppers, dill, and sweet gherkins. Three to 4 pint baskets, placed around the table, will provide 12 hungry mouths with plenty of "munchies."

PREPARATION TIME: 15 MINUTES

| |
|---|
| 1 head green or red cabbage |
| 1 large jar mild pickled peppers, chilled |
| 1 large jar midget dill gherkins, chilled |
| 1 large jar midget sweet gherkins, chilled |
| 3 or 4 pint baskets (from strawberries or cherry tomatoes) |

Shred cabbage and drain off any excess moisture by allowing to stand in a colander. (At this point, you

can crisp up cabbage in a plastic bag, overnight, in the refrigerator.)

Just before serving, line baskets along the bottom and up the sides with shredded cabbage. Arrange an assortment of pickled peppers, dill gherkins, and sweet gherkins in the center of each basket. Place baskets on plates (in case they drip), and set out on the table so that 3 to 4 children will be easily within reach of each basket.

## BO PEEP'S SHEEP

Sheep seem to be the predominant characters in nursery rhymes. There was Baa Baa Black Sheep, Mary's little lamb, and Bo Peep's whole herd. These ice cream versions come in vanilla and chocolate, just like their fuzzy friends.

You will need both a regular ice cream scoop and something that will give you smaller scoops.

PREPARATION TIME: 35 MINUTES

| 2 packages shredded coconut, one toasted (see note) |
| 1 quart vanilla ice cream |
| 1 quart chocolate ice cream |
| 12 white or offwhite construction-paper ears (see patterns, page 181) |
| 12 brown construction-paper ears (see patterns, page 181) |
| Thick fudge sauce (any brand or homemade, as long as it gets very firm when chilled) |
| 12 cupcake liners |

Spread toasted coconut in a pie plate. Open second package of coconut and place in another pie plate. Working with one flavor of ice cream at a time to avoid melting, and starting with vanilla, use about two thirds of the quart to make 6 scoops with a regular-size ice cream scoop. Place scoops on tray covered with waxed paper, and return to freezer. Repeat this same process with chocolate ice cream, returning unused ice cream to freezer when not working with it.

(a)

(b)

fig. 6

Remove tray of vanilla ice cream balls and roll in *untoasted* coconut. Place each ball in the middle of a cupcake liner. Take unused portion of vanilla ice cream from freezer and make 6 small scoops. Press a small scoop firmly on top of each large scoop and insert a white paper ear on each side of the "head," tilting downward like a lamb's ears (fig. 6a). Return this tray to freezer, and repeat the same process with the chocolate ice cream, rolling in the toasted coconut and inserting brown paper ears.

Fit a pastry bag with a writing tip; fill with about ½ cup fudge sauce. Pipe eyes, nose, and mouth as shown (fig. 6b) on both vanilla and chocolate lambs. Return to freezer until serving time.

Note: These can be covered tightly with plastic wrap and frozen up to 2 weeks in advance.

Note: Toast 1 package of the coconut on a baking sheet in a 400°F oven for 10 minutes, or until a rich golden brown; stir coconut about 3 times while baking. Cool completely.

## THERE-WAS-AN-OLD-WOMAN-WHO-LIVED-IN-A-SHOE CAKE

You needn't be an architect or a cobbler to create this cake, fashioned after the famous nursery rhyme. A surprising ingredient makes this cake amazingly simple—mayonnaise!

PREPARATION TIME: 1 HOUR 15 MINUTES
BAKING TIME: 40 TO 45 MINUTES

| |
|---|
| 3 tablespoons instant coffee |
| 6 tablespoons unsweetened cocoa powder |
| 2⅓ cups flour |
| 2 teaspoons baking powder |
| 2 teaspoons baking soda |
| ¼ teaspoon salt |
| 1⅓ cups *real* mayonnaise (do not use salad dressing) |
| 1 cup plus 1 tablespoon cold water |
| 1 tablespoon vanilla extract |
| 1⅓ cups sugar |
| Vanilla Frosting (recipe follows) |
| Chocolate Frosting (recipe follows) |
| Chocolate sandwich cookies or chocolate wafers, red hots, red licorice laces |
| 2 chocolate bars (select any brand that can be broken in sections) |

Preheat oven to 350°F.

Blend first 10 ingredients together in a large mixing bowl and beat until smooth. Line two 9 x 5 x 3-inch loaf pans with buttered aluminum foil. Pour equal amounts of batter into pans and bake for 40 to 45 minutes, or until a toothpick inserted in center of cakes comes out clean. Cool completely.

Remove cakes from pans and peel away foil. (Cakes may be wrapped and frozen at this point or completely assembled, frosted, and

kept frozen until the morning of the party.) If your loaf pans are not straight sided, level off sides of cakes by making thin slices around edges, and level any "hump" from tops of cakes. Place one loaf on serving plate or tray. Stand second loaf upright, against horizontal loaf. Cut corners of upright loaf to form a peaked roof, and trim a rounded toe for end of shoe (fig. 7).

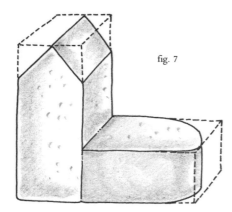

fig. 7

Frost shoe completely with vanilla frosting. Overlap cookies in rows across roof to resemble shingles, and use chocolate frosting to create a saddle-shoe effect (see photo opposite page 12). (This is a lot easier if you use a pastry bag to apply chocolate frosting to the specific area, then gently smooth over the frosting with a small metal spatula or knife.) Pipe a line of chocolate frosting around base of shoe to resemble edge of sole. Create eyelets and shoelaces with red hots and licorice laces (see photo). Break the candy bars into sections and use to fashion windows and a door.

# VANILLA FROSTING

| 1 cup butter, softened |
| --- |
| ½ cup milk |
| ½ teaspoon salt |
| 2 pounds confectioners sugar |

Beat butter, milk, salt, and 2 cups of the sugar until fluffy. Add remaining sugar gradually and beat until smooth and creamy. Reserve one fourth of the frosting for Chocolate Frosting (see below).

Note: You may need to add a little more milk to achieve the desired spreading consistency.

# CHOCOLATE FROSTING

| 1 tablespoon butter, softened |
| --- |
| ¼ cup unsweetened cocoa powder |
| Reserved Vanilla Frosting (see above) |

Beat butter and cocoa until smooth. Blend into reserved frosting.

## RUB-A-DUB TUB LEMONADE

A clever touch for serving lemonade, or your child's favorite beverage, is in a galvanized washtub. Allow about 1 quart per every 3 children. Freeze an additional quart of the beverage in an ice cube tray or ring mold. Use instead of ice and the drinks won't become watered down as the ice melts.

# POOH BEAR PICNIC

The adventures of A. A. Milne's little stuffed bear have been delighting children and their parents for generations. This is a "blustery day" picnic, which can be held indoors as well as out.

## MENU

**PINEAPPLE OWL AND FRESH FRUIT KEBABS**

**CHRISTOPHER ROBIN'S EGG SALAD**

**POOH BEAR PO'BOYS**

**PINK PEPPERMINT PIGLETS**

**TIGGER CAKE**

**"HUNNY" POT PUNCH**

**FEATURES:** Pooh's Party Hats, Bee Bags

**GAMES:** Roo Race, Heffalumps and Woozles, Pin the Tail on Eeyore

**INVITATIONS:** Christopher Robin's Kite

## INVITATIONS

These oversized invitations, in the shape of bright yellow kites with blue ribbon tails, can be hand delivered or mailed in large envelopes.

12 INVITATIONS
PREPARATION TIME: 1 HOUR

| |
|---|
| 2 bright yellow poster boards (20 x 30 inches each) |
| 6 yards ¼-inch-wide blue ribbon |
| Opaque blue felt-tip marker |
| 12 white envelopes (9 x 12 inches each; check with your nearest office supply) |
| Scissors, ruler, hole punch |

Cut 12 "kites" from poster boards, cutting pieces that are 11 inches long and 8½ inches wide. The kite should measure 6½ inches each side of the upper part and 7½ inches on each side of the lower part.

*Pink Peppermint Piglets (recipe pages 38-39)*

*Tigger Cake (recipe pages 39-41)*

Cut ribbon in 18-inch lengths and knot at 2-inch intervals.

Punch a hole at bottom tip of each kite, ½ inch from edge. Thread one end of each ribbon through a kite. Secure with a knot on back of kite.

Write (print) invitation on front of each kite according to the model.

*MODEL*

*[Name of child invited]*
*is requested to join*
*Christopher Robin and Winnie the Pooh*
*at*
*The Hundred Acre Wood*
*[your address follows]*
*on [date] at [time]*
*for a blustery day picnic*
*in honor of*
*[your child's name] birthday*

These invitations can be mailed in the large envelopes or delivered in your child's classroom, or around the neighborhood.

large tree or the overhang of a patio (fig. 1a). Indoors, you can hang them from the ceiling of the porch, recreation room, or wherever the party takes place. Turn helium balloons into Pooh, Piglet, Owl, Tigger, and Eeyore. Color on faces with felt-tip markers and tape construction-paper ears on each side of the balloons to create animal heads (fig. 1b). Use appropriate colors of balloons and paper for each character. Tie balloons to the backs of chairs, so that children may take them home as favors.

(a)

## DECORATIONS/HATS

A Pooh Bear Picnic can be held outdoors in The Hundred Acre Wood, or indoors at The House at Pooh Corner. It all depends on the season and cooperative weather. Aside from the standard balloons and streamers, there are 2 motifs that run throughout A. A. Milne's stories—kites and umbrellas. Either can be hung from the branches of a

(b)

fig. 1

# POOH'S PARTY HATS

Pass these bear hats out at the door or set them at each child's place on the table.

PREPARATION TIME: 1¼ HOURS

---

2 brown poster boards (20 x 30 inches each)

---

2 packages (40 sheets; 20 x 30 inches each) brown crêpe paper

---

4 sheets (9 x 12 inches each) pink construction paper

---

Small mixing bowl

---

Scissors, compass, ruler, glue or rubber cement, stapler

---

Cut out twelve 2 x 26-inch strips of brown poster board, twenty-four 4-inch circles of brown poster board, twenty-four 3-inch circles of pink construction paper, and twelve 12-inch circles of brown crêpe paper. Wrap a band of poster board around your own child's head. (This is your best model for size of a particular age group.) The fit should be comfortable, slightly loose—never too tight. (Remember that a small head can wear a large hat more easily than a large head can wear a small one). Hold band in place with your fingers, remove from head, and staple together.

Glue pink circles on brown circles off center, so that edge of both circles touch at one point (fig. 2a).

Make a small, ¾-inch clip at base of each ear. This makes it easier to fold.

Crease each ear *just at the base* by pinching it together, using the clip as your fold. Do not fold entire ear in half.

Staple an ear securely on each side of the band. (Ears should be attached from the inside of the bands at the folded base of the ear.) Ears will stand up (fig. 2b).

Center a crêpe paper circle over a small mixing bowl (to make contouring a crown much simpler) and slip band over bowl (fig. 2c).

Hold crêpe paper and band in place as you lift it off bowl. Staple crêpe paper around band, easing it in where necessary. Repeat this same process on all 12 hats.

Note: After the first couple of hats, this goes very quickly.

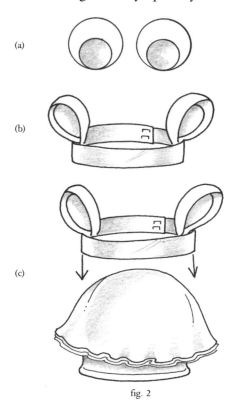

(a)

(b)

(c)

fig. 2

# INSTANT INVOLVEMENT

When the children start arriving at the party, gather them into a game of Bee Bag—similar to bean bag, only with bees. Children congregate around a large basket, or "hive," and practice throwing their "bees" from progressively further distances. The bees are made of yellow tissue, stuffed with a wad of more tissue and a miniature chocolate bar (this acts as a weight). After all of the children are present (and they've had enough time to practically exhaust this activity) tell them to open up their bees. Watch the delight as they find the surprise inside (if they haven't already discovered it!).

These Bee Bags are so simple to make, you're practically finished before you start. Even tots can help you with crumpling paper and twisting pipe cleaners.

PREPARATION TIME: 40 MINUTES

| |
|---|
| 24 sheets yellow tissue paper (20 x 30 inches each) |
| 12 miniature chocolate bars |
| 12 fuzzy black or brown pipe cleaners |
| 2 rolls of black or brown plastic tape |

Wad 12 sheets of tissue into tight balls, each around a chocolate bar. Fold remaining sheets in half and place a tissue ball in center of each.

Gather paper around balls and twist with pipe cleaners, making them resemble antennae. Wrap 3 rows of tape around bodies to look like bee stripes (fig. 3).

fig. 3

# GAMES

## ROO RACE

This is essentially a relay-style sack race, only the players are "kangaroos." The children are equally divided between 2 teams, with one potato sack per team. Each potato sack has the addition of a felt pocket or "pouch" stitched on the front. Inside each pouch is a baby Roo (a stuffed sock with felt ears and shoe button eyes and nose).

The object of the game is for each player to hop over to whatever you designate as his or her goalpost, circle it, and come back to the next member of the team. He or she climbs out of the sack and gives it to the following child, who repeats the same procedure.

If at any time Roo falls out of his pouch, the player must stop, turn around, and go back for him before continuing. The winning team is the first to have all players complete the relay.

Note: If there are an uneven number of children at the party, you'll need to find a volunteer from the "short" team to jump twice.

## KANGAROO BAG

PREPARATION TIME: 30 MINUTES

| 2 potato sacks (ask your grocer or produce market) |
| 2 squares (9 x 12 inches each) brown felt |
| Yarn needle and brown yarn |
| Scissors |

(a)

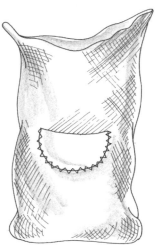

fig. 4

Have your child stand in a potato sack. If it's way too large, you may have to trim it down so that it comes up to your child's chest. (If it ravels too much, you can turn under a narrow hem on a sewing machine).

Trim felt rectangles so that the bottom edges are rounded like pockets. Save scraps for Roos' ears. With yarn needle and brown yarn, stitch pockets in the center of potato sacks (fig. 4a).

## BABY ROO

PREPARATION TIME: 35 MINUTES

| 2 brown boy's socks |
| Stuffing (cotton, fiberfill, even shredded tissue) |
| Yarn needle and brown yarn |
| Sewing needle and brown thread |
| 6 black shoebuttons |
| Reserved felt scraps from Kangaroo Bag pockets (see left) |
| Scissors |

Push a small wad of stuffing into the toe of each sock. Wrap a piece of yarn around each sock (underneath the wad of stuffing in the toe) and tie off in a bow. This will be the head.

Stuff rest of sock to within 3 inches of opening. Tie off with another piece of yarn. This forms the body.

Sew 2 shoebuttons on the head for eyes, and one for a nose (fig. 4b).

Cut 4 ears out of reserved felt scraps; set 2 aside. Pinch bottom

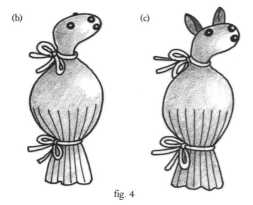

(b) (c)

fig. 4

edges of remaining ears together, to give ears a fold, and stitch one ear on each side of head (fig. 4c).

Repeat same process with other sock, using remaining ears.

## HEFFALUMPS AND WOOZLES

It's hard to know exactly what a "Heffalump" or "Woozle" looks like, because Pooh never actually saw one—except in his imagination. That's what makes this game all the more fun.

The children are divided into 2 lines: Heffalumps wear a trunk over their nose. Woozles wear big teeth over their mouth. The Heffalumps stand with their backs toward the Woozles. The Woozles quietly sneak up behind the Heffalumps. One child is selected to play Pooh. When the Woozles are within a few feet of the Heffalumps, Pooh cries out, "The Woozles are coming!" The Heffalumps turn quickly and run after the Woozles, catching as many as they can. Those caught join up with the line of Heffalumps. The next time, the Woozles turn their backs and the Heffalumps creep up on them. Pooh calls "The Heffalumps are coming," and the Woozles try to catch them. The game continues like this until all the children are in the same line.

## HEFFALUMP TRUNKS AND WOOZLE TEETH

PREPARATION TIME: 30 MINUTES

| |
| --- |
| 6 knee socks |
| 12 mask bands |
| 6, 2½" circles cut from pink felt |
| magic marker, needle & thread |
| 1 sheet (20 × 30 inches) white poster board |

String knee socks on mask bands to be worn over nose. Make "nostrils" on pink circles with magic marker. Sew circles to the toe of each sock, like an elephant's trunk (fig. 5a). Cut Woozle teeth out of white poster board, follow picture (fig. 5b). String a mask band through each corner of the teeth, to be worn across mouth (fig. 5c).

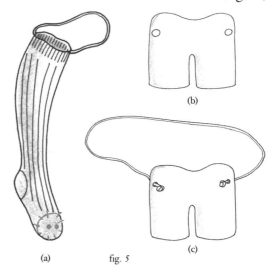

(a)  fig. 5  (b) (c)

# PIN THE TAIL ON EEYORE

This game is similar to the classic Pin the Tail on the Donkey. The main difference is that this donkey is made of gingerbread! Instead of hanging in a vertical position on a wall, the donkey lies horizontally on a low table or platform (depending on the age and size of the children playing).

Each child is given a licorice whip tail on a different colored frilly toothpick. When the child's turn comes up, he or she is blindfolded with an opaque scarf and led around the table 3 times by a parent or another child. After being released, it's up to the child to decide where the appropriate end of the donkey is to attach the tail. Once the child sticks the toothpick into the donkey, the blindfold is removed and everyone can enjoy seeing where it ends up. After first, second, and third prizes have been awarded (for each child who comes respectively closest to the "target"), the donkey is divided among all of the children to eat. There are no losers in this game.

## RECIPES

## GINGERBREAD EEYORE

PREPARATION TIME: 1 HOUR
BAKING TIME: 10 TO 12 MINUTES

| 1 cup butter |
| --- |
| 1 cup brown sugar, firmly packed |

| 1 cup dark molasses |
| --- |
| ½ cup water |
| 5 cups flour |
| 1 teaspoon salt |
| 1 teaspoon baking soda |
| 1½ teaspoons ground ginger |
| 1 teaspoon ground cinnamon |
| ½ teaspoon freshly grated nutmeg |
| ¼ teaspoon ground allspice |
| Shiny Glaze (recipe follows) |
| Chocolate Icing (recipe follows) |
| Large piece of heavy cardboard |
| Gold or colored foil |
| Donkey Tails (instructions follow) |

Preheat oven to 350°F. Cover a very large baking sheet with foil, shiny side down.

Melt butter, molasses, and the ⅓ cup water together in a saucepan. Cool slightly. Mix dry ingredients together in a large bowl. Pour molasses mixture over flour mixture and blend to form a smooth dough. Shape, roll, and pat dough with your hands to form a large donkey on the prepared baking sheet (fig. 6a). (This is just like working with modeling clay—if dough is a little soft, chill it briefly.) Use a flattened rope of dough along crest of neck for a mane, and score it with a knife. (Remember that gingerbread expands in the oven, so make Eeyore a little skinnier than you want him to look.) Bake for 15 to 20 minutes, or until golden brown.

(Use the upper half of your oven so it won't burn on the bottom). Cool completely. (Chilling the cookie makes it easier to carefully lift off the foil, peeling foil away.) Transfer to a large piece of cardboard (at least as big as the baking sheet) that has been covered with gold or colored foil.

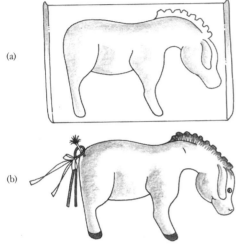

(a)

(b)

fig. 6

## SHINY GLAZE

| ¼ cup light corn syrup |
| --- |
| 2 tablespoons water |
| 1 large marshmallow |

Bring corn syrup and the 2 tablespoons water to a boil in a small saucepan. Remove glaze from heat and brush over surface of gingerbread. Slice marshmallow in half and press one piece of it (cut side down) against the gingerbread where the eye should be. Allow glaze to cool slightly while you prepare the chocolate icing.

## CHOCOLATE ICING

| 1 ounce unsweetened chocolate |
| --- |
| 1 tablespoon butter |
| 1 cup confectioners sugar |
| 1 to 2 tablespoons hot water |
| ½ teaspoon vanilla extract |

Melt chocolate and butter in a saucepan; cool slightly. Beat in sugar, 1 tablespoon hot water, and vanilla. If icing is too thick, thin it with another tablespoon of water. Fit a pastry bag with a medium-size writing tip; fill with icing. Pipe a pupil on the marshmallow for an eye. Pipe lines for a mouth, mane, and hooves (see fig. 6b).

## DONKEY TAILS

| 12 very long licorice whips |
| --- |
| 5 yards ribbon, cut into 15-inch lengths |
| Frilled party toothpicks of different colors |

Cut each licorice whip in half. Hold halves together and bend them in half again to form a loop in the middle. Tie a bow with a 15-inch strip of ribbon to secure the loop. Use frilled party toothpicks through the loop as you would thumbtacks to pin the tail on Eeyore.

Note: If your licorice whips are on the short side, use 24 and don't split them in half.

## PINEAPPLE OWL AND FRESH FRUIT KEBABS

Who would think that an upside-down pineapple looks just like an owl? Well, it does, and it makes a perfect centerpiece for a platter of fruit kebabs

PREPARATION TIME: 30 MINUTES

| |
|---|
| 1 large pineapple (choose one that's more yellowish than green) |
| 2 large lemon slices |
| 2 large purple or dark red grapes |
| 1 wedge of orange, with skin attached |
| 2 cinnamon sticks |
| Toothpicks |
| Lettuce (optional) |

Imagine that the top of the pineapple is an owl's head and the stem is the tail. Turn it upside down, at an angle, so that the tail will stick out in back. Plan on inserting the 2 cinnamon sticks as legs to form a sort of "tripod" (between legs and tail) for support. Use an apple corer to make holes in pineapple and insert cinnamon sticks. Use lemon slices to form 2 big yellow eyes and hold in place with a toothpick. Cover the end of each toothpick with a large grape for pupils. Attach orange wedge for beak with a toothpick (skin side out, with narrow edge against the pineapple). Place Owl in middle of a large platter or lettuce-lined basket. Surround with fruit kebabs.

## FRUIT KEBABS

| |
|---|
| 1 large pineapple, peeled, cored, and cut into large cubes |
| Seedless red or green grapes |
| Cantaloupe balls (from 1 melon) |
| Fresh strawberries (about a pint) |
| 12 to 18 wooden kebab skewers |

Thread the fruits on wooden skewers, alternating according to color. Arrange in a "sunburst" fashion around the pineapple owl.

Note: With very young children, it's frequently a good idea to remove any sticks as the food is served to them, after they've had an opportunity to see it. Simply slide the fruits off the kebab with a fork onto each serving plate.

## CHRISTOPHER ROBIN'S EGG SALAD

PREPARATION TIME: 30 MINUTES

| |
|---|
| 12 eggs |
| 4 tablespoons vinegar |
| Food coloring (4 drops blue and 1 drop green) |
| ½ cup boiling water |
| 1 cup mayonnaise |
| 2 tablespoons sugar |
| 2 teaspoons celery seed |
| 1 teaspoon dry mustard |
| 1 teaspoon salt |
| 2 cups shredded cabbage |

| 2 cups julienned cucumber (discard seeds and pulp) |
| --- |
| 2 cups julienned zucchini |
| 1 cup julienned carrots |
| Bibb or Boston lettuce cups |

Hard-cook eggs. While eggs are cooking, combine 2 tablespoons of the vinegar, food coloring, and boiling water in a coffee cup. When eggs are done, immediately immerse, one at a time, into dye and hold there just long enough for the egg to turn a delicate robin's-egg blue. Dry eggs in the egg carton, then chill until serving time.

Combine mayonnaise, sugar, remaining 2 tablespoons vinegar, celery seed, mustard, and salt in a small bowl. Toss cabbage, cucumber, zucchini, and carrots in a large bowl with dressing. Chill several hours or overnight.

To serve, spoon a heaping ½ cup of salad onto each lettuce cup. Make a well in the center (like a bird's nest) and place egg in the middle. Serve on each lunch plate, along with the Pooh Bear Po'Boys (recipe follows).

## POOH BEAR PO'BOYS

Rapid-rise yeast makes the delightful little bear buns used in the sandwiches quick to make. Each child is given a personal Winnie the Pooh to fill with a choice of cold cuts. Arrange the sliced meats and cheese on a platter and pass around the table.

Note: Very young children should have their sandwiches preassembled.

PREPARATION TIME: 1 HOUR 10 MINUTES
RISING TIME (FOR BUNS): 1 HOUR TO 1 HOUR 15 MINUTES
BAKING TIME (FOR BUNS): 30 TO 35 MINUTES

| 2 packages active dry yeast (rapid-rise variety) |
| --- |
| ⅓ cup warm water |
| ¼ cup honey |
| 2 tablespoons sugar |
| 2 teaspoons salt |
| 6 cups flour |
| 4 tablespoons butter, melted |
| ¾ cup buttermilk |
| ½ cup hot water |
| 3 eggs |
| Cornmeal |
| Raisins |

Dissolve yeast and water in a large mixing bowl. Add honey, sugar, and salt and stir until blended. Stir in 3 cups of the flour, the butter, buttermilk, water, and 2 of the eggs. Beat until smooth, then blend in remaining flour to make a smooth dough. Cover bowl with plastic wrap and allow to rise in a warm, draft-free place until doubled in bulk; this should take 30 to 45 minutes.

Meanwhile, grease 2 cookie sheets and dust with cornmeal.

Punch dough down and turn out on lightly floured surface. Knead the dough a little, just until it's no longer sticky. Divide dough into 12 equal parts. Shape each bear as follows: Make a large oval for the body and a ball for the head (fig. 7a). Make smaller balls for the nose, ears, and legs; use raisins for eyes (fig. 7b). Place on cookie sheets and brush with remaining egg beaten with a little water. Allow to double in bulk, about 30 minutes. Preheat oven to 375°F. Bake for 30 to 35 minutes, or until golden brown. Cool. (Bears may be frozen at this point.)

fig. 7

## PO'BOY FILLINGS

| 8 ounces sliced boiled ham |
| --- |
| 8 ounces sliced turkey roll |
| 8 ounces sliced bologna |
| 8 ounces each Swiss and American cheese |
| Sliced tomatoes |
| Pickles, mustard, mayonnaise, Russian dressing |

On a platter, arrange the meats, cheeses, and tomatoes; accompany with pickles, mustard, mayonnaise, and Russian dressing. Carefully split each bear bun in half crosswise and serve with the platter of meats and cheeses. (fig. 7c).

## PINK PEPPERMINT PIGLETS

This adorable dessert can be made in just minutes and frozen for a few hours or a few weeks. You'll need a regular-size ice cream scoop and a miniature.

PREPARATION TIME: 15 MINUTES
FREEZING TIME: ABOUT 1 HOUR

| 2 quarts pink peppermint ice cream (see note) |
| --- |
| 24 miniature marshmallows |
| Thick fudge sauce (any brand, or homemade, as long as it gets very firm when chilled) |
| Pink cupcake liners |
| Pink construction paper |

(a)

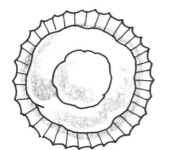

(b)

(c)

fig. 8

Cut 24 ears out of pink construction paper, as shown (fig. 8a). Set aside while you make ice cream Piglets.

Spread open cupcake liners and place a large scoop of ice cream in center of each. Top each large scoop with a small scoop (this is Piglet's nose) (fig. 8b). For each pig, insert 2 marshmallows for eyes, pushing down into ice cream, and 2 construction paper ears, creasing them down the center to give them more body before inserting. Return to freezer for at least an hour.

Fit a pastry bag with a writing tip; fill with about ½ cup of fudge sauce. Remove ice cream from freezer. Pipe pupils on marshmallow eyes and nostrils on nose of each pig (fig. 8c). Return to freezer until serving time.

Note: Use only *pink* peppermint ice cream. Some peppermint ice creams are pink with flecks of green mint or white with pink ripple. If you can't find pink peppermint, then use strawberry ice cream.

## TIGGER CAKE

"Bouncy" Tigger is in a position to pounce right on the plate. A nut-and raisin-filled orange cake is baked in two 9-inch round layers, then sculpted, with the help of orange buttercream frosting, into a chocolate-striped tiger.

PREPARATION TIME: 1 HOUR 15
MINUTES
BAKING TIME: 30 TO 35 MINUTES

| ½ cup butter, softened |
| --- |
| ¼ cup solid vegetable shortening, softened |
| 1½ cups sugar |
| 1½ teaspoons baking soda |
| ¾ teaspoon salt |
| 3 eggs |
| 2½ cups flour |
| 1½ cups buttermilk |
| 1 tablespoon grated orange zest |
| 2 teaspoons vanilla extract |

| 1 cup chopped golden raisins |
| ½ cup chopped nuts |
| Orange Frosting (recipe follows) |
| Chocolate Frosting (recipe follows) |
| 2 large marshmallows |
| Large piece of heavy cardboard |
| Gold or silver foil |

Preheat oven to 350°F. Line two 9-inch cake pans with foil (along bottom and against sides).

Cream butter and sugar together until light and fluffy. Add baking soda and salt. Beat in eggs. Add remaining ingredients and beat for 3 minutes at medium speed. Pour batter into prepared pans and bake 30 to 35 minutes. Cool layers completely in pans.

Turn cooled layers out on a rack and gently peel foil from sides and bottom. Cut cake as shown (fig. 9a).

Fit a pastry bag with a large writing tip; fill with orange frosting. "Sandwich" together the body sections and head sections of cake, and arrange on a foil-covered board. Sculpt head as shown, using scraps to fill in back of the neck (fig. 9b). Attach ears, tail, and paws with toothpicks or plastic straws (fig. 9c). "Crumb coat" cake (see page 10). Use remaining frosting to build up shape and define legs and paws. Insert marshmallows for eyes. Fit another pastry bag with a medium writing tip; fill with chocolate frosting. Pipe pupils for eyes. Pipe a nose, mouth, stripes, and claws (see photo opposite page 29).

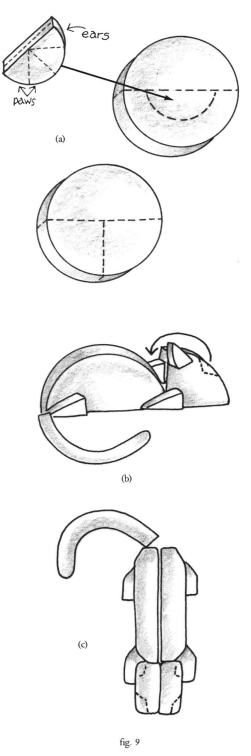

fig. 9

# ORANGE FROSTING

| |
|---|
| 1½ cups butter, softened |
| 3 pounds confectioners sugar |
| 3 tablespoons fine grated orange zest |
| 3 egg yolks |
| 3 tablespoons lemon juice |
| 6 tablespoons light cream, or as needed |
| 2 tablespoons vanilla extract |
| Few drops of red and yellow food coloring, to desired shade of orange |

Cream butter and sugar together well. Beat in orange zest and egg yolks, then lemon juice, cream, and vanilla. (Add more cream if frosting is too stiff.) Tint frosting with food coloring.

# CHOCOLATE FROSTING

| |
|---|
| ½ cup butter, softened |
| 3 ounces unsweetened chocolate, melted and cooled slightly |
| 3 cups confectioners sugar |
| 2 teaspoons vanilla extract |
| 4 tablespoons milk, or as needed |

Cream butter, chocolate, sugar, and vanilla together well. Beat in milk until smooth and creamy. (You may need to add more milk.)

# "HUNNY" POT PUNCH

Pooh's honey jar was his most prized possession, and "a useful place to put things." What more delicious thing could a bear put in it than a refreshing, honey-sweetened punch. All you have to do is find a large ceramic or glass crock or cookie jar. Paint the word HUNNY on it with red nail enamel. (Don't worry—it will come off later with nail polish remover.)

PREPARATION TIME: 15 MINUTES

| |
|---|
| 2 quarts lemonade |
| 3 quarts unsweetened pineapple juice |
| ⅔ cup honey |
| 1 pint fresh strawberries |

Combine lemonade, pineapple juice, and honey in pitchers or large plastic jugs. Wash strawberries and place one in each section of 2 ice cube trays. Pour punch over strawberries and freeze until firm. Chill punch until serving time.

To serve, fill "Hunny" Pot with half of the punch and a tray of strawberry ice cubes. (Reserve the rest for refills.) Ladle into cups.

# VALENTINE TEA WITH THE QUEEN OF HEARTS

**M**any children see Valentine's Day as an excuse for eating chocolate or who can collect the most heart-shaped cards from their classmates. By inviting them to a tea with the Queen of Hearts, you've introduced a creative new concept to this occasion and a classic children's fantasy: *Alice in Wonderland*.

## MENU

QUEEN OF HEARTS TARTS

RED RADISH ROSEBUSH

DILLY DEVILED EGG DIP

COOKIE CARDS

CHOCO-CHERRY
CHESHIRE CAT CAKE

WHITE RABBITS AND
MARCH HARES

PINK PEPPERMINT
FLAMINGO MERINGUES

"EAT ME" TEA CAKES

"DRINK ME" TEA

**FEATURES:** Mad Hatter Top Hats

**GAMES:** Crazy Croquet, Painting the Roses Red, "Off with Her Head!"

**INVITATIONS:** "Card" cards

## INVITATIONS

This is no ordinary Valentine, but an invitation to a royal reception. Since the occasion is a tea with the Queen of Hearts, it's only appropriate that each card contain a "card." You can purchase an inexpensive deck from your local dime store to glue right on the front, along with a doily and ribbon.

12 CARDS
PREPARATION TIME: 45 MINUTES

12 sheets (9 x 12 inches each) red construction paper

12 heart-shaped doilies (no wider than 6 inches)

12 playing cards from a *red* suit (preferably hearts)

Red ribbon (satin-type or curling ribbon)

White ink or opaque marker

12 envelopes to fit 6 x 9 cards

Scissors, glue, stapler

Fold sheets of paper in half to make 6 x 9-inch cards. Glue a doily on the center front of each card. Glue a card, face up, in center of each doily.

Cut twelve 6-inch lengths of ribbon. Staple ribbon at the point of each heart doily and tie in a bow (fig. 1). On the inside of each card, write the following message in white ink:

*WELCOME TO*
*WONDERLAND*
*HER ROYAL HIGHNESS*
*THE QUEEN OF HEARTS*
*REQUESTS YOUR PRESENCE*
*FOR TEA WITH ALICE*
*ON [date, time] AT [your address]*
*R.S.V.P.*
*[or Regrets Only]*

These invitations can be mailed, although Valentines are frequently hand delivered.

fig. 1

## DECORATIONS

Because Alice shrinks and grows, the oversized-undersized environment is a major motif in the story. This can be reflected in party decorations as well. You can re-create Wonderland on the walls of a room.

Doors were a major dilemma for Alice; they were either too large or too small, or she didn't know which to take at all. Giant paper doors with huge keyholes can be taped up around the room alongside tiny doors only 12 inches high (fig. 2a). Doll furniture will also help to enhance this illusion.

Signs were another problem for Alice; in search of the White Rabbit, she found directions leading her every which way (fig. 2b).

(a)

"Dummy boards" (freestanding cutouts) of characters can also be placed in the setting: Tweedle Dum and Tweedle Dee, the Dormouse, the March Hare, the Mock Turtle, or the Mad Hatter, just to mention a few. Surveying the scene is the omnipresent Cheshire Cat. His smile will seem to be invisibly suspended in air because it will be literally "hanging by a thread" (fig. 2c).

Decorate a white paper tablecloth with cutouts of red hearts and diamonds and black spades and clubs. You can even "slip cover" the backs of chairs with a sandwich of 2 white poster boards that resemble cards (fig. 2d). The threshold, doorway, or entrance to the room can be turned into a rose trellis by taping up rows of red tissue pompons.

(b)

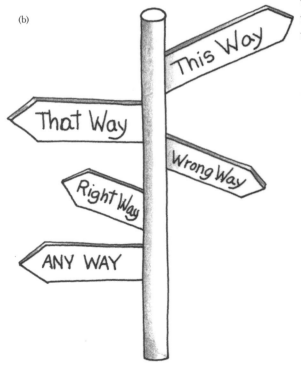

(c)

(d)

fig. 2

*Choco-Cherry Cheshire Cat Cake (recipe pages 52-54)*

*Pink Peppermint Flamingo Meringues (recipe pages 55-56)*

## INSTANT INVOLVEMENT

Hat making may be a dying art, but you can bring it back to life at the same time you get the party off to a lively start. Hang up a sign, THE MAD HATTER'S MILLINERY SHOP, over some designated work area. There should be a large table with chairs or enough noncarpeted floorspace for all of the children to work comfortably, constructing hats. All you have to do is supply the pre-cut pieces—the kids will take care of the rest (a real time saver!). As soon as guests arrive, direct them toward the "millinery shop" and watch the fun begin as each child expresses his or her individuality as a Mad Hatter.

The traditional Mad Hatter's hat is usually depicted as a classic dove-gray top hat. You should by no means feels limited to any particular color. After all, *Alice in Wonderland* is make believe, so why not make the hats any color your child chooses? However, for the purist, dove gray can be decorated with pink, red, or white hat bands, paper hearts, and ribbon for a striking Valentine "chapeau."

PREPARATION TIME: 30 MINUTES (FOR CUTOUTS)

---

6 sheets (20 x 30 inches each lightweight poster board or construction paper (all the same color)

---

Crêpe-paper streamers or ribbon (in contrasting colors for hat bands)

---

Decorations (sequins, feathers, doilies, etc.)

---

Hat elastics (optional)

---

Scissors, compass or pot lids, glue, tape or stapler

---

Two of the sheets of poster board or construction paper will be used for making the brims and tops of the hats, while the rest will be used for the sides. You'll need to measure 10- and 6¼-inch circles. This can be done by using a compass. However, you'd be surprised how many cake pans and pot lids are just the right size to make a perfect pattern. Trace six 10-inch circles on each sheet (you should have a total of 12). Center a 6¼-inch circle in the middle of each 10-inch circle and draw around it. Cut out the 10-inch circles, and carefully cut out the center 6¼-inch circles, preserving these round discs for the hat tops (fig. 3a). Cut the remaining sheets into twelve 10 x 20-inch strips (each sheet will yield 3 strips). Mark off a 1-inch line along the top and bottom of each strip, and cut through to the line at about 1-inch intervals (fig. 3b).

From this point, the rest of the construction can be done by the kids, unless they are very young. In this case, you may want to preassemble the hats and let them apply decorations. For each hat, both ends of a 10 x 20-inch strip are brought together to form a cylinder; join together with a ½-inch overlap (fig. 3c). The bottom tabs are folded out and the top tabs are folded in (fig. 3d).

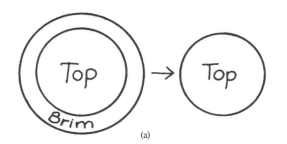

(a)

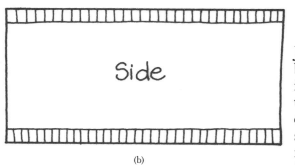

(b)

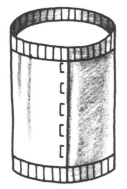

(c)

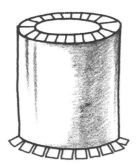

(d)

fig. 3

(e)

Join brim and top to tabs (tabs will be concealed). Now it's time for imagination to take over and transform each hat into a designer original. The more trimmings you set out, the more intriguing the results (fig. 3e). Since it's hard for a hat to stay on the head of a moving child, you may want to attach elastic bands that will hold a hat in place by strapping it underneath the chin.

## GAMES

### CRAZY CROQUET

While in Wonderland, Alice seemed to be constantly confronted with the bizarre. The Queen of Hearts invited her to join in a game of croquet, but this was no ordinary match—the Court was swinging away with pink flamingos for mallets and roly-poly hedgehogs for balls. You can recreate this crazy game right in your basement, recreation room, or living room. The simplest way is to make a few minor embellishments on a standard croquet set, but don't worry if you don't have one; you can still use short golf clubs, even baseball bats. Most croquet sets contain 8 mallets and 8 balls, stakes, and wickets, but since there will be 2 teams, you really need only 2 mallets.

Turn a mallet into a flamingo by pulling a thick pink sock (which has been stuffed with a wad of 2 or 3 rolled-up socks) over the end of the handle. Secure in place with a rubber band and tie a ribbon around the rubber band to conceal it. Cut out a beak from black felt (see pattern, page 181), punching out holes for nostrils. Curve beak slightly, so that it stands out straight, and stitch in place, along with 2 black buttons for eyes (fig. 4). Playing indoors, you may prefer the added safety factor of using tennis or foam-type balls over the hard wooden croquet balls.

Many sets come with wicket holders for indoor games. If you have them, use them. However, the structure of this game is similar to miniature golf. The obstacle course should be "wacky," so just let your imagination run wild. Use tunnels of coffee cans and oatmeal boxes, make ramps and slides out of boards or books, erect a maze out of Tinker Toys or even knock the ball under the legs of a silly stuffed animal. As long as there's a start and a finish, that's all that matters.

Divide the players into 2 teams. Each player takes turns hitting their ball through the course, one shot at a time. As soon as one player reaches the goal, it's his next teammate's turn. The first team to have all of its players finish the obstacle course wins.

fig. 4

## PAINTING THE ROSES RED

Only ruby-red roses could grow in the royal garden, so the royal gardeners scurried about trying to camouflage white rose bushes with cans of red paint. This can be turned into a team sport by hanging two 5-foot-long black-and-white murals on opposite walls. Use wide rolls of white drawing or freezer paper to create a larger-than-life coloring book. Draw outline roses with black felt-tip marker or crayon. Make as many roses, of whatever size, as you want, as long as both murals have the same amount.

Divide children into 2 teams. Give each child a red crayon (a purist can supply them with red paint—however, the house may suffer the consequences!). The teams start simultaneously, and the first to finish filling in all the roses wins.

## "OFF WITH HER HEAD!"

The Queen had quite a temper and was often subject to irrational outbursts of "Off with her [or his] head!" (This ritual was so routine that it's doubtful anyone was ever really decapitated.) In any event, it makes an amusing premise for an action-packed card game.

In order to play, all of the "face" cards are removed from the deck except for the Queen of Hearts and the Joker. One child is selected as the Queen of Hearts, and another as the Joker. The remaining children sit in a circle on the floor, facing the Queen, who sits on a "throne" (a chair). Meanwhile, the Joker hovers around the outside of the circle and deals out a card to each player. The Joker goes around and around until every card has been passed out. Each hand of cards is kept face down in front of the player until the Queen snaps her fingers. All hands must then be turned face up and shown to the Joker. When the Queen of Hearts card is discovered, the reigning Queen decrees: "Off with her (or his) head!" The player is led away by

the Joker and the circle grows smaller. The Joker becomes the new Queen and the old Queen takes her place among the players. The player who drew the Joker card becomes the next Joker. The game resumes and the cycle continues. Eventually, the game dwindles down to one player who is proclaimed the winner.

Note: In the event that one player should happen to have a hand with both the Queen and Joker cards, the highest card rules—in which case, the player is banished from the circle and the present Queen and Joker continue in the next round.

## RECIPES

## QUEEN OF HEARTS TARTS

Little cheese tarts, topped with pimiento hearts—most proper for Valentine tea with the Queen. These can be baked in muffin cups, fluted 2-inch tart pans, or even heart-shaped tart pans.

PREPARATION TIME: 20 TO 25
  MINUTES
CHILLING TIME (FOR PASTRY):
  1 HOUR
BAKING TIME: 20 TO 25 MINUTES

| |
|---|
| 1 cup butter, chilled |
| 3½ cups flour |
| ¼ teaspoon salt |

| |
|---|
| 4 eggs |
| ¼ cup vegetable oil |
| ½ cup cold water |
| 1 cup sour cream |
| ¼ cup chopped scallions |
| ½ teaspoon onion salt |
| Dash of freshly grated nutmeg |
| 1¼ cups grated Swiss cheese |
| 2 jars (4 ounces each) whole pimientos |

Slice butter into cubes and cut into flour and salt with a pastry blender or in a food processor until mixture resembles oatmeal. Beat one of the eggs into a measuring cup with oil and water mixture. Pour into flour mixture and stir with a fork until mixture forms a ball and clings together. Divide in half, wrap in plastic, and chill at least 1 hour.

Roll out one ball of dough at a time on a lightly floured surface. Cut into 3-inch circles and fit into pans (heart-shaped pans will require trimming). Chill while preparing filling. (Tart shells may be prepared way in advance and frozen.)

Preheat oven to 375°F. Beat remaining 3 eggs with a fork or wire whisk. Blend in sour cream, scallions, onion salt, and nutmeg. Stir in Swiss cheese. Spoon filling into tart shells. Use a small, heart-shaped biscuit or aspic cutter to cut tiny hearts out of pimiento. Center hearts in the middle of each tart. Bake for 20 to 25 minutes, or until puffy and golden. Serve warm.

# RED RADISH ROSEBUSH

"A rose is a rose" unless it's a radish! Two dozen long-stemmed beauties make an edible arrangement for the center of the table. When these buds blossom, you can tell from the white inside that the Queen had them painted red.

PREPARATION TIME: 20 MINUTES, PLUS OVERNIGHT SOAKING TIME

| |
|---|
| 24 red radishes |
| 24 scallions |
| 24 long wooden bamboo skewers |
| 1 head green cabbage |
| Fresh parsley or watercress (optional) |
| Flower pot or glass bowl |

Cut root ends off each radish. Use a thin paring knife to make petal-shaped cuts along sides of radishes. Soak radishes in a bowl of ice water overnight so they'll "bloom," or open up.

Insert skewers through the shaft of each scallion, pushing up through the green leafy tip. Spear a radish "bloom" on the end of each stem (fig. 5a). Slice off a large hunk of cabbage and place in your flower pot or bowl. Arrange roses by sticking end of each stem into cabbage, anchoring them in place (fig. 5b). Shred remaining cabbage and fill up pot or bowl as if you were filling a basket with Easter grass (fig. 5c). If desired, you can add some foliage to this arrangement with parsley or watercress.

(a)

(b)

(c)

fig. 5

Note: This bouquet will fade fast in a warm, dry room. A good way to keep radish roses fresh is by spraying them with cold water. (Just use a clean empty spray or pump bottle.)

## DILLY DEVILED EGG DIP WITH CUCUMBER CATERPILLARS

When Alice was no bigger than a weed (at least that's what the flowers thought of her), she met a haughty caterpillar. He told her that she could grow larger by taking a bite from his magic mushroom. Sliced cucumbers make convincing caterpillars and a refreshing teatime snack.

# CUCUMBER CATERPILLARS

PREPARATION TIME: 30 MINUTES
CHILLING TIME (FOR SCALLION "ANTENNAE"): AT LEAST SEVERAL HOURS

| 4 scallions |
|---|
| 2 English cucumbers (seedless cucumbers, often called "burpless") |
| 4 whole cloves |
| 1 medium-size head red cabbage |
| Red leaf, green leaf, or salad bowl lettuce |
| Dilly Deviled Egg Dip (recipe follows) |
| 2 dozen snow-white, fresh mushrooms |
| Toothpicks |

First make scallion "antennae": trim off ½ inch from root end of scallion and cut off most of the green stem so you have four, 4-inch segments. Make 2 deep gashes through each scallion, crisscrossing each other and cutting halfway down. Soak scallions in ice water for several hours, until ends spread open like tassels.

Cut a diagonal slice 3 inches from one end of each cucumber; these will be caterpillar heads. Slice remaining cucumbers into ¼-inch slices, keeping them aligned together. Insert a toothpick through base of each scallion antenna. Attach antennae to heads of caterpillars and insert cloves for eyes (fig. 6a).

Hollow out center of red cabbage to form a "bowl," leaving a thick wall around edge. Cut thin gashes about ¾ inch deep, all around outside of cabbage. Spread open gashes to form a "blossom."

Line a large oval or round platter with lettuce leaves. Place red cabbage carnation in center of platter and fill cavity with dip. Arrange a curving caterpillar along each side of cabbage by spreading out overlapping slices of cucumber and placing the heads at the ends (fig. 6b). Garnish with mushrooms.

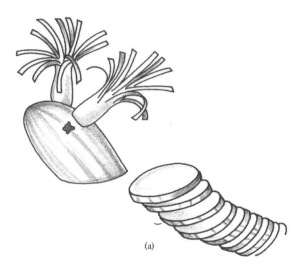

(a)

(b)

fig. 6

# DILLY DEVILED EGG DIP

| ¼ cup mayonnaise |
|---|
| 1 package (3 ounces) cream cheese, softened |
| 1 tablespoon milk |
| 1 tablespoon prepared mustard |
| ¼ teaspoon onion salt |
| ⅛ teaspoon pepper |
| 1 tablespoon chopped fresh dill or 1 teaspoon dried |
| 1 teaspoon chopped fresh chives |
| 4 hard-cooked eggs, chopped |

Beat mayonnaise, cream cheese, and milk until smooth. Stir in mustard, onion salt, pepper, chives, and eggs. Chill.

## COOKIE CARDS

Whether it's a full house or a royal flush, deal out a deck of cookie cards for a teatime treat.

PREPARATION TIME: 1 HOUR
BAKING TIME: ABOUT 8 MINUTES

| 1 cup butter, softened |
|---|
| 1 cup sugar |
| 2 eggs |
| 1 tablespoon vanilla extract |
| 3 cups flour |
| ½ teaspoon baking soda |
| ½ teaspoon salt |
| Decorator's Icing (recipe follows) |

Cream butter until light and fluffy. Beat in sugar, eggs, and vanilla extract. Combine flour, soda, and salt and blend into butter mixture, making a soft dough. Wrap in plastic wrap and chill dough for about 1 hour.

Preheat oven to 375°F.

Roll out dough, on a lightly floured surface, ¼ inch thick. Use a ruler or yardstick to cut into 2 x 3-inch card-shaped rectangles and place 1 inch apart on a lightly greased baking sheet. Bake for 5 to 8 minutes, or until cookies are barely browned around the edges. Cool cookies completely.

Glaze cookies with white icing, smoothing with a metal spatula. Allow icing to "set" for a few minutes. Divide remaining icing in half. Stir cocoa into one part (thinning with cream if necessary), and tinting the other part a rich red. Fit 2 small pastry bags with round writing tips; fill with the red and chocolate icing. There are 52 cards in a deck (you may or may not have that many—don't worry about it). The 2 red suits (hearts and diamonds) will be decorated with red frosting, and the 2 black suits (spades and clubs) will be decorated with chocolate icing. Each suit contains 10 "spot" cards that number 1 (ace) through 10, and 3 "face" cards: Jack, Queen, and King. Use real playing cards as models to pipe designs and numerals. When it comes to the face cards, just make stylized versions of the actual figures.

## DECORATOR'S ICING

| 3 cups confectioners sugar |
| 4 to 5 tablespoons light cream |
| 1 tablespoon vanilla extract |
| 2 tablespoons unsweetened cocoa powder |
| Red food coloring |

Blend confectioners sugar, vanilla, and cream together to make a smooth icing.

## CHOCO-CHERRY CHESHIRE CAT CAKE

The elusive Cheshire Cat's ever-present grin never seemed to fade. He followed Alice everywhere, watching over everything. This captivating cake is the focal point of the party.

PREPARATION TIME: 1 HOUR
BAKING TIME: 30 TO 35 MINUTES

| 2¼ cups flour |
| 1⅔ cups sugar |
| ⅔ cup shortening |
| ¾ cup milk |
| ½ cup maraschino cherry juice |
| 3½ teaspoons baking powder |
| 1 teaspoon salt |
| 5 egg whites |
| 1 teaspoon almond extract |
| ½ cup miniature semisweet morsels |

| 24 maraschino cherries, well drained and cut into eighths. |
| Cherry-Chocolate Frosting (recipe follows) |
| Large yellow gumdrop |
| Large black gumdrop |
| Black licorice whips or laces |
| Miniature marshmallows |
| ¼ cup unsweetened cocoa powder |
| 1 tablespoon milk |

Preheat oven to 350°F. Line the bottoms of two 9-inch round cake pans with foil or baking parchment.

Beat flour, sugar, shortening, milk, cherry juice, baking powder, and salt in a large mixing bowl until combined (about 30 seconds). Beat at medium speed for 2 minutes. Add egg whites and almond extract and beat at high speed for 2 minutes longer. Fold in chocolate morsels and cherries.

Pour batter into prepared pans. Bake 30 to 35 minutes, or until a wooden toothpick inserted in center comes out clean. Cool completely in pans.

Turn layers out of pans and peel foil or parchment paper away from bottoms.

Cut cake layers as shown (fig. 7a) and arrange on a 15 x 20-inch foil-covered cardboard to resemble a cat (fig. 7b). Frost cake with some of the frosting. Set 1 cup of the frosting aside; fit a pastry bag with a plastic coupling nozzle (no need to use a decorating tip) and fill with any remaining frosting. Pipe frosting to form brow, bridge of

nose, cheeks, and paws, building up frosting and sculpting with a small spatula (fig. 7c). Slice yellow gumdrop in half and flatten each half between wax paper with a

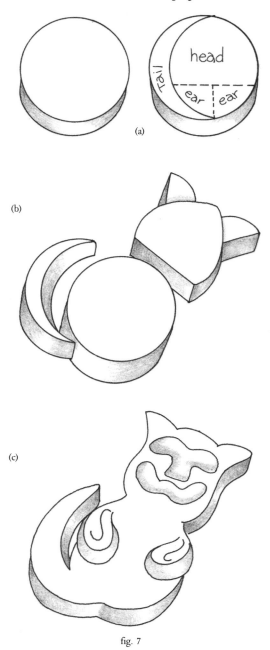

fig. 7

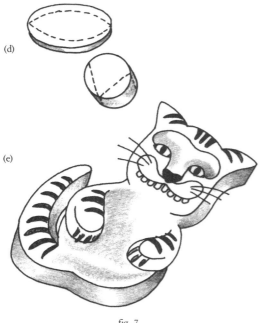

(d)

(e)

fig. 7

rolling pin. Cut into teardrop shapes for eyes and place below brow (fig. 7d). Cut black gumdrop into a wedgelike triangle and set in place for the nose. Cut licorice into 4-inch lengths and insert in cheeks for whiskers.

Blend ¼ cup cocoa powder and 1 tablespoon milk into reserved 1 cup frosting to make a smooth, dark chocolate frosting. Fit a small pastry bag with a round writing tip; fill with the darker frosting; use to pipe pupils on eyes, claws on paws, mouth line and stripes on body. Slice miniature marshmallows in half, so they look like pillow shapes (not across in round slices). Arrange cut side down along mouth line to form a "grinning" set of teeth (see photo opposite page 44).

Note: This cake can be prepared in advance and frozen.

## CHERRY-CHOCOLATE FROSTING

| 1 cup butter, softened |
| --- |
| 6 cups confectioners sugar |
| ¾ cup unsweetened cocoa powder |
| 1 teaspoon almond extract |
| 6 tablespoons maraschino cherry juice |

Cream butter until light and fluffy. Blend in remaining ingredients, beating to a creamy smooth consistency.

## WHITE RABBITS AND MARCH HARES

Once again, the basic ice cream ball is the perfect party dessert because it can be transformed into any type of animal. With the help of coconut jelly beans and paper ears, vanilla and chocolate ice cream become the White Rabbit and the March Hare. What better way to celebrate an "un-birthday"!

PREPARATION TIME: 30 MINUTES

| 1 pint vanilla ice cream |
| --- |
| 1 pint chocolate ice cream |
| 2 cups flaked coconut |
| 1 tablespoon unsweetened cocoa powder |
| 36 pink jelly beans |
| 36 cupcake liners (pink, white, or red) |
| Pink poster board or heavy construction paper |

Cut pink poster board or pink heavy construction paper into 24 ears according to pattern on page 181. Crease along fold line; set aside.

Working with one flavor of ice cream at a time, scoop each pint into 6 ice cream balls. Return to freezer while you prepare coconut.

Divide coconut in half. Combine one half with cocoa in a small bowl; use a fork and stir until coconut is completely tinted a rich chocolate color, then transfer mixture to a dish or pie plate. Put white coconut in another dish or pie plate. Roll chocolate ice cream balls in chocolate coconut, and vanilla ice cream balls in white coconut. Place each ice cream ball on a flattened cupcake liner. Use jelly beans for eyes and nose—remember that a rabbit's eyes are slightly on the side of its head. Insert ears and return to freezer until serving time.

## PINK PEPPERMINT FLAMINGO MERINGUES

The Queen played croquet with pink flamingos for mallets—very unconventional. This meringue version of pink flamingos takes a little patience, but the results are exquisite. The real secret is in leaving them alone while they bake! That means keeping the oven door shut for 8 hours.

PREPARATION TIME: 35 TO 40 MINUTES
BAKING TIME (FOR MERINGUES):
  8 HOURS
COOLING TIME (FOR
MERINGUES): 2 HOURS

| 6 egg whites |
| ½ teaspoon cream of tartar |
| 1½ cups plus 6 tablespoons superfine sugar |
| Red food coloring |
| ¼ cup chocolate-flavored morsels (see note) |
| Peppermint Cream (recipe follows) |

Preheat oven to 200°F.

Beat egg whites and cream of tartar until foamy (almost soft peaks). Gradually beat in the 1½ cups sugar, 1 tablespoon at a time. Continue beating at high speed until meringue forms stiff, glossy peaks (about 20–35 minutes, or until very stiff).

Beat in enough food coloring to tint meringue a delicate shade of pink. Gently fold in the 6 tablespoons superfine sugar (do not overmix, or you'll deflate meringue). Line 2 baking sheets with parchment paper. (This is an absolute *must*; nothing else can be substituted.) Fit a large pastry bag with a *large* round writing nozzle; fill with meringue. On one baking sheet pipe 24 egg-shaped ovals. On the second sheet, pipe 24 S-shaped necks (you'll only need 12 necks, but because they're very fragile some will break).

Place 2 oven racks evenly spaced in the center of the oven, with at least 5 inches between. Put the sheet with ovals on the rack above the sheet of S shapes. Bake at 200° to 225°F (somewhere in between) for 8 hours. (The easiest way is to just do it overnight.) Turn off oven and allow meringue to cool in oven for 2 hours.

Remove sheets from the oven, and *very gently* loosen shapes from the parchment paper with a thin metal spatula, so as not to break meringue. Melt chocolate-flavored baking chips over very hot (not boiling) water. Use a small paint brush to paint chocolate eyes and beak on S-shaped necks to create a flamingo face (fig. 8a).

Fill a pastry bag fitted with a large star-tip nozzle with the peppermint cream. Use to sandwich a neck between the 2 ovals that form each body (fig. 8b). Refrigerate until serving time.

Note: Do not refrigerate assembled flamingos longer than 24 hours. However, meringue shapes can be baked ahead of time, in dry weather, and stored in an airtight container for several weeks.

Note: Chocolate-flavored morsels are preferred to real chocolate morsels because they will not "bloom" when melted and rehardened. Because the cocoa butter has been replaced with palm kernel oil, gray discoloration and streaking don't occur.

## PEPPERMINT CREAM

| 1½ cups heavy cream |
| --- |
| ½ cup confectioners sugar |
| 1 teaspoon peppermint extract |
| Red food coloring (optional) |

Whip cream, confectioners sugar, peppermint extract, and 2 drops of red food coloring until stiff peaks form.

## "EAT ME" TEA CAKES

Throughout the story of *Alice in Wonderland*, Alice is constantly tempted into consuming something that causes her to change size. When Alice takes a bite from that infamous cake marked EAT ME, she literally grows into a house.

The tea cakes, pale pink in color, may be decorated with either white or red writing. It's really a matter of personal preference. Contrast is important and really depends on the shade of pink that you tinted the dough.

(a)

(b)

fig. 8

PREPARATION TIME: 25 MINUTES
CHILLING TIME: 1 HOUR
BAKING TIME: 20 TO 25 MINUTES

| 1 cup butter, softened |
| 2/3 cup confectioners sugar |
| 1 teaspoon vanilla extract |
| 2 cups flour |
| 1/4 teaspoon salt |
| Red food coloring |
| Decorator's Icing (recipe follows) |
| 24 cupcake liners (pink, white, or silver) |

Cream butter, sugar, and vanilla extract until light and fluffy. Blend in flour and salt. Beat in enough red food coloring to tint dough an appetizing shade of pale pink. Shape dough into a log or cylinder about 2 inches in diameter. Roll up in wax paper and chill about 1 hour, just until slightly firm.

Preheat oven to 350°F. Line twenty-four 2½-inch muffin cups with cupcake liners.

Slice dough into 24 equal sections. Place each round in a lined muffin cup. Press on dough lightly with bottom of a small glass (about the same size as the muffin cup). This will help even the surface and push dough into the crevices of the cupcake liner. Bake 20 to 25 minutes. (Don't overbake; they should never brown.) Cool completely.

Fit a small pastry bag with a round writing tip; fill with icing. Write EAT ME on top of each tea cake.

## DECORATOR'S ICING

| 1 cup confectioners sugar |
| ½ teaspoon vanilla extract |
| 1 to 2 tablespoons milk or light cream |
| Red food coloring (optional) |

Blend sugar and vanilla with enough milk to make a smooth, creamy icing. If desired, tint icing red with food coloring.

## "DRINK ME" TEA

Alice chased the White Rabbit down a hole and found herself in a strange room, face to face with a curious bottle labeled DRINK ME. She took one sip and shrank into one of the best loved children's stories. For an authentic adventure in Wonderland, a tea party should begin with little bottles of DRINK ME tea.

PREPARATION TIME: 15 MINUTES
CHILLING TIME: AT LEAST 1 HOUR

| 4 quarts water |
| 16 tea bags |
| ½ cup lemon juice |
| 4 cinnamon sticks |
| 1/3 cup honey |
| 1/3 cup sugar |
| 2 tablespoons vanilla extract |
| "Drink Me" Bottles (directions follow) |

Bring water, tea bags, lemon juice, cinnamon sticks, honey, and sugar to a boil. Remove from heat and let stand 5 minutes. Remove cinnamon sticks and stir in vanilla. Pour tea into two 2-quart pitchers and chill until ice cold.

Just before serving, pour tea into bottles, using a funnel. Keep the second pitcher of tea chilled for refills.

## "DRINK ME" BOTTLES

| 12 Perrier bottles (6½ ounces each) |
| --- |
| 6 plain white cards (3 x 5 inches each) |
| Pink felt-tip marker |
| Pink ribbon |

Soak bottles in warm sudsy water until labels come off. Rinse and dry. Cut each card into two 3 x 2½-inch cards and punch a hole in the corner of each. Use marker to draw a border around card and print the words DRINK ME. String ribbons through the holes in cards and tie one, with a bow, around neck of each bottle.

# A BIRTHDAY CIRCUS

**E**very child has a secret desire to join the circus and swing from a trapeze, walk a tightrope, and tame the lions. When the circus comes to town, it's time to pitch a tent (indoors or out) and have a birthday under the Big Top.

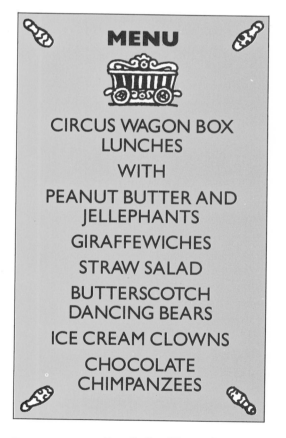

## MENU

CIRCUS WAGON BOX LUNCHES

WITH

PEANUT BUTTER AND JELLEPHANTS

GIRAFFEWICHES

STRAW SALAD

BUTTERSCOTCH DANCING BEARS

ICE CREAM CLOWNS

CHOCOLATE CHIMPANZEES

**FEATURES:** Bar Bells, Clown Ruffs, Clown Hats, Three-Ring Circus

**SIDE SHOW ACTS:** Tightrope Walking, Lion Tamer, Trained Seals

**INVITATIONS:** Free admission to your special circus

## INVITATIONS

Send your guests tickets to your birthday circus party. This is such a simple invitation to make. All you really do is photocopy tickets onto colored paper, cut them apart, and mail them. Many copy centers (or your local library) will be glad to open their machine and insert your 8½ x 11-inch colored paper. They may even have colored paper available that you can use.

12 INVITATIONS
PREPARATION TIME: 45 MINUTES

2 sheets (8½ x 11 inches each) typing paper

Pink, blue, or green 8½ x 11-inch paper—1 sheet for every 2 invitations

Black felt-tip marker

Regular letter-size envelopes

Ruler, typewriter (optional)

Every envelope contains 4 tickets as follows:

*Free Admission* BIRTHDAY
CIRCUS PARTY
*[Address, date, time, phone, regrets or R.S.V.P.]*

*Free refreshments* GOOD FOR ALL
CONCESSIONS
*Unlimited Use*
*Not Valid After [date of party]*

*Free makeup* GOOD FOR CLOWN PAINT,
HAT, AND RUFF
*Please Retain Ticket*
*Present at Makeup Tent*

*Free sideshow* TIGHTROPE, LION
TAMER, AND TRAINED
SEAL ACTS
*Please Retain Ticket*
*Present at Sideshow Tent*

Every child receives a ticket for admission, food and refreshment, clown makeup, and sideshow acts. Tickets are to be presented at the door for admission, but this is strictly to create the circus spirit. Remember, if a preschooler shows up empty handed, it's not a big deal. Have some spare tickets ready to pass around.

Fold typing paper lengthwise in half, into a 4½ x 11-inch strip. Then fold in half crosswise (to 4½ x 5 inches), then fold again (to 4¼ x 2¾ inches). Unfold paper and you should have eight 4¼ x 2¾-inch sections. Mark off sections with a ruler and pen, making "scrolly" lines around the borders of tickets. Type or write in the 4 varieties of tickets. Photocopy enough tickets onto colored paper so that you have one page for every 2 children. Cut tickets apart and include the correct combination of tickets in each envelope.

## DECORATIONS/HATS

The best circuses are always held in a tent. The aura of The Big Top is much more glamorous than an auditorium. Creating a tent indoors or out really depends on how large you want to make it and what materials are available to you. The cheapest and most colorful tent materials you can find are paper party tablecloths. The largest sizes are the best because you won't have to do a lot of taping together. Bright colors and stripes are the most effective. Some people seem to have a surplus of bed sheets and don't mind hanging them up all over the house or the backyard. However, plain white sheets can be a little drab unless they are perked up with plenty of balloons and streamers. As with tablecloths, colored or striped sheets make the best tents.

Indoors, you can drape your tent from 4 sides of the wall, gathering in the middle from a lighting fixture or chandelier (which is also an excellent place to hang balloons from). Or, you can

*Butterscotch Dancing Bears (recipe pages 67-69)*

*Ice Cream Clowns (recipe pages 69-70)*

stretch a rope of clothesline under the tablecloth or sheet "pup-tent" style. Outdoors, decorations are usually handled in the latter fashion. The clothesline can be strung from post to post or tree to tree. Use stakes and string to anchor the sides down (fig. 1a). If you're short on tent material, a small tent can simply canopy the top of the party table (fig. 1b).

The soda stand is an essential entertainment element to this party. Children use their refreshment tickets to purchase cold sodas and receive chocolate coins for their change. The stand can be made from any large box covered with striped wrapping paper. A paper awning can be placed over the top, supported by covered wrapping-paper tubes (fig. 1c).

Peanuts and popcorn can be "sold" from a portable stand strapped around the neck of a child or parent. A large traylike box is covered with striped paper and has a long strap of sturdy ribbon tied through 2 ends (fig. 1d). Fill the box with cups of peanuts and caramel corn.

A trapeze and fishnets can also be suspended from ceilings or the roof of the tent. Wrapping-paper tubes covered with paper and swinging from streams of ribbon make a perfect trapeze.

Set up table like a "Three-Ring Circus," using a large round platter for each dessert. You can even make a poster-board wall, 2 inches high, around platters. Make Clown Ruffs and Clown Hats (instructions follow) for the guests.

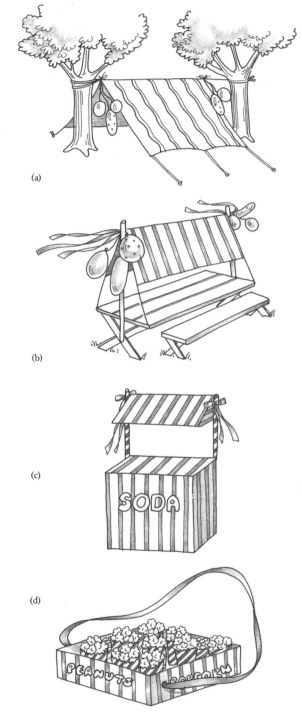

(a)

(b)

(c)

(d)

fig. 1

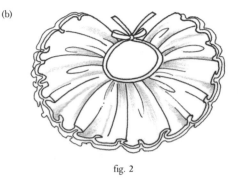

## CLOWN RUFFS

(b)

Crêpe paper ruffs are gathered onto ribbon bands that tie around each child's neck. They can easily be whipped up on a sewing machine with a long basting stitch.

fig. 2

PREPARATION TIME: 1 HOUR

2 packages (20 sheets each) 20 x 30-inch yellow crêpe paper

12 strips (36 inches each) ¾-inch-wide ribbon

Sewing machine threaded with yellow thread

Use 3 sheets of crêpe paper, stacked together, for each ruff. Fold sheets in half lengthwise into a 10 x 30-inch strip. Crease. Unfold sheets and baste down the center of crease using long stitch on sewing machine. Gather crêpe paper until center measures 12 inches. Center ruff on a strip of ribbon, allowing 12-inch streamers on each side. Sew in place with 2 rows of normal machine stitching about ½ inch apart (fig. 2a). Repeat with remaining paper and ribbon.

(You'll have 4 sheets left over; use them for the hat pompons on the next page.) Tie each ruff around a child's neck with a big bow at the back (fig. 2b).

## CLOWN HATS

These are made of poster board cones, crowned with crêpe-paper pompons. Mask bands help to keep the clown hats on the "clown" heads.

PREPARATION TIME: 1¼ HOURS

3 sheets (20 x 30 inches each) poster board (1 red, 1 green, 1 blue)

3 sheets (20 x 30 inches each) yellow crêpe paper

2 sheets (9 x 12 inches each) yellow construction paper

12 pipe cleaners

12 mask bands

Scissors, stapler, Scotch tape, glue or paste, hole punch

Cut 2 circles 15 inches in diameter out of each poster board. Cut each circle into 2 semicircles. (Each

(a)

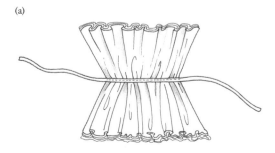

fig. 2

board will yield 4 hats.) Roll semicircles into cones, adjusting to the size of your child's head, and staple in place. Take a sheet of crêpe paper and roll into a 20-inch-long, tight "log." Cut into 4 pieces at 5-inch intervals. Twist a pipe cleaner around the middle of each 5-inch section. Fold in half, spreading ends open like a tuft or pompon (fig. 3a). Cut a small tip from end of each hat, making a hole to pull pompon base through. Insert pompon through hole. Anchor in place from inside of hat, using tape. Repeat with remaining crêpe paper and hats.

Cut 36 circles 1½ inches in diameter out of yellow construction paper. Paste a row of 3 "buttons" down front of each hat. Punch holes at base on each side, and string with mask bands (fig. 3b).

(a)

(b)

fig. 3

## CIRCUS WAGON BOX LUNCHES

In these box lunches on wheels, circus wagons are filled with sandwiches cut into the shapes of circus animals and buckets of "straw" salad, all resting on beds of snowy popcorn or crunchy potato chips—and the circus wagons double as take-home toys. If you don't happen to have a dozen empty shoeboxes for the wagons, just ask around. You'll probably discover that one of your neighbors is a chronic collector with a whole closetful.

As for the sandwiches, unlike those filled with mayonnaise-based spreads or with raw vegetables like lettuce and tomatoes, these are designed with freezability in mind. If you decide to prepare them in advance and store them in the freezer, wrap them tightly with plastic wrap. Place a few slices of fresh apple or orange on the tray to help sandwiches retain their moisture.

To make the sandwiches, you'll need to locate an elephant and a giraffe cookie cutter. This shouldn't be at all difficult. There are menageries of cookie cutters now available in most cookware shops, cake and party shops, as well as department stores. Look for sturdy metal cutters with sharp enough edges to cut and not "mash" bread. When selecting bread, you'll probably find that the animals don't quite fit standard slices. Look for a bakery that will put whole loaves of unsliced bread

on their slicing machine *lengthwise*. You will also notice that it takes more bread to make cut-out sandwiches than you usually plan on for feeding 12 children. This is because of all the "waste" that is unused. However, scraps can always find their way into homemade bread crumbs and croutons.

PREPARATION TIME: 1 HOUR 15
  MINUTES

| 12 shoeboxes |
| --- |
| Striped wrapping paper |
| 48 very small (4–5 inches), colored paper cocktail plates (If you can't find any, substitute 48 circles 4 inches in diameter cut from poster board) |
| 48 brads |
| 4 to 8 yards thick colored yarn |
| Scotch tape, scissors, hole punch |

Remove lids from boxes and wrap boxes with paper and Scotch tape so the tops remain open (fig. 4a).

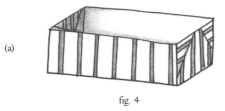

(a)

fig. 4

Punch brads through centers of plates or "wheels" and insert near the bottom corners of each box. Punch a well-centered hole at one end of every box. Cut twelve 12-inch lengths of yarn. Tie a knot in one end. String yarn through

hole in each box, then tie a knot in the other end (fig. 4b). (This makes a pull for the circus wagon.)

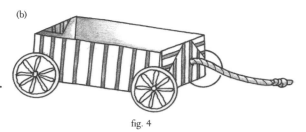

(b)

fig. 4

## INSTANT INVOLVEMENT

Set up some kind of ticket booth at the front door. (A card table, draped with a bright paper tablecloth and a box marked TICKETS, is just fine.) As soon as a child arrives, tell him or her to give you the admission ticket and keep the rest. If the child doesn't have a ticket, give the child an assortment from your "spare ticket reserve." Have your child and any early guests usher newcomers to the Makeup Tent—a room or other area you've set aside—to have their faces made up as circus clowns and be issued clown ruffs and hats. The makeup should be undertaken by a parent or adult assistant, with some makeup skills, who is also made up like a clown. If too many children arrive at once, there may be a little "backup." Pass out paper and crayons, asking children how they'd like to see themselves look. Toddlers may scribble something totally unrecognizable as a face, but their efforts should be acknowledged by questions like "Oh, what color

are your eyes?" or "Is that a red or blue nose?" Try to accommodate each child's expression of individuality in his or her makeup request.

## GAMES

Any of these games are suitable for very young children. Balancing and jumping skills may not have fully developed yet, but even toddlers are anxious to try. Invite the children into a special area designated as the Side Show, and let the circus acts begin. Calliope music, which is available from your children's public library on sound effects records, adds a lot of atmosphere to the fun.

## TIGHTROPE WALKING

Here each child takes turns walking down an eight foot two by four board. It's a balancing act, and if the child falls off (which is a 2-inch drop), he or she is out. The game progresses until only one child is left.

## LION TAMER

This game is similar to Simon Says. The Lion Tamer is like Simon, and the other children sit up in a ring of chairs like a lion act. The lions must do whatever Lion Tamer says unless "Lion Tamer says" isn't said first. Then, whichever child completes the action, erroneously, becomes the next Lion Tamer.

## TRAINED SEALS

In this game children take turns jumping through a hula hoop. The hoop is progressively raised after each round. If one child knocks down the hoop, he or she automatically becomes the hoop holder, and the game starts over again with the hoop held at ground level.

## RECIPES

### PEANUT BUTTER AND JELLEPHANTS

PREPARATION TIME: 30 MINUTES

| |
|---|
| 2 loaves of white bread, sliced lengthwise |
| 1 jar (16 ounces) peanut butter, smooth or chunky |
| 1½ cups strawberry jam |
| 2 packages (8 ounces each) cream cheese, softened |
| Red food coloring (optional) |
| 12 to 16 raisins (for eyes) |
| Elephant cookie cutter |

Using your elephant cookie cutter, cut as many elephants as you can from the bread slices. You should be able to get anywhere from 24 to 36 cutouts. Place half of the elephants on a work surface or tray, facing them all in the same direction. Spread a layer of peanut butter on each one. Place the other half of the elephants on a work surface or tray, facing the *opposite* direction. Spread a layer of strawberry jam on each one, reserving ½ cup. Sandwich peanut butter- and jam-sided elephants together.

Beat cream cheese and reserved ½ cup of jam together until smooth and fluffy. If desired, tint with a few drops of red food coloring to achieve a deeper shade of pink. Fit a pastry bag with a large round writing tip; fill with the cream cheese mixture. (Using a pastry bag in this manner makes the spread much easier to apply—no broken trunks or legs!) Pipe the cheese mixture on the surface of sandwiches. Gently smooth over ridges with a spatula. Now you can go back and use the writing tip to decorate ears and trunks. Use raisins for eyes.

## GIRAFFEWICHES

PREPARATION TIME: 30 MINUTES

| 2 loaves whole-wheat, rye, or pumpernickel bread, sliced lengthwise |
| --- |
| 1 container (16 ounces) cold-pack cheddar cheese spread, softened |
| 2 packages (8 ounces each) cream cheese, softened |
| ¼ cup pimientos, drained |
| 1 teaspoon onion powder |
| 1 can (16 ounces) pitted jumbo ripe olives, drained |
| Giraffe cookie cutter |

Using your giraffe cookie cutter, cut as many giraffes as you can from the bread slices. You should be able to get anywhere from 24 to 36 cutouts. Put cheddar cheese, cream cheese, pimientos, and onion powder in the bowl of a food processor. Process until mixture is very smooth and soft. Fit a pastry bag with a large writing tip; fill with cheese mixture. Place half the giraffes on a work surface or tray, facing them all in the same direction. Pipe a layer of cheese, completely covering surface of giraffes. Sandwich together with remaining halves of giraffes. (You should have about 12 to 18 sandwiches, all lined up and facing the same direction). Pipe rest of cheese on top of sandwiches, completely covering surface. Smooth with a spatula. Slice olives into "rings." Arrange slices on giraffes to resemble large spots. Use a chunk of olive for each eye.

## STRAW SALAD

This vegetable slaw of yellow squash will remind children of buckets of straw. What else would you feed a circus wagon full of Peanut Butter and Jellephants and Giraffewiches?

PREPARATION TIME: 25 MINUTES

| 4 large yellow summer squash |
| --- |
| 2 carrots, peeled |
| 1 teaspoon prepared mustard |
| ½ teaspoon onion salt |
| 1 tablespoon white or tarragon vinegar |
| 1 tablespoon sugar |

| ¼ cup mayonnaise |
| --- |
| ¼ cup sour cream |
| 12 large (3-ounce size) nut cups or aluminum foil soufflé-type cups |
| 12 colored pipe cleaners |

Split squash in half lengthwise and scoop out seeds. Grate into long shreds. Grate carrots in long shreds, too. Combine mustard, onion salt, vinegar, sugar, mayonnaise, and sour cream. Toss dressing, squash, and carrots together in a large bowl. (This can be prepared a day in advance and refrigerated overnight.) Pierce holes on each side of nut cups and fasten pipe cleaners through them to resemble bucket handles. Just before serving, fill cups with salad and place alongside sandwiches in circus wagons.

## TO FILL CIRCUS WAGONS

| 1 to 2 quarts popped but unbuttered popcorn or 1 large bag potato chips |
| --- |
| Peanut Butter and Jellephants, Giraffewiches, Straw Salads (recipes on pages 65 and 66) |
| Celery sticks or scallion "barbells" (3-inch sections of scallion with a pitted ripe olive at each end) |
| Aluminum foil |
| 12 large paper napkins |
| 8 yards thick colored yarn (optional) |

Line bottom and sides of each box with a piece of foil, followed by a large paper napkin. Make a 1-inch layer of unbuttered popcorn or potato chips across the bottom. Rest a Peanut Butter and Jellephant and a Giraffewich on top, with a bucket of Straw Salad nestled alongside. Garnish with celery sticks or scallion "barbells" (scallion sticks with pitted ripe olives on both ends).

If you wish, make a "yarn cage" for tops of boxes after you fill them. (This treatment is very effective, but can become tedious for large parties. Yarn is strung through slits in the side of each box, stretching across the top like bars of a cage. Children simply "unlace" the yarn to reach their lunch.) Cut yarn into 24-inch lengths. Cut about 8 equally spaced gashes, ½ inch deep, along both sides of each box. Fill boxes as described. Tie a knot at one end of each piece of yarn, and string across top from slot to slot. Tie end of yarn securely with a knot and trim excess.

## BUTTERSCOTCH DANCING BEARS

Cream-puff dough is used to create these incredibly cute pastries. It's hard to believe anything that looks this complicated isn't. One word of warning—some children may mistake them for teddy bears and take them home to bed!

PREPARATION TIME: 1 HOUR 15 MINUTES

BAKING TIME: 35 MINUTES

| 1½ cups water |
| --- |
| ¾ cup butter |
| 1½ cups flour |
| 6 eggs |
| Peanut Brittle Filling (recipe follows) |
| Butterscotch Glaze (recipe follows) |
| ⅓ cup chocolate-flavored chips (see note on page 56) |

(a)

(b)

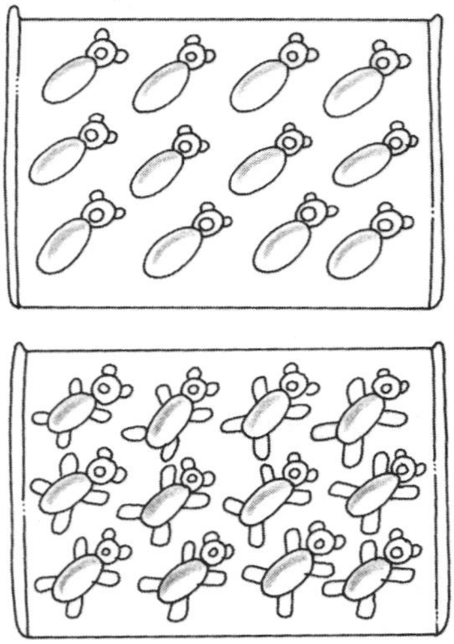

fig. 5

Preheat oven to 400°F.

In a large saucepan, bring water and butter to a boil. When butter melts, remove saucepan from heat and add flour all at once. Return saucepan to heat and beat with a wire whisk until dough forms a ball. Remove from heat and beat in eggs, one at a time, with wire whip or electric mixer. Dough should be smooth and lump free. Spoon dough into a very large pastry bag fitted with a large writing tip. On a large baking sheet, pipe 12 well-spaced "egg shapes" (about 3 x 1½ inches). Smooth any ridges with a spatula. Pipe a large "blob" for each head, and small "blobs" for ears and noses (fig. 5a). Pipe arms and legs on bodies (fig. 5b). Bake for 35 minutes, or until puffed and golden. Cool completely, then carefully slice off "stomachs" (oooh—that sounds awful!) and remove any soft dough inside.

Fit another pastry bag with a large plain tip; fill with peanut brittle filling, and pipe into bears. Replace stomachs on bears, making sure you match the right stomach to the right bear. Spoon butterscotch glaze evenly over each bear, smoothing with a spatula. (Hold each bear over double boiler or bowl of glaze to catch "drips" while working). Set bears on a rack to dry.

When glaze hardens, melt chocolate over hot water (or for 2 minutes in the microwave). Use a paint brush to paint chocolate eyes, noses, and mouths on bears. Chill until ready to serve.

Bears can be prepared 2 weeks in advance and frozen. If desired, you can pipe "tutus" on the bears with pink buttercream or decorator's frosting. Melt 2 ounces of white chocolate (or use white royal icing) and pipe on "whites" to the eyes before adding pupils (photo opposite page 60).

# PEANUT BRITTLE FILLING

| 2½ cups heavy cream |
| --- |
| 5 tablespoons dark brown sugar, firmly packed |

| 1 tablespoon vanilla extract |
| ½ cup finely crushed peanut brittle |

Beat cream with brown sugar and vanilla until stiff peaks form. (Do not overbeat or mixture will separate.) Fold in peanut brittle.

# BUTTERSCOTCH GLAZE

| 1 package (12 ounces) and 1 package (6 ounces) butterscotch morsels |
| 5 tablespoons corn or vegetable oil |

Place butterscotch morsels and oil in the top of a double boiler over hot tap water (never boiling). Let stand, covered, for 10 minutes, then stir until morsels are melted and mixture is smooth. (Butterscotch morsels may also be melted in a glass bowl in the microwave. Cook for 2½ minutes, stirring twice until melted.)

## ICE CREAM CLOWNS

This treatment of ice cream is such a classic that you're probably quite familiar with it by now. No wonder why it's so popular—nothing could be easier to prepare. Scoops of ice cream become the clown face, with an inverted cone for a hat. Tinted buttercream frosting is used to decorate hair and hats. Chocolate chips, licorice, and red cherries make funny faces.

PREPARATION TIME: 25 MINUTES

| 3 pints ice cream (choose your child's favorite flavors) |
| 12 sugar cones |
| Buttercream Frosting (recipe follows) |
| Chocolate chips |
| Red licorice laces |
| 12 red candied cherries |
| Colored paper cupcake liners |

Scoop out 12 balls of ice cream, and place each ball on a spread-open cupcake liner. Place inverted cones on top of ice cream balls, tipped back at a slight angle. Place balls on a tray and return to freezer while preparing frosting.

Using pastry bags fitted with star tips, pipe orange hair on clowns. Pipe yellow or blue ruffs around base of each head and hat. Pipe yellow or blue pompons on hats. Press chocolate chips into ice cream for eyes, cherries for noses, and pieces of licorice laces for mouths (see photo opposite page 61). Return clowns to freezer until serving time.

Note: These may be frozen up to 2 weeks in advance.

# BUTTERCREAM FROSTING

| 4 tablespoons butter, softened |
| ¼ cup milk |
| 1 pound confectioners sugar |
| ¼ teaspoon salt |
| 1 teaspoon vanilla |
| Food coloring |

Cream butter until light and fluffy. Blend in milk and half of sugar. Add remaining sugar, salt, and vanilla. Beat until smooth. Divide frosting into thirds and tint one part orange, one part blue, and one part yellow.

## CHOCOLATE CHIMPANZEES

Chocolate-dipped frozen bananas are a favorite among children. Imagine their enthusiasm when the bananas become monkeys!

PREPARATION TIME: 30 MINUTES
FREEZING TIME: ABOUT 1 HOUR

| |
|---|
| 1 package (12 ounces) chocolate-flavored morsels (see note on page 56) |
| 3 tablespoons vegetable oil |
| 6 large bananas, unpeeled |
| Sliced almonds (24 slices) |
| 12 miniature marshmallows, split in half |

Combine chocolate-flavored morsels with oil in top of double boiler. Place over very hot tap water (never boiling). Let stand, covered, for 10 to 15 minutes, then stir until chips are melted and mixture is smooth. (Chocolate can also be melted in a glass bowl in the microwave. Cook 2 to 3 minutes, stirring twice until chocolate is smooth and melted (do not overheat).

Slice bananas crosswise in half, then cut completely through skin (but not the banana) all the way around, about 1½ inches from each end. Peel skin away from each end to where skin was scored with knife (fig. 6a). Insert 2 almond slices on each side of end to look like ears. Dip ends of bananas in chocolate, allowing chocolate to cover some of the peel. Allow to harden for several minutes.

Think of the bananas as "monkeys," with the face the side of the banana curving backwards. Use a small paintbrush dipped in chocolate to "glue" marshmallow halves to face for eyes. Dot

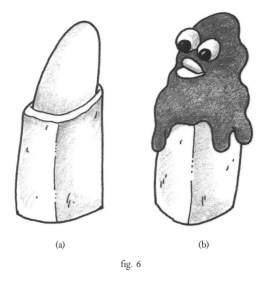

(a)                    (b)

fig. 6

marshmallows with chocolate for pupils. Cut a mouth into banana (fig. 6b). Stand in freezer until firm, at least 1 hour.

Note: These can be prepared several days in advance.

**AGE: 3–7**

# BEATRIX POTTER EASTER BRUNCH

Peter Rabbit is probably the world's best-loved bunny. This Easter brunch features Peter and all his friends from Beatrix Potter's timeless tales.

## MENU

### PETER RABBIT PEARS

### "RABBIT EGGS" IN EASTER BASKETS

### BENJAMIN BUNNY BISCUITS WITH STRAWBERRY BUTTER

### FLOPSY, MOPSY, AND COTTON-TAIL CAKES

### PUDDLE-DUCK ICE CREAM

### JUICE BAR

**FEATURES:** Henny Penny Hand Puppets, Assorted Animal Ears, Egg Baskets

**GAMES:** Mr. McGregor's Garden, The Roly-Poly Pudding, The Pie and the Patty Pan

**INVITATIONS:** *The Tale of Peter Rabbit* storybook

## INVITATIONS

These invitations are very similar to the storybook cards for the Mother Goose Party, only they're Beatrix Potter books with Peter Rabbit on the covers.

12 INVITATIONS
PREPARATION TIME: 1 HOUR 15 MINUTES

| |
|---|
| 12 sheets (9 x 12 inches each) pale yellow construction paper |
| 1 sheet (8½ x 11 inches) typing paper, for photocopies |
| 3 sheets (9 x 12 inches each) brown construction paper for Peter Rabbit cutouts |

| Materials |
| --- |
| 1 sheet (9 x 12 inches) blue construction paper for jacket cutouts |
| 1 sheet (9 x 12 inches) orange construction paper for carrot cutouts |
| 4 cotton balls |
| Green and black felt-tip markers |
| ¼-inch-wide ribbon, or use curling ribbon, green or blue (to match jacket) |
| 12 envelopes that will accommodate a 4½ x 6-inch card |
| Scissors, glue or paste, stapler |

Fold sheets of yellow paper in half to 9 x 6 inches. Fold again, like a book, to 4½ x 6 inches; folds should be on the left and across the top. Cut out 12 Peter Rabbits from brown paper (see pattern, page 183). Paste a rabbit on front of each card, centered about 1 inch from bottom (fig. 1a). Cut out jackets from the blue paper (see pattern, page 183) and paste a jacket on each rabbit. Cut out 12 "carrots" from the orange paper (see pattern, page 183) and paste a carrot in each rabbit's paw.

Pull each cotton ball apart into 3 smaller sections and wad up into

---

(first page)

Once upon a time there were five little rabbits, and their names were . . . .

Flopsy

Mopsy

Cottontale

Peter

and [Your child's name].

[Your child's name] thought it would be great fun to have a big party and invite all of their friends. Peter agreed and said:

"Let's talk to Beatrix Potter, she always knows what to do."

(second page)

So, [Your Child's name] and Peter went to Miss Potter's house and asked for her permission to have a party. She was delighted with the idea. . . .

"Why we'll have a brunch right in the middle of Mr. McGregor's garden, where there are plenty of good things to munch on. We can borrow some eggs from Henny Penny, Ribby can bake one of her patty-pan pies, and Benjamin Bunny can make the invitations."

And that's exactly what they did.

fold → lines

(third page)

(back)

Please join us for a

Beatrix Potter Brunch

at [time] on [date]

in

Mr. McGregor's Garden

[Your Address]

R.S.V.P.

[your phone number]

Sincerely,
Benjamin Bunny

balls (you will have 12). Paste in place of a tail. Draw in detail with a black felt-tip marker; use a green felt-tip marker to make carrot "greens," a little grass around Peter Rabbit's feet, and to write across the top of the card THE TALE OF PETER RABBIT. Type or write invitation as on page 72. (Some pages will be upside down until folded. Do not draw dotted lines, or else they will be photocopied— they're simply guides for folding.)

Have 12 photocopies made of the page. Fold pages (print side out) in the same fashion as the book cover. Bind with 3 staples down the spine and the center page of the book. Cut ribbon into 12-inch lengths and tie across binding as shown (fig. 1b). Close books and slip into envelopes.

(a)

(b)

fig. 1

## DECORATIONS/HATS

Beatrix Potter's Easter Brunch should have elements from all of her stories in the decorations. Begin by blowing up "bunny balloons." Fill balloons with helium and tape lightweight paper rabbit ears to the top; draw on faces with a felt-tip marker. Tie balloons to the back of chairs. Recreate Mr. McGregor's garden indoors: Paint a white picket fence with poster paint on a roll of brown paper (long enough to go around the room). Paint vegetables along the fence. Make a cabbage patch in one section, add vining vegetables (peas, green beans, pumpkins and squash, and tomatoes) in another section. Root vegetables (carrots, radishes, beets, and potatoes) have only their green tops exposed. Label vegetable groups with seed packages glued to popsicle-stick stakes. Glue sticks directly against paper (fig. 2a).

At the center of attention is Jane and Lucinda's red brick doll house from *The Tale of Two Bad Mice.* This can be built from any size box you want. Cut away one side to expose the interior, like a doll house. Use additional sheets of cardboard (cut from another box) to add a roof and make room divisions. Cut out windows. Line the walls with a small print or striped wrapping paper. Furnish with real or paper doll furniture, paintings, and rugs (fig. 2b). For the exterior of the house, "cement" pink sugar wafer "bricks" against the cardboard with Royal Icing (recipe follows).

fig. 2

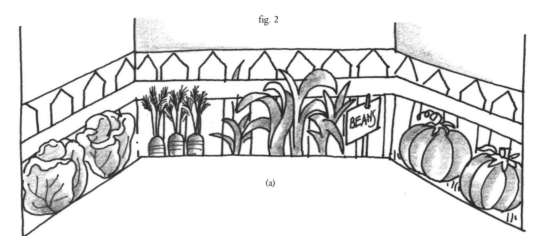

(a)

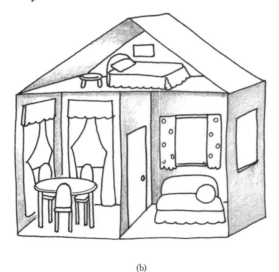

(b)

(c)

Use chocolate-covered sugar wafers for roof shingles and window shutters (fig. 2c). Now you have a house just waiting for Tom Thumb and Hunca Munca to mess up. Make "mouse marker" place tags just like them out of colored Easter eggs. Pierce each eggshell with colored pipe cleaners, making loops for ears and a long tail; draw on a face and whiskers with a felt-tip marker, and write the child's name on its side (fig. 2d).

(d)

## ROYAL ICING

| 6 egg whites |
| --- |
| 2 tablespoons lemon juice |
| 2 pounds confectioners sugar |

In a large mixing bowl (use an electric mixer), beat egg whites and lemon juice until foamy. Slowly beat in sugar. Continue beating until frosting forms very stiff peaks.

## ASSORTED ANIMAL EARS

Beatrix Potter's stories revolved around the lives of small animals. There were many interesting characters, from Mrs. Twiggy-Winkle the hedgehog to Jeremy Fisher the frog. There was even a Sir Isaac Newton the newt. However, the major protagonists tended to be rabbits, cats, and mice. For hats, you can provide an assortment of animal ears and the hat bands to attach them to. Ask the children when they arrive what animal they would like to be. Then, simply staple on the appropriate pair of ears.

PREPARATION TIME: 35 TO 40
MINUTES

| 3 brown, beige, or gray poster boards (20 x 30 inches each) (any of those colors will work for rabbits, cats, and mice) |
| --- |

| 2 sheets (20 x 30 inches each) pink construction paper or several sheets (9 x 12 inches each) pink construction paper |
| --- |
| Scissors, stapler, glue |

Cut one sheet of poster board into twelve 2 x 20-inch strips (use leftover poster board for ears). Cut remaining poster board into animal ears, according to pattern (see page 183; use rabbit ear pattern above dotted line for cat ears). (Use poster board as efficiently as possible to eliminate waste; you should be able to get anywhere from 8 to 12 pairs each of rabbit, cat, and mouse. There's really no predicting which will be the most popular when children are offered a choice. Undoubtedly, you'll be left with extras, because you have more ears than bands.) Cut ear linings out of pink paper (see patterns). Staple bands together, overlapping slightly, using your child's head to gauge measurement. Glue linings to insides of ears. When ready to assemble, staple ears at the base on the insides of bands (fig. 3).

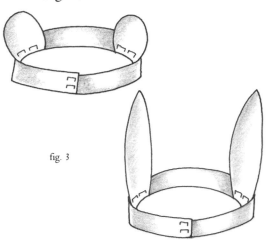

fig. 3

## INSTANT INVOLVEMENT

When the children arrive at the party, bring them into the chicken coop of Sally Henny Penny. In the center of a table, place about 2 or 3 dozen snowy white hard-cooked eggs in a large straw basket lined with Easter grass. Pass out an assortment of bright-colored watercolor markers and hen hand puppets. Each child can decorate eggs and their puppet at the same time, giving it feathers and wings.

PREPARATION TIME: 40 MINUTES

| |
| --- |
| 12 squares (12 inches each) of white felt |
| Black and red watercolor felt-tip markers |
| Scissors, fabric glue |

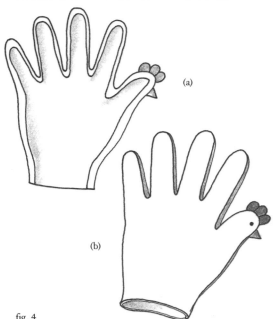

(a)

(b)

fig. 4

Have your child place his or her hand on a piece of paper, spreading fingers apart. Trace around hand. Draw an additional ⅝-inch seam around the traced line. Draw a beak and chicken comb at the thumb (fig. 4a). Use this as a pattern to cut out 24 felt shapes; you should get 2 to each square. Glue 2 together to form a sort of "glove" using a thin line of adhesive all around the edge. Let dry several hours to be sure the seams are good and set. Use a black marker to make eyes on each hen, and a red marker to make a comb (fig. 4b).

## GAMES

### MR. McGREGOR'S GARDEN

Peter Rabbit's and his cousin Benjamin Bunny's favorite form of entertainment was eating out of Mr. McGregor's garden. Sometimes he'd catch them, other times they'd get away, but they never stopped coming back for more. In this game, a large, shallow cardboard box becomes the vegetable patch. Naturally, the vegetable patch is filled with vegetables: carrots, cucumbers, potatoes, and celery stalks (about 2 dozen of each).

A volunteer is selected to be Mr. McGregor, who stands guard over the vegetable patch. The rest of the players form a large circle around Mr. McGregor, standing with their backs to him. At the sound of a

*"Rabbit Eggs" in Easter Baskets*

*Flopsy, Mopsy, and Cotton-Tail Cakes*

whistle (or a bell), the players turn around and rush toward the box and grab a vegetable. With vegetable now in hand, each player dashes back to his or her original place. Mr. McGregor tries to tag them as they flee. If one is caught, they must freeze in that spot. Once they return to their place, they're "safe." The "frozen" players must return their vegetables to the vegetable patch and go back empty-handed. The last player to be tagged must trade places with Mr. McGregor.

The game continues like this, until all of the vegetables have been raided from the box. The player with the most vegetables "stashed" away at their place becomes the victorious Peter Rabbit.

## THE ROLY-POLY PUDDING

Once upon a time there was an old cat called Mrs. Tabitha Twitchit, who was an anxious parent. She used to lose her kittens continually, and whenever they were lost, they were always in mischief!

On baking day she determined to shut them in the cupboard.

She caught Moppet and Mittens, but she could not find Tom.[1]

Tom Kitten was always into trouble. This time he was investigating the chimney when he was taken captive by 2 rats in the attic. Samuel Whiskers was an old

---

[1]Reprinted from THE BEATRIX POTTER GIANT TREASURY by Beatrix Potter. Copyright © 1984 by Crown Publishers, Inc. Used by permission of Derrydale Books, distributed by Crown Publishers, Inc.

fat rat and his wife, Anna Maria, was very skinny. They both decided that Tom would make a fine "kitten dumpling roly-poly pudding." After much preparation (tying up Tom and stealing butter and dough from the pantry), the rats were stopped (just in the nick of time) by Tabitha Twitchit, her cousin Ribby, and John Joiner (the carpenter dog).

The game follows a similar scenario. The children are divided into 2 teams of 6 players. Three players on each team assume the characters of Tom Kitten and the rats, Samuel Whiskers and Anna Maria. The other 3 players on both teams assume the characters of Tabitha Twitchit, her cousin Ribby, and John Joiner.

Each group of rats take "their" Tom Kitten to some hiding place where they intend to turn him into a "roly-poly pudding." Obviously, they'll have to hide in different hiding places. Meanwhile, 2 search parties form. Each consists of a Tabitha Twitchit, cousin Ribby, and John Joiner. The object of both search parties is to find "their" Tom Kitten first. In other words, the team that is first to reunite Tom with Tabitha Twitchit wins.

What happens if one team's search party finds the other team's Tom Kitten? Then they, too, become prisoners of the rats until they are freed by the other team's search party. The game progresses in this manner for as long as the children like; they can switch teams, change roles—even rewrite the plot.

# THE PIE AND THE PATTY PAN

A "patty pan" is one of those Edwardian English expressions that now needs translating. Most children (and adults) are baffled by this basic element in Beatrix Potter's story. Patty pans are tin funnels used to raise up the top crust in a meat pie, allowing the juices and steam to escape. In *The Pie and the Patty Pan*, Ribby, the cat, invites Duchess, the dog, over for tea and pie. Ribby is serving mouse and bacon pie, which Duchess dislikes intensely. Duchess decides to swap a veal and ham pie when Ribby isn't looking. The plot thickens when Duchess panics at the thought that she might have swallowed the patty pan (because she can't find it in the pie).

The game is similar to the old nutshell trick in a magician's act. A "patty pan" (you can just use a small, funnel-shaped pastry nozzle or cake-decorating tip) is placed under one of 3 inverted pie plates. A volunteer is selected to play the "shuffler." The players line up in front of the pie plates, which are on a smooth-surfaced table or floor. The shuffler sits behind the pie plates. The first player spins around in place 3 times. As long as the player is turning, the shuffler rearranges the pie plates. When the player comes to a stop, so does the shuffler. The player gets one chance to guess which pie plate the patty pan is hiding under. If the player is right, he or she is awarded another turn. But an incorrect guess results in the player taking the place of the shuffler, and the shuffler joins the end of the line.

The player who stays up the longest (for the most turns) is the winner.

## RECIPES

## PETER RABBIT PEARS

Peter Rabbit's mother could never keep Peter out of mischief and Mr. McGregor's garden. In this fresh pear salad he's even munching on a cheese carrot, straight out of the garden patch.

PREPARATION TIME: 20 MINUTES

| |
|---|
| 12 small ripe pears |
| Lemon juice |
| Raisins |
| Slivered almonds |
| 12 lettuce leaves or lettuce cups |
| 1 cup cottage cheese |
| 1 cube or chunk (6 to 8 ounces) of sharp (orange) cheddar cheese |
| 12 small fresh parsley sprigs |

Cut 2 lengthwise slices from bottom of each pear. Cut very bottom slices into V-shaped ears. (You won't be using second slices; they're just for leveling off bottom of pears.) Rub all exposed cut surfaces with lemon juice to retard browning. Cut a wedge-shaped

(a)

fig. 5

(b)

gash at base of each "head" and carve base of ears to fit notch (fig. 5a). Insert raisin eyes, nose, and almond whiskers.

Place pears on lettuce leaves and make "tails" with small scoops of cottage cheese. Make cheese carrots by cutting 1½ x ½-inch wedges of cheese that come to a point like a carrot and insert a parsley sprig in the back end for greens (fig. 5b).

Note: These shouldn't be prepared too long before serving or the pears will discolor.

## "RABBIT EGGS" IN EASTER BASKETS

"**G**olden Buck" or "Welsh rarebit" is often referred to in England as "rabbit." By any name, it's a dish consisting of a rich cheddar-cheese sauce. This rabbit is combined with eggs and served in an edible cream-puff Easter basket.

PREPARATION TIME: 40 MINUTES
BAKING TIME (FOR BASKETS): 35 MINUTES

| |
|---|
| ¼ cup butter |
| ¼ cup flour |
| ½ teaspoon onion salt |
| ½ teaspoon dry mustard |
| 1 teaspoon Worcestershire sauce |
| 1½ cups milk |
| 2 cups (8 ounces) shredded cheddar cheese |
| 12 hard-cooked eggs |
| Easter Baskets (recipe follows) |
| Fresh parsley sprigs |
| Paprika |

Melt butter in a large saucepan. Blend in flour, onion salt, mustard, and Worcestershire sauce. Cook over low heat, stirring constantly until smooth and bubbly. Blend in milk and cook, stirring, until sauce thickens. Stir in cheese, blending until it's smooth and melted. Slice eggs in half and remove yolks (set aside). Cut up egg whites into chunks or cubes (not too small) and fold into sauce.

Just before serving, gently reheat sauce in the top of a double boiler, or over very low heat. Spoon into baskets and line edges between filling and baskets with parsley sprigs (to resemble Easter grass). Crumble or grate egg yolks and sprinkle over filling. Top each with a dash of paprika. When serving, advise children to remove toothpicks and then collect them to avoid accidents.

## EASTER BASKETS

| 1 cup butter |
| --- |
| 2 cups water |
| 2 cups flour |
| 8 eggs |

Preheat oven to 400°F. Butter twelve 6- to 8-ounce custard cups and place in freezer so that dough will adhere to sides (this only takes a few minutes). (Many people don't have 12 custard cups. If you are one of them just bake baskets in 2 batches and reuse your set.)

Bring butter and water to a rolling boil in a large saucepan. Add flour and beat vigorously with a wire whisk over medium heat until mixture forms a ball. Remove from heat and beat in eggs with an electric mixer until smooth. Place about 2 heaping tablespoons of dough in each chilled custard cup and spread evenly with a metal spatula, coating sides completely.

Fit a pastry bag with a large round tip; fill with remaining dough. Pipe 12 or more (in case of breakage) U-shaped ribbons of dough for basket handles on a very *lightly* greased baking sheet. Bake baskets 35 minutes, handles 20 minutes. Cool slightly.

Carefully slide spatula under handles to remove from sheet. Lift baskets out of custard cups. Attach handles to baskets with toothpicks.

Note: These may be prepared a day ahead, wrapped in foil and rewarmed in a low oven before filling.

## BENJAMIN BUNNY BISCUITS

Benjamin Bunny was Peter Rabbit's cousin and accomplice to Peter's regular raids on Mr. McGregor's garden. The 2 were quite close, so it's only natural to serve Benjamin Bunny Biscuits with Peter Rabbit Pears. The beauty of this traditional cream biscuit dough is that you can throw aside a pastry blender and rolling pin. All you do is stir and shape.

PREPARATION TIME: 20 MINUTES
BAKING TIME: 12 TO 15 MINUTES

| 4 cups flour |
| --- |
| 1 teaspoon salt |
| 2 tablespoons baking powder |
| ½ cup plus 2 tablespoons sugar |
| 2¼ cups heavy cream |
| 6 tablespoons butter, melted |
| 1 tablespoon ground cinnamon |

| 3 candied cherries, quartered |
| Raisins |
| Slivered almonds |
| Strawberry Butter (recipe follows) |

Preheat oven to 425°F. Combine flour, salt, baking powder, and sugar in a mixing bowl. Stir in cream, mixing just until dough holds together (add a tablespoon or more of cream only if dough seems very dry and crumbly—flours differ). Place dough on a floured surface and gently knead about 1 minute. Pat dough out to a thickness of about ½ to ¾ inches and cut with a 2-inch round cutter into 24 circles.

Cut 12 circles into semicircles (for ears). Spread ears apart in a V shape on a baking sheet lined with foil (shiny side down). Be sure to allow at least 2 inches between biscuits. Moisten lower ends of ears and place circles on top of moistened portion, pressing together. Brush biscuits with melted butter. Mix sugar and cinnamon together and sprinkle over biscuits; press raisin eyes, cherry nose, and almond whiskers firmly into place (fig. 6). Bake for 12 to 15 minutes, or until light golden. Lift biscuits off foil very *carefully* (ears break off easily). Serve warm with strawberry butter, piped into halves of empty egg shells or small ramekins.

Note: These can be prepared in advance, wrapped tightly in plastic wrap, and frozen. Defrost before baking, or increase baking time.

fig. 6

## STRAWBERRY BUTTER

| ½ cup strawberry preserves |
| 1 cup butter, softened |
| 1 tablespoon confectioners sugar |
| 12 empty eggshell halves or small ramekins |

Beat strawberry preserves, butter, and sugar together until light and fluffy. Fit a pastry bag with a star-tipped nozzle; fill with strawberry butter. Pipe into eggshell halves or ramekins and serve alongside biscuits.

## FLOPSY, MOPSY, AND COTTON-TAIL CAKES

The famous siblings of Peter Rabbit are here in a trio of coconut cakes: Flopsy is fluffy and white, Mopsy is mocha, and Cotton-Tail is caramel.

PREPARATION TIME: 1¼ HOURS

BAKING TIME: 30 TO 35 MINUTES

| |
|---|
| 1¾ cups sugar |
| ⅔ cup butter, softened |
| 1½ teaspoons vanilla extract |
| 2 eggs |
| 2¾ cups flour |
| 2½ teaspoons baking powder |
| ½ teaspoon salt |
| 1¼ cups milk |
| Fluffy White Frosting (recipe follows) |
| Mochonut Frosting (recipe follows) |
| Caramel Coconut Frosting (recipe follows) |
| Pink jelly beans |
| Black jelly beans |
| 2 cups shredded coconut |
| Few drops green food coloring |
| Easter eggs |
| Pink paper ears (see page 75) |
| Tray or platter (20 or more inches in diameter) |

Preheat oven to 350°F. Line three 8-inch cake pans with baking parchment or foil.

Beat sugar, butter, vanilla, and eggs on medium speed until well blended (about 30 seconds). Beat at high speed, scraping bowl occasionally, for 5 minutes. Combine flour, baking powder, and salt; beat in alternately with milk on low speed.

Pour batter into prepared pans and bake 30 to 35 minutes. Cool completely.

Remove layers from pans and peel away paper or foil. If you don't have a tray or platter about 20 inches in diameter, make one by covering a piece of cardboard with foil. (It can be round or square, as long as it will accommodate 3 cakes.) Each cake will be cut and decorated in the same manner, using the appropriate flavor of frosting and "coconut fur."

Prepare each cake as follows: Cut round layer into semicircles. Standing 2 semicircles on cut edge, hold together and cut a notch from both at one end (fig. 7a). Use one piece of the notch for a tail and arrange cake on serving tray; sandwich pieces together with a little frosting. Carve contours into cake to form neck, head, and body (fig. 7b). Frost cake with remaining frosting and sprinkle all over with coconut. Insert paper bunny ears, a pink jelly bean for nose, and black jelly beans for eyes.

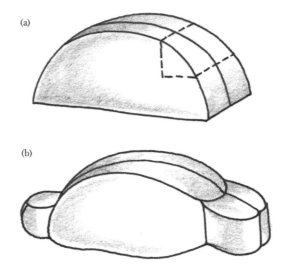

fig. 7

Repeat process with other 2 cakes, arranging them on the platter either side by side, or back to back in a circle—this depends on the shape of your serving tray (see photo opposite page 77).

Tint 2 cups shredded coconut by shaking it in a jar with a few drops of green food coloring. Use as you would Easter grass around the bunnies on the tray. Garnish with real or candy Easter eggs.

## FLUFFY WHITE FROSTING (FLOPSY)

| 2 egg whites (¼ cup) |
| --- |
| 1½ cups sugar |
| ¼ teaspoon cream of tartar or 1 tablespoon light corn syrup |
| ⅓ cup water |
| 1 teaspoon vanilla extract |
| 1 cup shredded coconut |

Combine egg whites, sugar, cream of tartar, and water in top of a double boiler; beat with a hand-held electric mixer for 1 minute. Place over boiling water (water should not touch bottom of pan); beat on high speed 7 minutes. Remove pan from over boiling water and add vanilla. Beat 2 minutes longer on high speed. Use frosting on cake and then sprinkle with coconut.

## MOCHONUT FROSTING (MOPSY)

| 2 egg whites (¼ cup) |
| --- |
| 1½ cups dark brown sugar, firmly packed |
| ¼ teaspoon cream of tartar or 1 tablespoon light corn syrup |
| ⅓ cup strongly brewed coffee |
| 1 teaspoon vanilla extract |
| ⅓ cup plus 2 tablespoons unsweetened cocoa powder |
| 1 cup shredded coconut |

Combine egg whites, sugar, cream of tartar, and coffee in top of a double boiler; beat with a hand-held electric mixer for 1 minute. Place over boiling water (water should not touch bottom of pan); beat on high speed 7 minutes. Remove pan from over boiling water and add vanilla. Beat 2 minutes longer on high speed. Sift the ⅓ cup cocoa over frosting and fold in gently. Shake coconut in a jar with the 2 tablespoons cocoa, until tinted chocolate brown. Use frosting on cake and then sprinkle with coconut.

## CARAMEL COCONUT FROSTING (COTTON-TAIL)

| 2 egg whites (¼ cup) |
| --- |
| 1½ cups light brown sugar, firmly packed |
| ¼ teaspoon cream of tartar or 1 tablespoon light corn syrup |
| ⅓ cup water |
| 1 teaspoon vanilla extract |
| 1 cup shredded coconut, toasted golden brown |

Combine egg whites, sugar, cream of tartar, and water in top of a double boiler. Beat with a hand-held electric mixer for 1 minute. Place over boiling water (water should not touch bottom of pan); beat on high speed 7 minutes. Remove pan from over boiling water and add vanilla. Beat 2 minutes longer on high speed. Use frosting on cake and then sprinkle with toasted coconut.

## PUDDLE-DUCK ICE CREAM

Poor Jemima Puddle-Duck just couldn't keep track of her eggs. She had little patience for sitting in a nest, and was easily distracted. The farmer's wife was well aware of Jemima's absentmindedness, and much to Jemima's dismay, let the hen hatch her whole brood. In this case, it must have been quite a "chilly" nest—for what should pop out of the eggs but a dozen ice cream ducklings!

PREPARATION TIME: 15 MINUTES
FREEZING TIME: ABOUT 1 HOUR

| 2 quarts lemon, banana, or French vanilla ice cream (select a flavor with a yellow or golden color) |
| --- |
| 12 whole blanched almonds, lightly toasted |
| 2 dozen chocolate chips, currants, or raisins (for eyes) |
| 12 paper or foil cupcake liners |

Make 12 large round scoops of ice cream and place each in a slightly flattened cupcake liner. Place a small scoop of ice cream on each large scoop, flattening slightly to form a neck. Place another small scoop on top of necks for heads. Insert an almond for a bill and chocolate chips, currants, or raisins (cut raisins in half) for eyes (fig. 8). Freeze until ready to serve.

fig. 8

Note: For even more animation, split some or all of the almonds in half lengthwise before inserting into ice cream. This creates the effect of an open, or "quacking" beak (photo opposite page 93).

## JUICE BAR

When it comes to breakfast, people are creatures of habit. Children, in particular, all seem to have a personal preference for their favorite fruit juice. The best solution is to set up a "juice bar" with beakers or bottles of assorted juices—orange, pineapple, grape, or tomato.

# DINOSAUR DAY

**T**he childhood infatuation with dinosaurs is at its peak in this age group. Even though they exist only in encyclopedias, children have a special relationship with these creatures that once walked the earth.

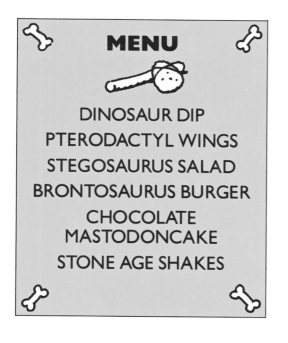

## MENU

DINOSAUR DIP

PTERODACTYL WINGS

STEGOSAURUS SALAD

BRONTOSAURUS BURGER

CHOCOLATE MASTODONCAKE

STONE AGE SHAKES

**FEATURES:** Cave Costumes, Archeologist Hats, Cave Painting

**GAMES:** Dizzy Dinosaurs, Boulder Busters, Fossil Hunt

**INVITATIONS:** A cardboard dinosaur bone "Announcing Dinosaur Day!"

## INVITATIONS

As any archeologist will tell you, finding a dinosaur bone is, indeed, like finding buried treasure. It's a key to unlocking a whole world of undiscovered wonders. A dinosaur-bone invitation is the perfect prelude to a prehistoric party.

The invitation includes a folded-up suggestion sheet for cavepeople costumes. Be sure to emphasize that costumes are optional by saying something like "For extra fun, come as a caveperson!"

PREPARATION TIME: 1 HOUR 15 MINUTES

| |
|---|
| 12 sheets (9 x 12 inches each) green construction paper |
| 4 sheets (9 x 12 inches each) light beige, eggshell, or off-white construction paper (bone color) |
| Brown felt-tip marker |

12 photocopies of costume
suggestion sheet

Scissors, stapler or Scotch tape

Fold sheets of green construction
paper into thirds *lengthwise*, as if
you were folding a letter the wrong
way. You should have 3 x 12-inch
folded papers to use as envelopes.

Fold bone-colored paper into 3 x
12-inch sections, too. Cut along
creases into 3 x 12-inch strips. On
one strip, draw a dinosaur bone
(fig. 1) that covers the entire
length of the strip; the mid-section
of the bone will be about 1½ inches
thick. Use this first bone as a
pattern for cutting out the rest.
(You can cut out several at a time by
stacking strips together.) Using
brown marker, write:

> Announcing Dinosaur Day!

On the reverse side of bone
write:

[Your child's name] Archeological Dig
[Your address, date, time]
Regrets [or R.S.V.P.]
[Your phone]

The bone is narrow, so try to
write in 3 long lines across. Crease
costume suggestion sheets in the
same fashion as envelopes (they'll
be slightly smaller). Unfold sheets
and place a bone in the center of
each. Fold sheets up around bone,
and fold construction-paper
envelopes around sheets (fig. 2).

## COSTUME SUGGESTION SHEET

*For Extra Fun, Come as a Caveperson!*

A caveperson costume can be made
out of anything that's fuzzy or looks
like animal skin. A piece of fake fur
cloth, animal print cotton (leopard,
tiger, or zebra), or even an old bath
or throw rug. No sewing necessary—
cavepeople didn't sew!

*Bath rug or fur cloth*
Cut a hole in the center, allowing
enough fabric to fall down the front
and back of the caveperson evenly,
and to drape around each side. Trim
with scissors if necessary. Tie
costume in place,
at the waist,
with a sash
or cord.

*Animal print fabric*
Tie a piece of fabric, wide enough to
drape around caveperson, in a knot
over one shoulder. Tie costume in
place, at the waist,
with a sash
or cord.

Have your caveperson wear solid
colored shirt and pants under
costume. Any questions? [Your
phone number]

*Note:* Children may wish to wear
swimsuits under costumes in warm
weather.

Staple or tape edges of envelopes, and address with brown marker.

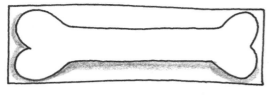

fig. 1

fig. 2

Write or type suggestion sheet according to model. Make 12 photocopies. At the bottom of each sheet, include the line "Any questions?" and your phone number. This enables confused or relatively uncreative parents to call and ask what they should do. If they call, assure them that it's nothing to fret or fuss over. A pair of old animal-print pajamas (leopard or tiger) or a fuzzy rabbit-fur hat can put the child into the spirit of the party. If the parent seems totally helpless, make a note of it and plan on providing something for the child to put on when he or she arrives. Chances are the parent will come up with some kind of prop, but it's nice to be prepared for such a situation.

A good backup or emergency costume idea is to let a child become an "archeologist." The child who might otherwise feel left out will feel special and of great importance. Archeological digs are usually located in hot, desertlike areas where head protection is needed from the brutal sun. Find some broad-brimmed straw hats that will fit a child's head. Cut out some 2-inch-wide construction-paper hat bands and staple them around the crown of each hat first, writing OFFICIAL ARCHEOLOGIST across each band with a felt-tip marker. (It's a big word, so write small.) Explain to the children how important the archeologist is and what one does. Without archeologists, no one would know that dinosaurs ever existed.

## DECORATIONS

Creating the ambience for Dinosaur Day isn't hard, if you just close your eyes and think of a swamp. The setting calls for an abundance of ferns, plants, pebbles, and rocks. Drape lots of green crêpe-paper streamers across the ceiling of the room. Make crêpe-paper ferns and hang from streamers. Tape ferns so that they dangle from the backs of chairs and the edges of the tablecloth. You can even decorate the tablecloth with dinosaur tracks or footprints. Set the table with pots of low-lying leafy plants, pebbles, and stones. (If you don't have any, check with your local nursery or garden center.)

Mark children's place settings with "personalized" rocks. Paint the child's name on the rock and stand a plastic dinosaur on top.

## CRÊPE-PAPER FERNS

PREPARATION TIME: 30 MINUTES

| |
|---|
| 6 packages green crêpe paper |
| Scissors |

Unwrap packages of crêpe paper, but keep them folded. Cut a large, long leaf through all thicknesses of paper, using entire width and length of paper. Cut gashes in leaves to form a feathery, fernlike effect. Separate leaves and stretch crêpe paper slightly, giving ferns interesting shape and more body.

## DINOSAUR TRACK TABLECLOTH

PREPARATION TIME: 30 MINUTES

| |
|---|
| 1 or 2 green paper tablecloths (large enough to cover your table or tables) |
| Brown finger paint (or powdered tempera paint that has been mixed a little thick) |

Get your child to help with this one. Make fists with hands. Do not pull thumb in with fingers (fig. 3a). Press clenched hands, palmsides down, into a pie plate that has been filled with a shallow layer of paint. Make an imprint of your hand on the tablecloth.

Repeat this, using both right and left hands in a "walking" pattern across the tablecloth (fig. 3b). Allow to dry thoroughly before setting the table.

Note: This can be done several weeks in advance, if cloths are folded carefully so the paint doesn't crack.

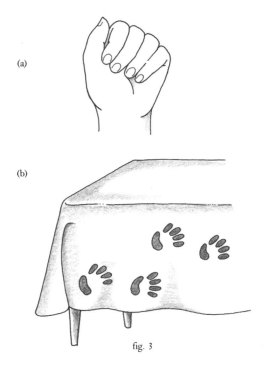

(a)

(b)

fig. 3

## INSTANT INVOLVEMENT

Art is a great icebreaker, and encourages children to get into the Dinosaur Day spirit. As soon as "cavepeople" start arriving, commission them to work on a cave painting (a record of prehistoric life that will be discovered by an archeologist and put in a museum). Of course, the mural has to be painted on the wall of a cave. A rec room, garage, basement, or screened porch is a good place for a cave. Tape wide rolls of brown wrapping paper completely around the walls of the room. If you don't mind the mess, cave painting is the most colorful when you provide cans full of tempera paint and brushes. However, many parents prefer thick, sturdy crayons (which won't spill). After all of the children are present and the mural is reasonably complete, the mural can be left in the room or transferred to the wall of the dining area. If you already planned to eat or play games in this room, then leave the mural where it is as a backdrop.

## GAMES

### DIZZY DINOSAURS

This game is based on the same principle as the classic Upset the Fruit Basket. Instead of Apples, Oranges, Strawberries, and Pineapples, children are divided into groups of Brontosauruses, Stegosauruses, Triceratops, and Pterodactyls. Enough chairs are placed in a large circle (facing toward the center) to accommodate all but one child, who will play It. The child who is It stands in the center of the circle and announces the dinosaur of his or her choice (from the four categories described above). Example: If It announces, "Triceratops!" all of the Triceratops must scramble to change their seats with one another, while It also rushes to grab an empty seat. If It fails to get a seat, he or she remains It for the next turn. If It is able to get to a seat, he or she becomes a Triceratops, and the displaced dinosaur becomes It.

### BOULDER BUSTERS

This is a form of "prehistoric piñata," where children break paper-bag "boulders" with a baseball bat "club." Each boulder is filled with shredded newspaper and candy, tied with a hemplike rope or packaging cord and suspended from the limb of a tree. (See modifications for playing indoors.) There are really 2 objects to this game: (1) to find the Golden Stone and become the next Boulder Buster; (2) to gather the most hard candy. If the party is small—12 or less—the ideal situation is to have enough boulders so that every child can have a turn. However, for large parties, this is impractical. In the case of 24 children, it's better to have only 6 boulders to break and fill them with twice as much candy. Even though only 6 children may win the position of Boulder Buster, there is still a great deal of sport in gathering the most candy.

The game begins by choosing a volunteer for the first Boulder Buster. The Boulder Buster is blindfolded and given a club (a plastic ball bat). The other children gather around in a large circle, allowing plenty of room for safe swinging. A parent acts as the operator, pulling the boulder up and down as the child swings at it. (It's important that an adult assumes this position. If a child is having difficulty hitting the boulder, the operator should try to make it easily within reach. With children under 5, it may be necessary to hold it at an almost stationary position within reach). As soon as the boulder breaks, the Boulder Buster drops the bat and the children rush in, sorting through shredded paper and gathering candy into their own sacks or bags. The child who finds the Golden Stone (a piece of candy wrapped in gold foil) becomes the next Boulder Buster.

The game continues like this until all of the boulders have been broken. No child can be a Boulder Buster twice. If he or she tries to grab a Golden Stone for the second time, the child must dump his or her candy back in the pile and start over.

## FOSSIL HUNT

This is a variation on the classic Easter egg hunt, replacing dinosaur cookies (recipe follows) for eggs. The cookies are wrapped in plastic wrap or cellophane and hidden around the yard or in specific rooms in the house.

## RECIPES

## DINOSAUR COOKIES

ABOUT 8 DOZEN
PREPARATION TIME: 1 HOUR

BAKING TIME: 8 MINUTES PER BATCH

| |
|---|
| 1½ cups (3 sticks) butter, softened |
| 3 cups brown sugar, firmly packed |
| 3 eggs |
| 4¼ cups flour |
| 1 tablespoon freshly grated nutmeg |
| 1½ teaspoons soda |
| Raisins |

Beat butter and brown sugar until fluffy. Beat in eggs, one at a time. Stir flour, nutmeg, and soda together in a separate bowl. Stir dry ingredients into butter mixture until well blended. Wrap in plastic wrap and chill 3 hours or more.

Preheat oven to 350°F.

Roll dough out on floured surface ¼ inch thick. Make cardboard patterns of dinosaur shapes (see patterns, page 182) and use to cut out cookies. Trace around patterns with a large needle to cut dough. (A needle turns corners better than a knife.) Gather up scraps, chill, and reroll. Give dinosaurs raisin eyes, and bake for 8 minutes.

## DINOSAUR DIP

Even self-proclaimed spinach haters will dig into a dip-filled dinosaur. The body is a sculpture of squash and zucchini.

PREPARATION TIME: 50 MINUTES

| 1 large, slightly elongated acorn squash |
| 2 long, narrow, curved zucchini |
| 4 small or miniature zucchini (each about 3 or 4 inches long) |
| 2 whole cloves |
| Bamboo skewers or sturdy toothpicks |

Set acorn squash on its side and slice off a section from the top couple of lobes (fig. 4a). Hollow out seeds and fiber to form a cavity for the dip. Use the small zucchini for legs by trimming tops to fit against curvature of squash body. Secure legs in place with skewers or toothpicks (fig. 4b), so that the dinosaur is standing firmly (without wobbling). Cut gash in one larger zucchini to make a head (fig. 4c) and secure in place with toothpick.

Use a knife to cut open mouth, and stick in 2 whole cloves for eyes. Trim neck and tail zucchini to fit against body (fig. 4d) and secure in place with toothpicks (fig. 4e). Wrap carefully in plastic wrap and refrigerate until ready to fill and serve.

## DIP

| 1 package (10 ounces) frozen chopped spinach |
| 1 cup mayonnaise |
| 1 cup sour cream |
| ½ teaspoon garlic salt |
| 1 tablespoon onion juice |
| ¼ cup chopped scallions |

Defrost spinach and squeeze to remove all moisture. Mix together with mayonnaise, sour cream, garlic salt, onion juice, and

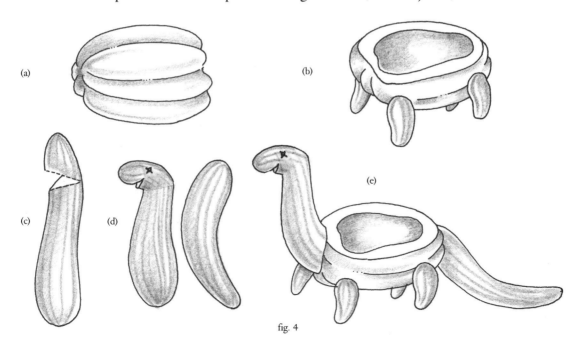

(a)  (b)  (c)  (d)  (e)

fig. 4

scallions. Pour into dinosaur as needed, keeping any remaining dip covered in the refrigerator.

## VEGETABLE DIPPERS

Some vegetables should be served raw, crisped in ice water (such as carrots, celery, and cucumbers). However, the color, taste, and texture of broccoli and cauliflower flowerets or strips of zucchini are much improved by blanching. Pour boiling water over a kettle of vegetables, and allow water to return to boil. Immediately drain vegetables in a colander and immerse in a bowl of ice water. Replace cold water after 15 minutes and soak 2 hours or overnight.

How much to allow for? The following assortment will feed up to 2 dozen children:

| |
|---|
| 1 bunch broccoli, broken into flowerets |
| 1 bunch cauliflower, broken into flowerets |
| 1 bunch celery, trimmed and cut into sticks |
| 1 bunch carrots, peeled and cut into sticks |
| 2 large cucumbers or zucchini, cut into sticks |
| 1 pint cherry tomatoes |

If your party is smaller, select a combination of any 3 vegetables.

To serve: Arrange dinosaur on a platter or tray lined with a decorative lettuce (such as red leaf or salad bowl), and fill cavity with dip. Surround dinosaur with vegetables and "cavepeople clubs" (small bread stick crackers or pumpernickel snack sticks).

## PTERODACTYL WINGS

Although chicken wings can be disjointed into drummettes, these are left whole to suggest the wingspan of a Pterodactyl. Allow 1 wing for 4- to 6-year-olds, 2 wings for 7- and 8-year-olds.

PREPARATION TIME: 25 MINUTES
BAKING TIME: 40 MINUTES

| |
|---|
| 4 eggs |
| ¾ cup peanut oil |
| ¼ cup prepared mustard |
| 1 tablespoon Worcestershire sauce |
| 2 dozen chicken wings |
| 4 cups crushed cheddar cheese crackers |

Preheat oven to 375°F.

Beat eggs, oil, mustard, and Worcestershire sauce together until smooth. Wash wings and pat dry with towel. Grab hold of wing tips and spread them enough so they look like they're ready to "fly." Dip wings in egg mixture and coat in cracker crumbs. Place on a large baking sheet lined with foil (shiny side down). Bake for 20 minutes. Turn wings carefully so as not to break the crust, and bake for another 20 minutes.

Note: These can be prepared a few days ahead of time and reheated in a 200°F oven for 20 minutes.

*Chocolate Mastodon Cake*

*Puddle-Duck Ice Cream (recipe page 84), from Beatrix Potter Easter Brunch*

# STEGOSAURUS SALAD

Even children with an acute aversion to "everything green" will get excited about avocados and endive in this Stegosaurus salad.

PREPARATION TIME: 25 MINUTES

| |
|---|
| 3 large ripe avocados |
| Juice of 2 large lemons |
| 4 to 6 heads endive |
| 12 large, broad lettuce leaves (romaine or red leaf) |
| 2 cucumbers |
| 6 pitted ripe olives, cut in half |
| Honey-Lime Dressing (recipe follows) |

Split and peel avocados, remove pits, then cut halves in half lengthwise to make quarters. Rub each with lemon juice to prevent discoloring. Wash endive and separate leaves. Trim leaves at base, so that leaf tips are 2 inches long. Place a lettuce leaf on each serving plate and set a slice of avocado on its side on top of lettuce. Gently insert or press the base of each leaf (use 5 to 6) along the crest or arch of the avocado slice. The tips should be sticking out to resemble the plates across a stegosaurus's back. Split cucumbers in half and scoop out seeds. Cut into ½-inch semicircle sections. Place 2 at each end of avocado for legs (fig. 5). Place half of a ripe olive on each head for an eye. Spoon dressing over salads, or pass around separately and allow children to serve themselves.

# HONEY-LIME DRESSING

| |
|---|
| ¼ cup fresh lime juice |
| ¼ cup honey |
| ½ teaspoon dry mustard |
| ¼ teaspoon salt |
| ¾ cup peanut or vegetable oil |

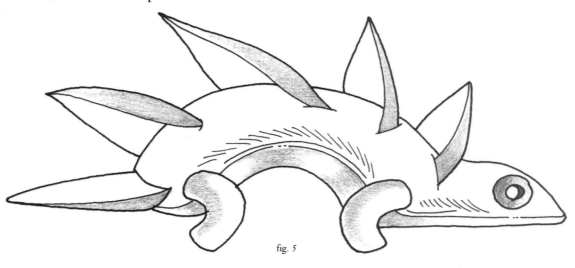

fig. 5

Combine dressing ingredients in a screw-top jar. Shake until blended. Chill. Shake again before serving.

## BRONTOSAURUS BURGER

What a mouthful! This gargantuan hamburger is actually a meatloaf in disguise. One alone will feed a dozen hungry cavepeople. If your party is larger, it's easier to make 2 or 3 than to keep making them bigger. Remember that meatloaf shrinks in the oven while bread expands. This is important to keep in mind, so that the end result will be a harmoniously matched hamburger patty and bun.

PREPARATION TIME: 1 HOUR
RISING TIME (BUN): 1 HOUR
COOKING/BAKING TIME: 1½ HOURS

| |
|---|
| Brontosaurus Burger (recipe follows) |
| Brontosaurus Bun (recipe follows) |
| ½ cup Special Sauce (recipe follows) |
| Salad bowl lettuce |
| ½ cup ketchup |
| 1 large tomato, thinly sliced |
| 2 *jumbo* dill pickles (deli kind) |

Warm burger patty in oven as described opposite. Open up bun. Spread bottom half with ¼ cup of the sauce. Cover with leaves of lettuce, creating a ruffled effect around the edge. Place patty on top of lettuce (you may have to slide it off a tray). Spread with ketchup and cover with tomato slices and pickles. Spread remaining ¼ cup sauce over tomatoes and pickles; cover with top of bun.

To serve, cut burger into pie-shaped wedges. Pass around dishes of extra ketchup, sauce, and pickles for children who like to add more.

## BRONTOSAURUS BURGER

The meatloaf patty can be prepared ahead of time and even frozen. To reheat, wrap fully cooked patty in foil and warm in a 300°F oven for 20 to 25 minutes.

| |
|---|
| 3 eggs |
| 1 bottle (1½ cups) chili sauce |
| ¼ cup instant minced onion |
| 2 tablespoons Worcestershire sauce |
| 2 teaspoons dry mustard |
| 1 teaspoon garlic powder |
| 1 teaspoon onion powder |
| 1 teaspoon celery salt |
| 2 cups herb-flavored stuffing mix |
| 4 pounds ground lean beef |

Preheat oven to 350°F.
Beat eggs, chili sauce, instant minced onion, Worcestershire sauce, dry mustard, and garlic,

onion, and celery salts together until thoroughly combined. Mix in stuffing and ground beef. Line a 12-inch round cake or springform pan with foil. Pat meatloaf patty evenly into pan. Bake for 1½ hours.

Cool patty 15 minutes. Carefully pour off fat around sides, then cool 30 minutes longer. Cover a baking sheet with foil and invert meatloaf onto sheet. Peel foil away from bottom of patty. Wrap and store in refrigerator or freezer until ready to reheat.

Note: Frozen patty must be completely defrosted before reheating.

## BRONTOSAURUS BUN

| 1 package rapid-rise active dry yeast |
| --- |
| ¼ cup warm water |
| 4 cups flour |
| ¼ cup sugar |
| 1½ teaspoons salt |
| ½ cup hot water |
| ½ cup milk |
| ¼ cup butter, softened |
| 1 whole egg and 1 egg white |
| 1 tablespoon sesame seeds |

Dissolve yeast in warm water in large bowl. Mix in 2 cups of the flour. Add sugar, salt, hot water, milk, butter, and whole egg until moistened. Beat 2

minutes with electric mixer until smooth. Stir in remaining 2 cups of flour by hand. Cover bowl with plastic wrap. Let rise in warm place until doubled (about 30 minutes).

Punch dough down. Turn out on a lightly floured board and knead until no longer sticky. Grease a large baking sheet and sprinkle with cornmeal. Trace an 11-inch circle on baking sheet (this can be done with a toothpick). Form dough into a large, round ball, place on the baking sheet and pat evenly into a flattened, 11-inch circle. Lightly beat the egg white and brush on dough. Sprinkle with sesame seeds. Let rise until double in bulk (30 to 35 minutes).

Preheat oven to 350°F.

Bake 30 to 40 minutes, or until golden brown. Bread should sound hollow when tapped, if it has been thoroughly baked. Cool. Use a bread knife to split open like a hamburger bun.

## SPECIAL SAUCE

| 1 cup mayonnaise |
| --- |
| ¼ cup prepared mustard |
| 2 tablespoons sugar |
| 1 tablespoon sweet India relish |
| ½ teaspoon onion salt |

Combine ingredients in a small mixing bowl and blend until smooth. Chill before serving. Makes about 1½ cups.

# CHOCOLATE MASTODON CAKE

This furry prehistoric pachyderm tastes like a moist chocolate macaroon. It's a fairly large cake, so if your party is for only 12, plan on having a few extra pieces. If you're having a large party, you can bake 2 Mastodons, or supplement the cake by baking a batch of cupcakes using the same batter and frosting.

PREPARATION TIME: 1 HOUR
BAKING TIME: 30 TO 35 MINUTES

| 4 cups sugar |
| 4 eggs |
| 2 cups milk |
| 2 cups unsweetened cocoa powder |
| 2 cups shortening (preferably butter-flavored) |
| 1 teaspoon salt |
| 4 teaspoons baking powder |
| 2 teaspoons baking soda |
| 2 teaspoons almond extract |
| 6 cups flour |
| 2 cups shredded coconut |
| 2 cups boiling water |
| Chocolate Cheese Frosting (recipe follows) |
| ½ cup toasted coconut (see note, page 26) |
| 1 cinnamon stick |
| 1 large marshmallow |
| 1 chocolate kiss |
| 1 piece (20 x 30 inches) heavy cardboard |
| Gold or silver foil |

Preheat oven to 325°F.

Measure all of the cake ingredients into a large mixing bowl, adding the boiling water last. Stir until smooth and thoroughly blended. Line a 9 x 13-inch sheet cake pan and two 9-inch round layer pans with baking parchment. Spoon batter evenly into pans and bake 35 minutes for sheet cake and 30 minutes for round layers, or until toothpick inserted into center comes out clean. Cool layers in pans 1 hour.

Invert cooled layers out of pans. Peel parchment away from bottoms of layers. (At this stage, you can wrap and freeze layers; or assemble cake and freeze until the day it's to be served.)

Cut rectangular layer and round layers as illustrated and identified in fig. 6a. Cover a 20 x 30-inch piece of cardboard with foil. Arrange pieces of cake as shown in diagram (fig. 6b). Frost cake with half of frosting (refer to page 10 for suggestions on frosting techniques). Fit pastry bag with large writing tip; fill with remaining frosting. Pipe "shaggy" frosting "fur" all over mastodon. Sprinkle with toasted coconut. Insert cinnamon stick for tusk and marshmallow for eye, using chocolate kiss for pupil. (See photo opposite page 92).

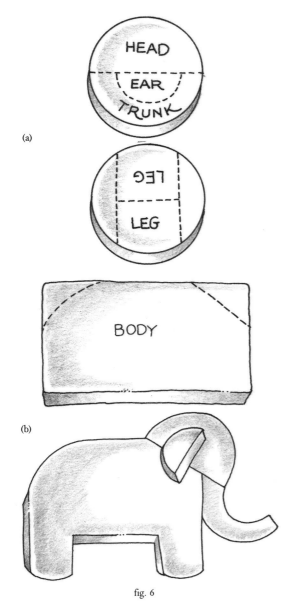

(a)

(b)

fig. 6

# CHOCOLATE CHEESE FROSTING

| ⅔ cup unsweetened cocoa powder |
| 1 cup butter |
| 1 package (8 ounces) cream cheese |
| 2 pounds confectioners sugar |
| 1 tablespoon almond extract |
| ¼ cup milk (optional) |

Cream cocoa and butter together until light and fluffy. Beat in cream cheese until smooth. Blend in confectioners sugar, adding milk if necessary to make a smooth, spreadable, but not too soft frosting.

## STONE AGE SHAKES

Frosty banana milkshakes double as a beverage and ice cream companion to cake. For that prehistoric touch, garnish with sprigs of fresh "swamp fern" (mint leaves). Because most blenders have about a quart capacity, you have to make 3 batches of this recipe. Each batch makes 4 generous servings.

PREPARATION TIME: 15 MINUTES

| 1 pint vanilla ice cream |
| 2 cups milk |
| 2 ripe bananas |
| 1 tablespoon lemon juice |
| 2 tablespoons superfine sugar |
| Mint leaves |
| Freshly grated nutmeg |

Mix ice cream, milk, bananas, lemon juice, and sugar in blender until smooth. Pour into tall glasses or paper cups and garnish with mint leaves. Sprinkle shakes with a dash of nutmeg.

# SPACE STATION STOPOVER

**M**essages from outer space summon aliens for a special mission: a party that's "out of this world"!

## MENU

SATURN SALAD

FLYING SAUCER SANDWICHES

MOON ROCKS

SOLAR SYSTEM CAKE

ICE CREAM SPACE CAPSULES

JUPITER JUICE

**FEATURES:** Space Suits, Unidentified Flying Object Factory

**GAMES:** Lost in Space, Moon Walking, War of the Worlds

**INVITATION:** A "Message from Outer Space"

## INVITATIONS

The novelty of this invitation is that it's incomplete. Part of the fun is in the follow-up.

12 INVITATIONS
PREPARATION TIME: 20 MINUTES

| 12 miniature plastic pillboxes |
| --- |
| Typing paper |
| 12 envelopes |

Small colored pillboxes can be found in most drug or dime stores. On the typing paper, type 12 of these one-line messages, all capitals, triple spaced:

THIS IS A MESSAGE FROM OUTER SPACE:
CALL [*your number*]

Cut messages apart in strips. Fold up each strip and place in a pillbox. Seal pillboxes in envelopes, address, and mail. Responses to the invitation will be your R.S.V.P.s. Invite them to your Space Station, giving them all of the details. Don't forget the most important ones—where and when!

## DECORATIONS/ COSTUMES

This is one of those party themes that's wide open to your imagination. Just about anything could be out there in outer space. There's so much unknown, and so much room for fantasy. Who's to say that Martians aren't green, or that aliens from other galaxies don't speak backwards? When was the last time you saw a good picture of a UFO? Chances are it looked like someone hung a Frisbee from the ceiling.

Christmas lights are extremely effective in creating an extra-terrestrial atmosphere. Colored lights can be hung around mirrors, doorways, and the dining table itself to recreate the interior of a space ship. Tape strings of miniature white lights to the ceiling in constellationlike clusters. You can also drape midnight blue or black streamers across the ceiling and hang foil-covered paper plates for flying saucers (fig. 1a), styrofoam-ball and pipe-cleaner satellites (fig. 1b), or crêpe-paper comets (fig. 1c). Balloons can be decorated to resemble planets (fig. 1d) or, with the addition of paper tail fins (fig. 1e), turned into rockets.

Make a Martian centerpiece with an empty fish bowl. Blow a green balloon up so that it's still smaller than the opening of the bowl. Draw a face with a magic marker, and tape pointed paper ears on each side of the head. Insert the head into

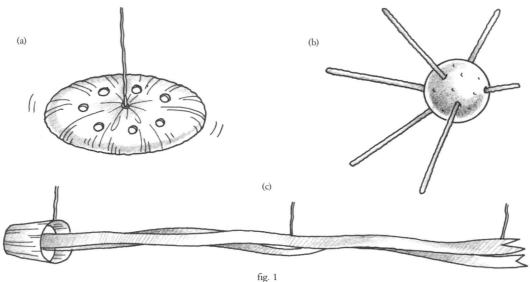

(a)

(b)

(c)

fig. 1

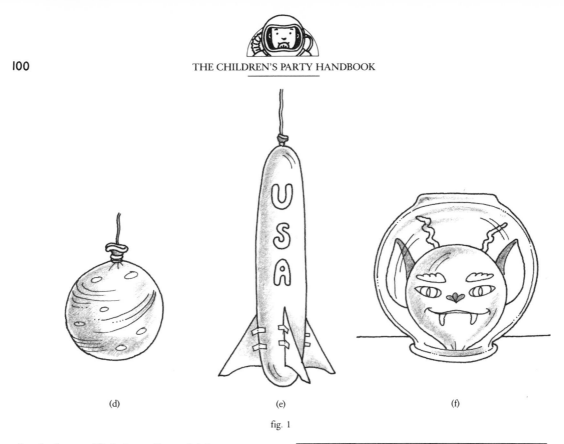

(d)                    (e)                    (f)

fig. 1

the helmet (fish bowl) and blow up completely. Tie off the balloon and secure in place with a cardboard base. Turn upside down in the center of the table (fig. 1f). This, and everything else, will look more dramatic in a dimly lit room.

## SPACE SUITS

Trash bag space suits are easy-to-make, inexpensive costumes that you can provide for every child. They're a little on the futuristic side, more appropriate on aliens than astronauts.

PREPARATION TIME: 1 HOUR

| 12 steel-colored plastic trash bags |
| Aluminum foil (lightweight) |
| 12 large paper bowls |
| 12 mask bands |
| 36 toilet paper tubes (optional) |
| Silver plastic tape |
| Scissors |

Use your child for a model in determining length of the space suits. Cut slits in a trash bag for neck and armholes. Slip over your child's head and mark where knee cap begins. Remove bag and trim that much from bottom. Reserve band and split open at one seam to make a tie belt. Repeat with remaining trash bags, trimming the same distance off each hem. To make helmets, place a paper bowl upside down in the center of a 40-inch sheet of foil. Mold foil into the concave of the bowl. Bring foil

up around sides, molding to figure of bowl and twisting ends together at the top. Wrap top twist into a spiral and attach a mask band on each side of helmet (fig. 2a). Repeat with remaining paper bowls.

For each "powerpack" (optional because some people don't seem to collect toilet paper tubes. However, if you ask around the neighborhood, you're bound to accumulate more than you'll ever need): Cover 3 toilet paper tubes with foil and strap together with silver plastic tape (fig. 2b). Costumes are worn by slipping bags over head and slipping arms through armholes. The sash is double wrapped and tied around the waist. Powerpacks are strapped to the back with plastic tape (fig. 2c). Space helmets are worn on top of the head, with mask bands strapped under the chin.

(a)

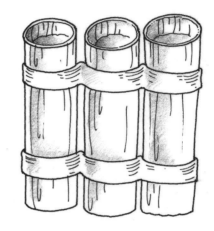

(b)

(c)

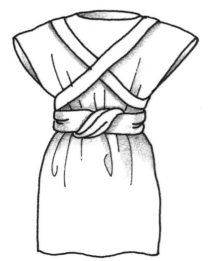

fig. 2

## INSTANT INVOLVEMENT

Upon arrival at the space station, every child is "issued" a costume. Most of them will need a little assistance when it comes to taping on the powerpacks. As soon as they're in costume, they can go into the Unidentified Flying Object Factory. This is a top-secret place where aliens can build models of the exact same space ships they arrived in. Set up a work area with paper plates, aluminum foil, construction paper, pipe cleaners, tin cans, paper tubes, sequins, glue, tape, and staplers. Just about anything can go into making a UFO. As soon as they're finished, you can hang them from the ceiling in the dining area (along with the rest of the solar-system apparatus).

## GAMES

### LOST IN SPACE

Children are divided into 2 groups: Earthlings and Aliens. The Aliens capture the Earthlings, blindfold them, and tie them together in a long chain. (A clothesline is wrapped around each child's waist, with about three feet of rope between them.) The Earthlings are led to some unknown planet (a particular spot in the yard or room, agreed upon by the Aliens). The Earthlings must then try to find their way back to Earth (home

base). In the meantime, the Aliens may call out instructions from the sidelines that either guide or confuse the Earthlings. As soon as the Earthlings find their home planet, they trade places with the Aliens, and the game begins again. There are no actual winners in this game. The enthusiasm for whether the Aliens help or hinder the Earthlings' journey home is hard to predict. It all depends on how anxious they are to be "Lost in Space"!

### MOON WALKING

This game seems to end as soon as it begins, but it's tremendous fun while it lasts. Each child blows up 2 balloons and ties about a yard of string on each one. Then they tie the ends of the strings around their ankles. Upon signal, every child tries to stamp out everyone else's balloons, without having his or hers broken. The winner is the one left with the last surviving balloon.

### WAR OF THE WORLDS

If you're familiar with Capture the Flag, this is the science-fiction version. It should be played in a large area or out of doors. Instead of flags, each team holds the other's planet. Try to find a world globe to use for Earth and a rubber ball for Mars. Divide children into Earthlings and Martians. There are 3 Zones in the game: Earthling Territory, Martian Territory, and No Man's Land (a

narrow strip of area between the 2 borders). The Capital, or goal, is where each planet is holding the other's hostage. A guard stands watch over it. The object of the game is for one team to infiltrate the other team's territory, rescue the planet, and return it safely home. If any of the "aggressing" team are tagged on "foreign" soil, they are taken prisoner along with the planet. When a planet is seized, any prisoners are simultaneously freed. However, the planet must be safely carried back into No Man's Land without being tagged, or they all return as prisoners. The winner, obviously, is the team who bring back both its planet and prisoners.

## RECIPES

## SATURN SALAD

You could say this is an "out of this world" way to serve fruit, with honeydew for the rings of Saturn and a peach or plum for the planet.

PREPARATION TIME: 25 MINUTES

| 2 large, ripe honeydew melons |
| 6 ripe peaches or plums (your preference) |
| 1 package (8 ounces) cream cheese, softened |
| ¼ cup apricot preserves (or use plum preserves if you're serving plums) |
| ½ teaspoon almond extract |

Slice whole melons into ¾- to 1-inch thick rings. Scoop out seeds and fiber. (Use only the center sections of melons, which produce the largest holes.) Place 12 slices of melon on individual salad plates. Put cream cheese, apricot (or plum) preserves, and almond extract in a food processor. Blend until smooth. Split fresh peaches (or plums) in half, discarding pits. Stuff cavity left by each pit with a heaping spoonful of the cream cheese mixture. Invert peaches (or plums) on each plate, skin side up, in the center of each melon ring.

## FLYING SAUCER SANDWICHES

Have your kids ever mistaken a pita pocket for a Frisbee? If so, you can probably understand how this bread stimulates young imaginations. Add some lights (our "laser beams") and landing gear, and you've created Flying Saucer Sandwiches. The dressing, by the way, is the kind that usually comes from a "Russian" satellite!

PREPARATION TIME: 45 MINUTES
CHILLING TIME (FOR "LASER
  BEAM" SCALLIONS): SEVERAL HOURS

| 12 scallions |
| 12 pita bread pockets |
| 4 cups shredded lettuce |
| 2 cucumbers, thinly sliced |

| Satellite Dressing (recipe follows) |
| 12 slices ham |
| 12 slices turkey |
| 12 slices Swiss cheese |
| 12 crisp-cooked strips bacon |
| 4 dozen *midget* sweet or dill gherkins |
| 8 dozen pimiento-stuffed green olives |
| 12 pitted ripe olives |
| 12 slices tomato (3 to 4 medium tomatoes) |
| Frilled party toothpicks |
| Wooden toothpicks (plain) |

Start by preparing scallions for "laser beams." Trim bulbs and green ends from scallions so that each remaining stalk is about 6 inches long. Slash one end of each stalk in 2 crisscross slices, each about 3 inches deep. Soak scallions in cold salted water (with ice) for several hours or overnight. (The cut ends of scallions should "bloom" and become very frilly.)

Make a slash in the side of each pita, and open up pocket. Fill with about ⅓ cup of shredded lettuce and 4 to 5 slices of cucumber. Drizzle with some dressing. Stack ham, turkey, cheese, and bacon on top of lettuce and close pocket.

To make "landing gear," select 4 gherkins of uniform length. Trimming if necessary, spear each at one end with a frilly toothpick. Insert at 4 points on bottom of one filled pita, so it can stand up. Spear olives with toothpicks and insert around sides of pita, pimientos facing out, to resemble lights. Repeat with remaining gherkins, olives, and sandwiches.

Drain scallions. Insert base of each in hole of a ripe olive. Insert a plain toothpick halfway into base of each scallion-stuffed olive. Center a tomato slice on top of each pita. Insert scallion-stuffed olives through tomatoes into pitas, anchoring tomatoes in place with the toothpicks (see photo opposite page 140).

## SATELLITE DRESSING

| 1 cup mayonnaise |
| ¼ cup chili sauce |
| 2 tablespoons sweet India relish |
| 1 tablespoon prepared mustard |
| 2 teaspoons paprika |
| 1 teaspoon onion salt |
| 1 hard-cooked egg, chopped |

Combine ingredients in a small bowl and blend until smooth. Chill before serving.

## MOON ROCKS

Lumpy, bumpy, funny-looking red-skinned new potatoes make a potato salad resembling "moon rocks."

PREPARATION TIME: *25 MINUTES*

| 3 to 4 dozen (3 to 4 pounds) small red-skinned new potatoes |
| 1 cup sugar |
| 1½ cups white, cider, or tarragon vinegar |
| 1½ cups corn or vegetable oil |
| 2 teaspoons dry mustard |
| 2 teaspoons celery seed |
| 1 teaspoon onion powder |
| 1 teaspoon garlic powder |
| 1 tablespoon fresh dill or 2 teaspoons dried |
| ¼ cup chopped fresh parsley |

Wash potatoes and place in a large kettle. Cover with water and boil until tender (20 to 25 minutes). (They should not fall apart.) Transfer warm potatoes to a large bowl.

Bring sugar, vinegar, oil, mustard, celery seed, and onion and garlic powders to a boil in a saucepan. Boil 3 minutes. Remove from heat and stir in dill and parsley. Pour dressing over potatoes. Cover bowl and chill for 2 to 3 days, stirring potatoes twice a day. Drain off excess dressing before serving.

## SOLAR SYSTEM CAKE

A cake as big as the solar system? Well, almost. Nine planets revolve around the sun on a large round card table, each in their own orbit.

PREPARATION TIME: 1½ HOURS
BAKING TIME: UP TO 35 MINUTES

This cake is so moist and simple to make that you'll never dream of using a mix again. The recipe must be doubled, but it's suggested that you mix a single batch at a time, so your bowl doesn't overflow. You'll also need to save 5 flat tuna cans (thoroughly washed) for baking 5 planets.

| 3 cups sugar |
| 6 eggs |
| 1½ cups vegetable oil |
| 1½ cups orange juice |
| 1 tablespoon grated orange peel |
| 3¾ cups flour |
| ½ teaspoon salt |
| 3½ teaspoons baking powder |
| 2 teaspoons vanilla extract |

Preheat oven to 350°F.

Line bottoms of three 8-inch round layer cake pans, one 9-inch round layer pan, and five 3-inch empty tuna cans with foil. Grease pans and dust with flour. Beat eggs and sugar in a large mixing bowl until light and fluffy. Blend in oil, orange juice and peel, flour, salt, baking powder, and vanilla. Beat until smooth, about 1 to 2 minutes. Pour batter into 3 of the 8-inch round pans and 4 of the tuna cans. Mix batter again (second batch). Pour into 9-inch round pan and remaining 8-inch round pan and tuna can. Bake 8-inch and 9-inch layers for 30 to 35 minutes, tuna cans 25 to 30 minutes. (Don't use more than one shelf in your

oven, to assure even baking. It's better to bake cakes in two shifts). Cook cakes 20 minutes. Invert cakes and peel foil away from the bottoms. Turn cakes right side up again. Cool completely. Note: Cakes may be baked several weeks in advance, and frozen before frosting.

## BUTTERCREAM FROSTING

This makes a single batch, but I suggest you double it because you'll need a lot of colors. It's always better to have extra frosting (which can be frozen) than to run short. As with the cake batter, it's easier to double this recipe in separate batches.

| |
|---|
| ½ pound butter (2 sticks) |
| ½ cup shortening |
| 3 pounds confectioners sugar |
| ¾ cup milk |
| ½ teaspoon salt |
| 1 tablespoon vanilla extract |
| food coloring (pastel colors are preferable) |
| ⅓ cup unsweetened cocoa powder |

Cream butter and shortening until light and fluffy in a large mixing bowl. Add 1 pound of the sugar and milk. Beat until smooth. Blend in remaining sugar until smooth, then add salt and vanilla. Take it slow or the confectioners sugar will fly all over the room.

Divide frosting into 4 parts. Tint one part yellow, one red, one orange, and one green. Prepare second batch of frosting and also divide into 4 parts. Tint one part light blue and one part purple. Cream 2 tablespoons butter with cocoa and tint another part of the frosting chocolate brown with this mixture. Divide remaining amount of frosting in half. Leave half white and tint the other half dark blue.

## ASSEMBLING THE CAKE

Planets will be set out, starting from the Sun, in their respective orbits. Smaller planets (Mercury, Venus, Earth, and Mars) can be placed closer together to allow more space for the larger planets. Don't concern yourself with the actual distance scale; if you did, half the cakes wouldn't even be in the house. If it helps you to keep track, draw the orbits into the foil. The large planets (Jupiter, Saturn, Uranus, and Neptune) should be spread out in their orbital positions to allow room for each other. Place one north, south, east, and west.

It's difficult to say exactly how many inches apart each planet should be, since that will vary depending on the size of your table. Cut and arrange the planets before frosting. Begin with Mercury and end with Pluto; if they seem too crammed to fit, simply scatter them around the table so that no two large planets are too close together. Here are the cutting and frosting instructions:

*Sun*—Cut notches 1½ inches deep into the edge of the cake completely around the outside of the 9-inch layer. Place in center of table and frost with yellow.

*Mercury*—Cover a 3-inch round with orange frosting.

*Venus*—Cover a 3-inch round with green frosting.

*Earth*—Cover a 3-inch round with light blue frosting. Make swirls of green and brown to resemble continents.

*Mars*—Cover a 3-inch round with red frosting.

*Jupiter*—Coat an 8-inch round with orange frosting. Run streaks of yellow and red frosting across the orange with a spatula; make a few whirlpool-like swirls.

*Saturn and Pluto*—Cut a 6-inch circle from an 8-inch round layer. The 6-inch circle will become Pluto. Leave the outer ring intact; this will become the ring around Saturn. (A 3-inch round cut from a tuna can will be the planet itself.) Place the remaining 3-inch round in the center of the 8-inch circle. Frost both parts light blue. Run streaks of purple and green across the blue planet and ring. For Pluto, frost the 6-inch round with purple.

*Neptune and Uranus*—Trim 1 inch from the edges of two 8-inch round layers to make two 7-inch planets. For Uranus, frost one round with chocolate; for Neptune, frost the other round with dark blue.

Fill a pastry bag, fitted with a small writing tip, with the white frosting. Pipe the name of each planet on the respective cake.

Note: These cakes should be assembled the day before the party. As soon as the icing sets, the whole table can be carefully covered with plastic wrap for protection until serving time.

## ICE CREAM SPACE CAPSULES

**M**artians and Earthlings orbit the planets of the Solar System cake in their ice cream cone space capsules.

PREPARATION TIME: 25 MINUTES
FREEZING TIME: 1 TO 2 HOURS

| |
|---|
| 1 pint peppermint or strawberry ice cream |
| 1 pint green mint chocolate chip or pistachio ice cream |
| 1 pint chocolate chip ice cream |
| 12 flat-bottomed wafer-type cones in assorted colors (4 red, 4 green, 4 plain or chocolate; see note below.) |
| Decorator's Frosting (recipe follows) |
| 12 foil cupcake liners |

Soften ice cream slightly. With a spoon fill red cones with peppermint or strawberry, green cones with mint chocolate chip or pistachio, and plain or chocolate cones with chocolate chip. Pack ice cream down into cones and return to freezer until firm.

Invert cones into foil cups, which have been flattened out. Fit pastry bag with a small writing tip;

fill with frosting (fig. 3). Decorate as desired. (*Suggestions:* Red capsules can be from Russia, marked U.S.S.R. Plain or chocolate capsules can be from America, marked U.S.A. with some stars and stripes. Green capsules can be from Mars, marked MARS. If you prefer, you can mark all of the capsules from planets only such as EARTH, VENUS, MARS, PLUTO, etc.) Return to freezer until serving time. Place around Solar System cake.

Note: These cones are available in an assortment of the colors.

fig. 3

## DECORATOR'S FROSTING

| 3 cups confectioners sugar |
| 2 to 3 tablespoons water, adding more only if necessary |
| Food coloring (red, blue) |

Blend water with sugar, adding just enough to make a smooth frosting that will still hold its shape when piped. Divide frosting in 3 parts. Leave one white and tint remaining frosting red and blue.

## JUPITER JUICE

Just as for the astronauts, "weightlessness" can be a problem for active children, too. Everything seems to fly through the air, especially liquids. Take a tip from NASA and serve beverages in plastic bags. The kids will love it, and so will your carpet.

PREPARATION TIME: 15 MINUTES, PLUS FREEZING TIME FOR ICE CUBES

| 4 quarts limeade (or other green beverage) |
| 12 plastic sandwich bags |
| 12 clear plastic tumblers |
| 12 plastic straws |
| 12 white plastic bag twists |

Freeze 1 quart of the limeade in ice cube trays until firm.

If your sandwich bags have "zip locks," trim them off with scissors; do not use bags with foldover flaps. Place a baggie in each cup, and fold excess from the opening over the sides. Fill cups three-fourths full of limeade ice and limeade. Place straws in cups and bring sides of bags back up around straws. Twist bags closed around straws with plastic twists and serve.

# WILD WEST ROUND-UP

**A**gathering like this is bound to bring in the "Best of the West": cowboys, Indians, outlaws, sheriffs, pioneers, prospectors, Daniel Boones, and Davy Crocketts.

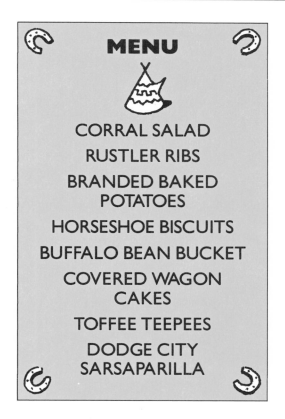

## MENU

CORRAL SALAD

RUSTLER RIBS

BRANDED BAKED POTATOES

HORSESHOE BISCUITS

BUFFALO BEAN BUCKET

COVERED WAGON CAKES

TOFFEE TEEPEES

DODGE CITY SARSAPARILLA

**FEATURES:** Olde Time Tin Type Gallery

**GAMES:** Calf Roping, Panning for Gold, Pony Express

**INVITATIONS:** "WANTED" poster

## INVITATIONS

In frontier times, the word "WANTED" could recruit riders for the Pony Express, summon pilgrimages of pioneers and prospectors, and bring back outlaws "dead or alive." A "WANTED" poster is also a great way to round up all of the above for your Wild West party. Copies of posters can be sent out as invitations. The paper can even be distressed with burns and "bullet" holes to look as if it spent several years nailed to a tree.

12 INVITATIONS
PREPARATION TIME: 1 HOUR

One 8½ x 11-inch sheet white typing paper

Black magic marker

Black felt-tip pen

12 sheets (8½ x 11 inches each) off-white or tan stationery

Cigarette, matches, sponge

12 legal-size envelopes

Write the following invitation poster-style, using the marker for bold-face printing and the felt-tipped pen for the rest of the copy:

*WANTED*
Pioneers, Prospectors
Pony Express Riders
Cowboys & Indians
—even outlaws—
for the
BIGGEST ROUND-UP THIS
SIDE OF DURANGO

*WILD WEST ROUND-UP*
IN THE [name of street or neighborhood] TERRITORY
ON [child's last name] RANCH
[address, date]
RSVP [phone]
COME DRESSED FOR THE WEST

Take your "model" poster to a copy center or a local library. Ask to have your stationery inserted in the machine for the photocopies.

Distressing the posters is fun and there is really no end to the methods you can use. The paper can be wrinkled, moistened, torn, burned, and shot with "bullet holes." Just remember to keep the important information legible.

After each invitation looks aged and weathered, it's ready to be sent. Fold posters as you would a letter and mail in envelopes.

## DECORATIONS/ COSTUMES

Maybe you don't have wild mustangs running across your lawn, but you can still re-create a ranch. Anchor 2 posts, one on each side, at the end of your driveway. Stretch a cloth or crêpe paper banner between them, announcing the name of your ranch. The name can be a variation on your child's first or last name; for example, Christina Gordon could call her ranch "The Christina Cross" or "The Gordon Gate." Just allow enough of a clearance, under the banner, for cars to pass.

Swinging doors are another Western motif that can be effective. Make them for saloons, banks, and sheriff's offices wherever there's a threshold or a doorway. Simply cut large flats of corrugated cardboard to resemble swinging doors. Paint with tempera, and tape each side to the doorway.

Red and white checked gingham is about as Western as Wyatt Earp. Use it as a traditional tablecloth for a chuck wagon. Gingham is easy to find, either in paper or real cloth. If you're looking for something a little more unconventional, cover the table as if it were a covered wagon. Use heavy 8- or 10-gauge wire to create "hoops" or arches and attach to the sides of the table.

fig. 1

This is the wagon frame, over which you can stretch a white sheet (fig. 1).

For centerpieces make pots of cucumber cacti. Stand 2 or 3 large cucumbers upright in a clay pot, and surround with sand. Insert rows of toothpicks for thorns. Shred 2 packages of golden or tan tissue by slicing them at ½-inch intervals on a paper cutter. Completely separate all strands of paper, then wad up the pieces to resemble tumbleweeds. Arrange cacti and tumbleweeds down the center of the table.

One of the refreshments on the menu is Dodge City Sarsaparilla, which is served at a "Soda Saloon." The bar can be any kind of long table or appliance box. Drape the counter with a dark cloth or paint the front of the box to resemble carved wood moldings. On the front, paint or tape the sign SODA SALOON. You can even make a brass rail by covering wrapping paper tubes with gold foil. Add a few stools for extra atmosphere.

This is one party where everyone will be able to come up with something, even if it's just a pair of jeans and a flannel shirt. Some children will arrive as cowboys, others as Indians. You may even see a few prairie dresses or coonskin caps. As with any party, it never hurts to be prepared for those who don't come in costume. Have a few cowboy hats or red bandannas handy as quick costumes.

## INSTANT INVOLVEMENT

When children walk through the door, they automatically become "deputized." Pass out star-shaped badges with each child's name on it. Next it's time for a photo session at the Olde Time Tin Type Gallery. Of course, one of the advantages you have over those early photographers is the Polaroid camera. For authenticity, try to locate black and white film, however for many cameras this is impossible. Set up an old-fashioned box camera with a black cloth and shoe box. Attach the box to a tripod, and cut a hole large enough for the lens opening. Staple the cloth to the back of the box so it can be draped over the photographer's head (fig. 2). The camera is held inside the box, while children pose in front of the Wild West sets. Make these out of cardboard flats, like the ones you see in movie lots. Use tempera paint to decorate buildings from a typical town. Cut swinging doors in a bank or saloon and a barred window in the jail. These make amusing backdrops for kids to stand in front of, and the photographs make great party favors to take home.

fig. 2

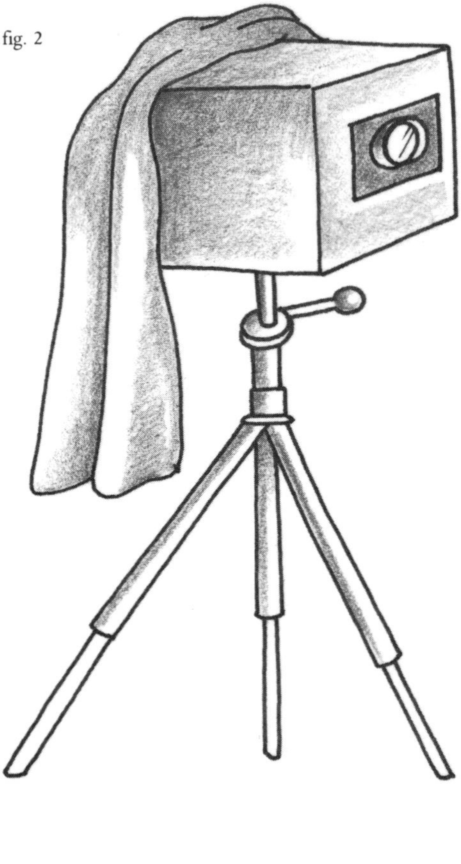

## GAMES

### CALF ROPING

This is basically an action game, with no definitive beginning or ending, winners or losers. It involves a lot of horse play and a lot of fun. A "lariat" or "lasso" is made by tying a clothesline rope to a hula hoop. Each cowboy takes a turn standing in the middle of a "cattle herd." The other children gallop in a circle around the cowboy, who tries to rope a calf in the hula hoop. The calf who gets caught trades places with the cowboy.

### PANNING FOR GOLD

In this game, children become prospectors in the San Francisco Gold Rush. Fill a small play pool (or sand box) with

sand. Buy a sack of pebbles from a nursery or garden center. Spread the pebbles out on some sheets of newspaper and spray them with a light coating of gold paint. When the stones are completely dry, mix into the sand. Make 2 sieves from wooden picture frames with some screen wire nailed to them.

Divide children into 2 teams and hand each one a sieve. The teams line up on opposite sides of the pool, and each child takes a turn at being a prospector. Each prospector is allowed to take one heaping scoop of sand and sift it. Any gold left in the sieve belongs to the team and goes into a communal bag. After everyone has had a turn, the teams count their gold, and the team with the most wins.

## PONY EXPRESS

Another relay game, this time it's a race to carry the U.S. Mail from St. Joseph to Sacramento. Children divide into 2 teams, with the exception of 2 who volunteer to play Indian and bandit. One team lines up at a point designated as St. Joseph, Missouri. The other team lines up at a point designated as Sacramento, California.

The object of the game is for each team to eventually get all of their original Pony Express riders to the other city. The territory each rider must cross contains 2 danger zones: outlaw country and Indian country. The bandit and the Indian patrol their respective

territories. The St. Joseph team starts the race by carrying the sack of mail. (The sack can simply be a brown paper bag marked U.S. MAIL and filled with blank envelopes.) The rider must carry the sack to Sacramento, where the next one in line takes the sack and returns it to St. Joseph. If a bandit or Indian should intercept the mail en route, then he or she trades places with the rider. When all of the riders have made an attempted journey, the team with the most *original* riders in the opposite city wins.

## RECIPES

## CORRAL SALAD

Serve this ranch-style salad from a celery corral filled with carrot-stick cattle.

PREPARATION TIME: 40 MINUTES

| 3 to 4 heads romaine lettuce |
| 3 bunches of celery |
| Ranch Dressing (recipe follows) |
| 1 pint cherry tomatoes |
| 1 cup grated Swiss cheese |
| 2 hard-cooked eggs, grated |
| Carrot Cows (recipe follows) |

Wash lettuce and spin dry thoroughly. Coarsely shred with a knife and spin dry again. Wash and cut longer celery stalks into ½ x 6-

inch sticks. (Chop short inner stalks and add to romaine in salad.) Just before serving, toss lettuce with dressing and pile into a large wooden salad bowl. Arrange celery sticks around the edge of the bowl, overlapping them "split-rail" style (fig. 3a). Top salad with tomatoes, grated cheese, and eggs. Place Carrot Cows in the center of corral.

# RANCH DRESSING

| |
|---|
| 1½ cups mayonnaise |
| ½ cup buttermilk |
| ½ cup sour cream |
| 1 clove garlic, crushed |
| 1 tablespoon dried chives |
| 1 teaspoon onion powder |

(a)

(c)

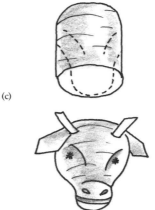

(b)

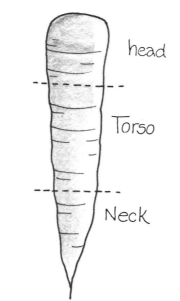

head

Torso

Neck

(d)

fig. 3

| 1 teaspoon garlic salt |
| 1 teaspoon dill weed |
| 1 teaspoon cracked pepper |
| 1 teaspoon Worcestershire sauce |
| 1 tablespoon sugar |
| ¼ cup grated Parmesan cheese |

Combine ingredients in a mixing bowl and blend until smooth. Store in a glass jar and chill for at least 4 hours before serving.

## CARROT COWS

| Large bunch of carrots |
| Cloves |
| Slivered almonds |
| Scallions |
| Toothpicks |

The number of cows you make really depends on the size of your carrots and the size of the bunch itself. Select the largest carrots for cow bodies. Clean carrots with a vegetable peeler and cut into neck, head, and torso sections (fig. 3b). Carve the head sections to resemble the contours of a cow's head. Use cloves for eyes, almonds for horns, and cut notches for mouths and nostrils. Use carrot trimmings to make ears and attach with pieces of toothpick (fig. 3c). Anchor neck, torso, and head together with toothpicks. Cut remaining carrots into sticks for legs. Attach legs with toothpicks (fig. 3d).

## RUSTLER RIBS

Children love finger food, but ribs can get messy so tie a big kerchief around the neck of each cowboy or cowgirl. Be sure there's a "watering hole" close by; this can be a large wash bucket with soap and towels alongside. Outdoors, you can put up a WATERING HOLE sign with an arrow pointing to the faucet on the side of the house. (Remember to disconnect the hose, though, unless you planned on having a sprinkler party!)

PREPARATION TIME: 30 MINUTES
COOKING TIME: 2 HOURS
   10 MINUTES, PLUS TIME TO
   REHEAT

| 2 cloves garlic, crushed |
| 1½ cups chopped onion |
| ½ cup finely chopped celery |
| 2 bottles (14 ounces each) ketchup |
| 1 bottle (12 ounces) chili sauce |
| 1½ cups strong coffee |
| ¼ cup red wine vinegar |
| ½ cup honey |
| ½ cup firmly packed brown sugar |
| 1 tablespoon Worcestershire sauce |
| 2 tablespoons chili powder |
| 1 teaspoon celery salt |
| Dash of Tabasco |
| 6–8 pounds spareribs |
| 2 cups tomato juice |

Combine all of the ingredients (except ribs and tomato juice) in a very large saucepan. Cover and simmer 30 minutes until onions are tender. Uncover and simmer, stirring occasionally, until sauce is slightly thickened. Reserve 2 cups sauce, then pour remaining into a large jar and set aside.

Preheat oven to 450°F. Cut spareribs into 2 sections. Place in a shallow roasting or large baking pan. Bake for 40 minutes.

Drain all the fat from ribs. Combine reserved sauce with tomato juice, then pour over ribs. Cover tightly with foil and bake 1 hour longer, until tender.

Remove ribs from pan, discarding drippings (the sauce will be full of grease). To serve, reheat ribs on the barbeque grill or in a 350°F oven, basting with fresh sauce until glazed. Pass the rest of the sauce at the table.

## BRANDED BAKED POTATOES

Each baked potato carries the brand of a child's initials. Serve piping hot with a lazy Susan of condiments.

PREPARATION TIME: 25 MINUTES
BAKING TIME: 1 HOUR
CHILLING TIME: 2 HOURS

| 12 baking potatoes |
| --- |
| 2 tablespoons molasses |
| 1 cup chopped scallions |

| 1 cup chopped crisp bacon |
| --- |
| 1 cup chive-flavored sour cream |
| Cheese Butter (recipe follows) |

Preheat oven to 400°F. Wash and lightly scrub potatoes. Using a linoleum cutter, wood chisel, or similiar tool, carve the initials of each child into a potato, so that they resemble ranch brands. For example, Barbara Boggs can be written with initials back to back like ꓭB. Other initials can be made upside down or with bars through or underneath them. Take a small paint brush and paint molasses into the grooves of the carved initials. Place directly on the rack of the oven (initials facing up), an hour before serving. Bake for 1 hour. Serve with Cheese Butter, scallions, bacon bits, and sour cream.

## CHEESE BUTTER

| 1 cup (2 sticks) butter, softened |
| --- |
| 1½ cups firmly packed grated cheddar cheese |
| ½ teaspoon paprika |
| Dash of Tabasco |

Put the ingredients in a food processor or blender and blend until smooth. Chill until 2 hours before serving, then allow to soften to room temperature.

Note: Tell the kids it's best to put the Cheese Butter on the potatoes first, while the potatoes are still piping hot.

## HORSESHOE BISCUITS

Whipped cream provides all the shortening these flakey biscuits need.

PREPARATION TIME: 20 MINUTES
BAKING TIME: 15 MINUTES

| 1 cup heavy cream |
| --- |
| 2 cups flour |
| 1 tablespoon baking powder |
| 1 egg, slightly beaten |
| 2 tablespoons sesame seed |

Preheat oven to 400°F. Beat cream until very stiff. Combine flour, baking powder, and sugar in a mixing bowl. Fold in heavy cream until thoroughly blended. Turn out onto a lightly floured board and knead 8–10 times until smooth. Roll into a 9 x 9-inch square. Trim sides evenly to make an 8 x 8-inch square. Cut into twelve ¾-inch strips. Shape strips into horseshoes and place on an ungreased baking sheet. Brush lightly with beaten egg and sprinkle with sesame seeds. Bake for 12–15 minutes, or until golden.

Note: If these are to be frozen, wrap in foil immediately from oven to preserve freshness. Heat biscuits when ready to serve.

## BUFFALO BEAN BUCKET

"Texacan" baked beans are served up campfire style in buckets. The crunchy corn tortilla topping adds a Southwestern flavor.

PREPARATION TIME: 25 MINUTES
BAKING TIME: 1 HOUR 20 MINUTES

| 2 cans (16 ounces each) pork and beans |
| --- |
| 1 can (16 ounces) pinto beans, drained |
| 1 can (16 ounces) red kidney beans, drained |
| 1 bottle (12 ounces) chili sauce |
| 1 jar (8 ounces) mild taco sauce |
| ½ cup molasses |
| ½ cup firmly packed brown sugar |
| 1 large onion, sliced |
| 3 cups cooked corn, drained |
| 2 cups grated cheddar cheese |
| 2 cups crushed tortilla chips |

Preheat oven to 350°F. Combine beans, chili sauce, taco sauce, molasses, brown sugar, and onion. Turn into a 4-quart casserole. Bake, uncovered, for 1 hour. Line 1 or 2 metal paint buckets (depending on what size you can find) with aluminum foil, crumpling some of the foil around the edge. Spoon beans into buckets.

Combine corn and cheese with half the crushed tortilla chips. Layer over the top of beans. Sprinkle with remaining crushed tortilla chips. Just before serving, bake at 400°F for 20 minutes, or until topping is golden brown.

Note: Carry bucket by the handle with a *hot pad*. Be sure to remind children not to touch the hot bucket when spooning out the beans.

# COVERED WAGON CAKES

This miniature wagon train is made from bars of caramel apple cake. For a dramatic presentation, arrange covered wagons in the traditional circle on a round platter. You could place the village of Indian Toffee Teepees in the center of the circle, however it might be more authentic to have them on the opposite end of the table. Use very flexible, lightweight poster board for wagon covers. A stiff, thick posterboard will crease, not bend.

PREPARATION TIME: 1¼ HOURS
BAKING TIME: 55 MINUTES

| |
|---|
| 1 cup vegetable or corn oil |
| ¼ cup butter, melted |
| 4 eggs |
| 2 cups sugar |
| 1 cup apple butter |
| ½ cup raisins |
| 1 cup chopped toasted walnuts |
| 3 cups flour |
| 2 teaspoons baking powder |
| 2 teaspoons baking soda |
| 2 teaspoons ground cinnamon |
| 1 teaspoon ground nutmeg |
| Caramel Frosting (recipe follows) |
| Chocolate Frosting (recipe follows) |
| 48 ginger snaps |
| 12 root beer candy cane sticks |
| 12 root beer barrel candies |
| Twelve 12-inch sections of black licorice whips or laces |
| Twelve 4 x 8-inch rectangles, cut from lightweight white posterboard |
| Scotch tape, toothpicks |

Preheat oven to 350°F. Line a 9 x 13-inch cake pan with baking parchment or buttered aluminum foil.

Combine the oil, butter, eggs, sugar, apple butter, raisins, nuts, flour, baking powder and soda, and spices in a large mixing bowl, and beat until smooth. Pour into prepared pan and bake for 50 to 55 minutes. Cool cake completely. Invert onto a baking sheet, and peel parchment paper or foil from the bottom. Cut cake into twelve 2 x 4-inch bars. (The cake will shrink to about 8 x 12 inches after baking.)

Frost top and sides of cake bars with caramel frosting. Spoon chocolate frosting into a pastry bag fitted with a small, round writing tip. Pipe "slats" on the sides of wagon cakes (fig. 4a). Pipe spokes on wheels and attach to wagons with frosting (fig. 4b). Stick root beer barrels on the rear ends of wagons. Insert a root beer stick and licorice whip at the front of each wagon for harness and reins (fig. 4c). On 4-inch sides of poster boards, tape 3 toothpicks along each edge (fig. 4d). Just before serving, arch each cover and anchor into sides of wagons (fig. 4e).

fig. 4

(a)

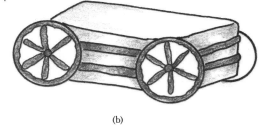

(b)

(c)

(d)

(e)

Note: Butter-based frostings have a tendency to "bleed" grease stains into paper; that's why you should never attach covers too far in advance.

## CARAMEL FROSTING

This recipe makes a generous amount. Reserve some for chocolate frosting.

| 1 pound butter |
| --- |
| 1 pound (4 cups) firmly packed dark brown sugar |
| 2 pounds (8 cups) confectioners sugar, sifted |
| 1 tablespoon vanilla extract |
| 1 cup milk |

Melt butter in a very large saucepan. Blend in brown sugar and cook, stirring constantly, over low heat for 2 minutes. Add milk and bring to a boil, stirring constantly until sugar dissolves. Remove from heat and cool to lukewarm. Beat in confectioners sugar and vanilla, adding enough milk (if necessary) to make a smooth, spreadable frosting.

## CHOCOLATE FROSTING

| 2 tablespoons unsweetened cocoa powder |
| --- |
| 1 tablespoon hot water |
| 1¼ cups reserved Caramel Frosting (previous recipe) |
| Milk |

Dissolve cocoa in hot water and then let cool slightly. Blend into the reserved frosting. If necessary, thin with a little milk until smooth and light.

## TOFFEE TEEPEES

Watch your tribe devour these toffee ice cream teepees, made from white chocolate-dipped ice cream cones.

PREPARATION TIME: 45 MINUTES, PLUS ABOUT 10 HOURS FREEZING

| 1 quart vanilla ice cream |
| --- |
| 1 cup crushed toffee bars |
| 12 ice cream sugar cones |
| White Chocolate Glaze (recipe follows) |
| ½ cup chilled fudge sauce (any brand or homemade) |
| Toothpicks |

Soften ice cream slightly, and mix in crushed toffee. (Don't let ice cream melt too much.) Quickly spoon ice cream into cones. Pack it down as gently as possible, then invert cones onto a foil-lined tray and return to the freezer immediately. Freeze 4 hours, or until firm.

Remove about 3 cones from the freezer at a time to work with. Hold each cone over a double boiler with the glaze, and spread on glaze, allowing the excess to drip back into the pot. As soon as glaze starts to set slightly (this will take a few seconds—the glaze no longer runs or drips), return to freezer tray. Repeat with all of the cones. Freeze for another 4 hours.

Carefully slice ½ inch from the tip of each cone with a sharp knife. Insert 3 toothpicks at the top of each teepee for supporting posts. Spoon fudge sauce into a pastry bag fitted with a small, round writing tip. Pipe a door and Indian designs on teepees (fig. 5). Freeze until serving time.

fig. 5

# WHITE CHOCOLATE GLAZE

| 12 ounces real white chocolate |
| --- |
| ¼ cup butter |
| 2 tablespoons light corn syrup |

Chop white chocolate into small chunks and place in the top of a double boiler over (not touching) very hot tap water. Add butter and corn syrup, then cover for 10 minutes. Remove lid and stir until smooth. If necessary, continuously change water to keep it hot, however never set over boiling water or chocolate may "tighten or seize."

## DODGE CITY SARSAPARILLA

Cream soda makes a big foamy head, so be sure to use tall glasses or paper cups.

PREPARATION TIME: 10 MINUTES

| ¾ cup grenadine syrup |
| --- |
| Angostura bitters |
| 12 cans cream soda, chilled |

Pour a tablespoon of grenadine syrup in the bottom of each of 12 glasses and add a dash of angostura to each. Pour cold cream soda into glasses and watch the surprise as the clear beverage becomes a pink, fruity drink.

# PIRATES' PLUNDER

**T**his is a gathering of "buccaneers," "swash-bucklers," and assorted "ruffians," so try to hold it outdoors or in a recreation room.

## MENU

**TREASURE ISLAND WITH GREEN ONION DILL DIP**

**STUFFED SEASHELLS**

**PIRATE SHIP PIZZAS**

**FROZEN FRUIT CARIBBEAN**

**JOLLY ROGER CAKE**

**CROCODILE COOKIES**

**GINGER BEER**

**FEATURES:** Buccaneer Hats, Buried Treasure

**GAMES:** Swashbuckling Breadsticks, Sinking Ship, Treasure Hunt

**INVITATIONS:** Messages in bottles

## INVITATIONS

What else would you expect? An invitation to a Pirates' Plunder Party is a message in a bottle! Ideally, this invitation is hand delivered; it's difficult to send even small glass bottles through the mail. (If you could locate a dozen miniature plastic bottles—like the kind they sell on airplanes—however, you might consider it. In this case, you would have to write HAND CANCEL on each envelope.) I find that 6½-ounce Perrier bottles make very authentic-looking vessels. Soak the labels off first, then roll up the invitations, stuff them into the bottles, and bring the bottles around to the children's houses.

12 INVITATIONS
PREPARATION TIME: 30 TO 40 MINUTES

| |
|---|
| 12 small bottles |
| 1 sheet 8½ x 11-inch typing paper |
| Felt-tip marking pen |

The fun part about this invitation is making a mythical map of your neighborhood. You can turn your street into a sea and your yard into an island. X marks the spot of your house on this treasure map. Of course, this newly charted territory should bear a reasonable resemblance to the actual geography; you wouldn't want your guests to get lost. After you've drawn a map on the order of the example (fig. 1), applying to your area, write the following message across the bottom.

Ship's Ahoy and Shiver Me Timbers! They say there's a Party of Pirates at Captain Billy's [your child's name] Hideaway. Calling all buccaneers, Barbary bandits, salty dogs, and sea scoundrels for great grub, games, and gold, [date, time, your address].

R.S.V.P. [your phone]

Come in a white, oversized shirt, dark rolled-up pants, and knee socks—the rest of the costume is waiting for you.

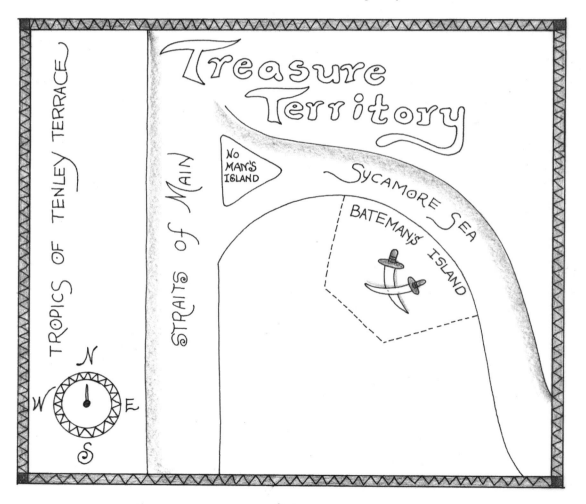

fig. 1

Take this sheet to a library or copy center and make about a dozen photocopies, fold sheets in half lengthwise, roll up, and stick into bottles.

## DECORATIONS/HATS

The atmosphere for a Pirates' party is created by combining nautical and tropical themes. Depending on the part of the country you live in, life preservers, fishnets, etc., may be easy to find. If you can get hold of some, they're great for hanging around the walls of the room. Import and party shops are an abundant source of luau supplies. There you can buy (or sometimes rent) yards of fishnetting, grass mats, coconut bowls, lanterns, seashells, even artificial fish. You can also make some of these yourself from construction paper or cardboard.

My favorite table treatment for this party is to turn it into a ship! This is done by standing masts with sails down the center of the table. You'll need 3 wooden posts or dowels. Two should be about 4 foot long for the foremast and mizzen mast; the other should be about 5 foot long for the mainmast. Prop the masts up by nailing them perpendicularly to a 1 x 5-inch board about as long as the table. The mainmast should be centered between the other two (fig. 2a). You can use white sheets to simulate sails, but this requires rigging up a

(a)

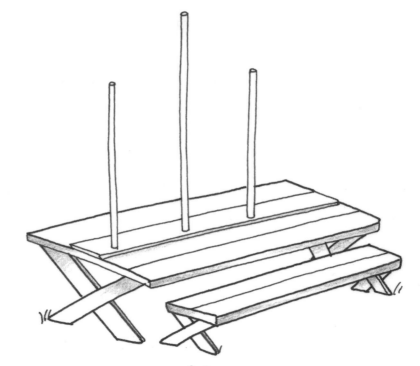

fig. 2

(b)

(c)

(d)

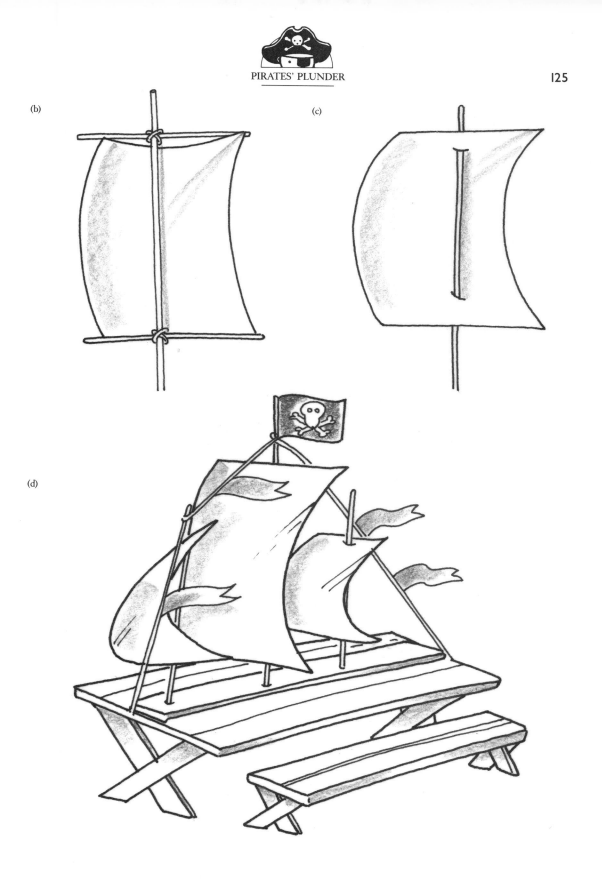

cross-dowel (fig. 2b). Perhaps the easiest way is simply to use bowed sheets of large white poster board (fig. 2c). After you've set up the sails, run clothesline or heavy twine over the tops of masts and down under the table. Tie securely in place. Use this rigging for flying streamers of crêpe paper flags, and don't forget the most important flag of all—the Jolly Roger (fig. 2d). This can be made on a black construction paper background, with a white skull and crossbones cut-out pasted on. You can even cut a cardboard anchor to hold down the ship. Suspend from some clothesline or twine over the end of the table, so that the anchor just touches the floor.

## BUCCANEER HATS

At a party such as this, the "pirates" arrive in basic costume and you provide the finishing touch. The invitation suggests that children wear white shirts (loose or oversized ones are very effective), dark pants rolled up at the cuffs, and white knee socks. These buccaneer hats are perhaps one of the easiest costume projects in this book. Remember the classic paper hats you used to fold out of newspaper? Well, these are essentially the same. Black tissue paper, bright marabou plumes, and gold seal "medallions" will make you feel like the milliner for an MGM movie.

PREPARATION TIME: 30 MINUTES

1 package (you'll only need 12 sheets) 20 x 30-inch black tissue paper

12 marabou feathers (available in packages at craft shops; choose bright colors: red, blue, yellow)

12 gold pressure-sensitive medallion seals about 1¼ to 1½ inches in diameter (available at stationery and office supply stores)

Stapler

For each hat, fold a sheet of tissue into a 20 x 15-inch rectangle. Now fold the rectangle into a 10 x 15-inch rectangle, with the major fold at the top. Fold the corners of each top side down 7 inches and crease. There should be about a 1-inch space at the top (fig. 3a). Fold bottom on each side up 1½ inches. Crease. Fold up 1½ inches again and crease. Turn hat over and repeat on the other side. Staple hat together at edges (fig. 3b). On right side of hat, slightly off center, staple a feather behind the cuff or "brim." Stick a gold medallion seal over the staple (fig. 3c).

## INSTANT INVOLVEMENT

After children have been greeted at the door, and you've taken their coats and presents, guide them into the "Wardrobe Department." This

(a)

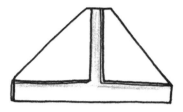

(b)

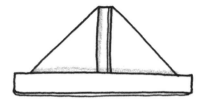

(c)

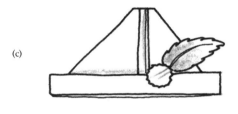

fig. 3

"make-up artist" can be on hand to apply moustaches with eyebrow pencils and scars with lipstick. As soon as each child is in costume, he or she can proceed to the "crow's nest." This is any window or vantage point that allows children to view arriving guests. A pair of binoculars or small telescope adds an aura of excitement. It's the duty of the pirates in the crow's nest to announce all newcomers by calling out their names, such as "Charlie Ahoy!"

## GAMES

## SWASHBUCKLING BREADSTICKS

The prospect of a sword fight erupting at a pirate party is as inevitable as it is undesirable. The idea of playing with toy swords, plastic daggers, or (especially) sticks can be dangerous and must be discouraged. The best way is to channel all of this energy and imagination into a battle of breadsticks. Obviously, if all the children were to participate at once, the chaos would come close to mutiny. There's more sportsmanship in organizing a one-on-one duel of formal fencing. The game commences with 2 pirates squaring off in the "On Guard" position, breadsticks crossed in an X like fencing foils. The object is to break down the opponent's breadstick, without damaging their

can be any designated room with a sign above the door. Whether you're casting for *Treasure Island*, *The Pirates of Penzance*, or *Peter Pan* is really up to the children. This party, after all, is a totally original production. Give out the buccaneer hats, along with various optional accessories such as eye patches, golden earrings, and sashes. A friend, serving as

own (or as little as possible). When one player's breadstick becomes so short that he or she can no longer use it, the player surrenders the stub and is forced to "walk the plank." (The plank can be either a real or make-believe board.) The remaining player is the champion, and must defend this position against a new challenger stepping in. Both begin the next match with fresh breadsticks.

There is one major rule: No breadstick should strike any part of the opponent's body, other than the arm. If a player does, he or she is automatically called out. The whole point is to break breadsticks with breadsticks, not over each other's heads. The champion who stays up the longest wins and is awarded a prize. However, this game is so engrossing that the kids will want to go for several rounds, so have plenty of breadsticks and prizes on hand.

For extra fun, you can turn this into a swashbuckling screen test à la Errol Flynn. Use your own, borrow, or rent a home movie or video camera. The latter allows you to enjoy an instant replay of the action, right at the party.

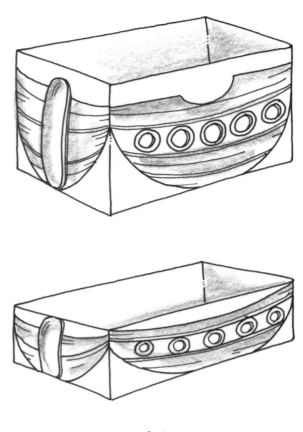

fig. 4

## SINKING SHIP

For this game, you'll need to locate a couple of refrigerator boxes from a large appliance store. If you can only get hold of one, just split it in half lengthwise to form 2 open-topped boxes. If you have 2 boxes, then cut open one of the sides for the top of each ship. At this point, you can decorate the boxes with tempera paint to resemble pirate ships (fig. 4), or simply leave it to the imagination. Divide the party into 2 teams for the crew on each ship. (If the party is larger than 12, you may have to play in 2 shifts.)

Position ships at opposite ends of the room, or about 12 to 18 feet apart. The crews stand or kneel in their ships, depending on the height of the box. The object of the game is to sink the other ship with

cannon (Ping-Pong) balls. The first round begins by giving one crew 2 dozen Ping-Pong balls. They barrage the opposing ship with a shower of balls, trying to land them inside the box. Each "cannonball" that makes a successful hit counts as a point for the offensive team. The only defense against attack is if a member of the defensive crew is able to catch a ball in mid-air. Then they have the chance to either throw it out of the ship (canceling a point made against them) or throwing it back into the offensive ship (scoring an instant point for their team). When the offensive team has used up all of their ammunition, a tally is taken of the score by counting the balls in the defensive ship. The balls are all collected and now it's the defensive team's turn to begin the battery of cannon fire. This battle continues for four rounds, with the winning crew making the highest score of hits, the sinking ship receiving the most cannonballs.

## TREASURE HUNT

A chocolate chest filled with candy coins is truly a prize for any pirate. This treasure hunt follows a series of clues that lead to the legendary "X marks the spot." You should gear your clues to the age group. The older the children, the greater the challenge. A game that gives hints in a riddle form will last longer than if the clues are quite obvious.

The "Treasure Territory" is somewhere in the tropics. This can be outdoors or in, as long as you have plenty of resourceful hiding places. There should be a total of 12 clues, 11 of them written on pieces of paper. The first clue is given to the crew of pirates by the Ancient Mariner (any adult present at the party). This could be something like, "Where the sea stands above the sand." The first children to catch on will discover the next clue under the bird bath, which might read, "Land-locked by a wooden wall." This will lead children to the fence, where the next clue is wedged in the latch of the gate. Of course, these are only examples. The clues that you create will have to apply to your setting. The final clue will be a little map that shows the "Treasure Territory" with an X on the spot of the chocolate chest. The first child who finds it keeps the chest but must share one coin with every pirate. It's a good idea to hide the chest in a cardboard box (so it won't get dirty) and away from the sun (so it won't melt).

## CHOCOLATE TREASURE CHEST

| |
| --- |
| 2 bags (12 ounces each) chocolate-flavored morsels (see note, page 56) |
| Gold or silver foil |
| Gold or silver dragées (metallic candy balls to match your foil) |
| Foil-covered chocolate coins |
| Paint brush or pastry brush |

Place chocolate chips in the top of a double boiler. Set over very hot tap water (never boiling), cover, and let stand 10–15 minutes. Change water and replace with more hot tap water. Stir chocolate until it's smooth and melted. (Never allow any moisture to make contact with the chocolate or it will not melt smoothly.) If you have a microwave, you can also melt the chocolate by pouring the morsels into a large ceramic bowl. Microwave on medium for 2 minutes, stir, and microwave 2 minutes longer. Stir until smooth and melted.

Spread the chocolate in a thick wall along the bottoms and sides of two 9 x 5-inch loaf pans. Reserve a little chocolate for patching or decorating. Chill the chocolate-filled pans in refrigerator until firm. (The chocolate will shrink from the sides.) Gently unmold the chocolate boxes from the pans. If there are any major cracks, fit pieces back into loaf pan mold and patch with melted chocolate. Chill again until firm and unmold.)

You should have a top half and a bottom half for the chest. Cut two 4 x 4-inch foil squares. Fold the squares into 1 x 4-inch strips, trimming ends to points (fig. 5a). Remelt some leftover chocolate and use the paint brush to apply it to one side of each foil strip. Press strips against back of chest to form "hinges" (fig. 5b). Stick rows of dragées to the chest with melted chocolate to form a design (fig. 5c). Set chest in the refrigerator and allow to harden. When chocolate is firm, gently open lid and fill with chocolate coins.

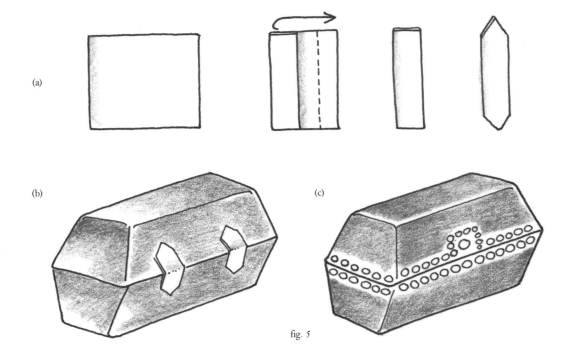

fig. 5

## RECIPES

## TREASURE ISLAND

Land Ho! Yonder lies an island shaded by green pepper palms, inhabited by carrot parrots, and surrounded by cucumber sharks and sea turtles. On shore, pirates can dip into a creamy pool of onions and dill.

PREPARATION TIME: 1 HOUR

| |
| --- |
| 1 very large, flat-shaped cabbage |
| Green Pepper Palm Trees (recipe follows) |
| Carrot Parrots (recipe follows) |
| Cucumber Turtles (recipe follows) |
| Cucumber Sharks (recipe follows) |
| Turnip Gardenias (recipe follows) |
| Green Onion Dill Dip (recipe follows) |
| Zucchini, celery, and carrot sticks |
| Bamboo or wooden skewers, toothpicks |

Make the decorations a day ahead, then assemble the island on the day of the party. Slice bottom off cabbage to make a level base. Set cabbage in the center of a large round platter and hollow out a large "well" in the middle to hold the dip. Take cabbage scraps and shred with a knife. Scatter shredded cabbage at base around cabbage head.

Anchor Palm Trees in place around island with skewers. Perch Carrot Parrots on top of cabbage. Use toothpicks to stick Cucumber Turtles around sides of island. Lay Turnip Gardenias around the base. Fill the hollow of the cabbage with dip to create a "pool." Arrange sticks of zucchini, carrots, and cucumbers around the edge of the platter (see fig. 6i).

## GREEN PEPPER PALM TREES

Peel 3 very large carrots and cut small gashes in rows up the sides (fig. 6a). Cut 3 green peppers so that each lobe looks like a jagged palm frond (fig. 6b). Soak carrots and green peppers overnight in ice water (they'll spread open). Attach green peppers to the tops of carrots with toothpicks.

## CARROT PARROTS

Peel 3 or 4 very small carrots. Cut 3 gashes about 1½ inches deep at the pointed end (fig. 6c). Soak in ice water overnight to make "tail feathers" spread. Attach snow peas on sides of carrots for wings. Insert cloves for eyes and slivered almonds for bills. Use toothpicks for legs (fig. 6d).

## CUCUMBER TURTLES

Slice 2 cucumbers in half lengthwise and cut into quarters. Carve sections into ovals and then into turtle shapes. Score with grooves to create a shell effect (fig. 6e).

## CUCUMBER SHARK

Cut a gash at one end of another cucumber for a mouth and 2 smaller gashes on each side for gills. Hollow out an eye. Cut slice from the bottom and rear sides of cucumber for fins. Trim fins to fit along sides and anchor with toothpicks, two on the top and one on each side (fig. 6f).

## TURNIP GARDENIAS

Slice turnip across in thin shavings and soak in ice water until slices curl. Skewer slices on a toothpick and spread out like a flower (fig. 6g). Use a chunk of turnip for stamen and cover toothpick with a scallion stem (fig. 6h).

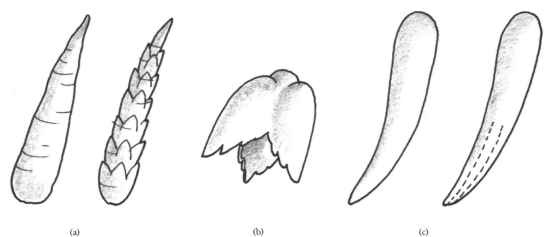

(a)

(b)

(c)

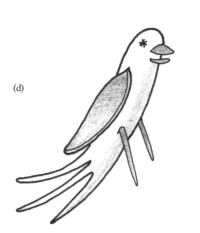

(d)

(e)

(f)

fig. 6

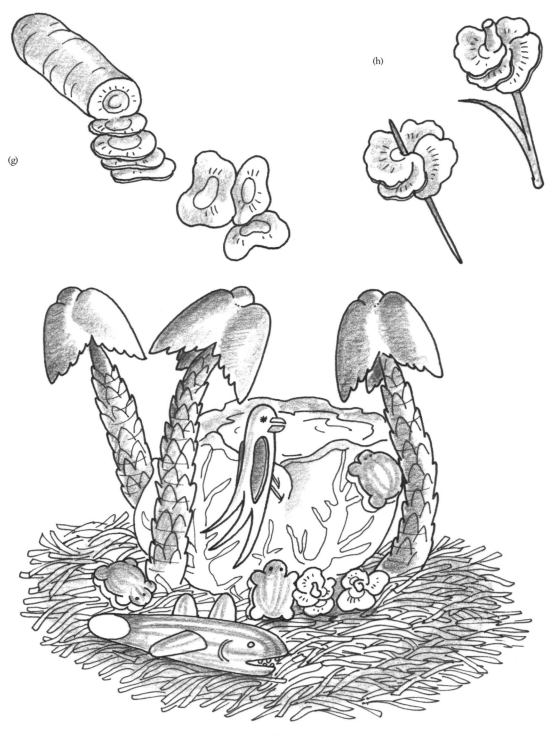

(g)

(h)

(i)

## GREEN ONION DILL DIP

| |
|---|
| ¼ cup chopped fresh parsley |
| ¼ cup chopped scallions |
| 1 clove garlic, minced |
| 1 tablespoon fresh dill or 1 teaspoon dried |
| 1 teaspoon herbed salt |
| ½ cup sour cream |
| ½ cup mayonnaise |
| 1 cup small curd cottage cheese |

Combine parsley, scallions, garlic, dill, herbed salt, sour cream, and mayonnaise in a food processor and blend until smooth. Stir into cottage cheese. Keep refrigerated until serving time. Refill pool as often as necessary.

## STUFFED SEASHELLS

Flaky pastry scallop shells are filled with tuna salad to make an irresistible seafood sandwich.

PREPARATION TIME: 30 MINUTES
BAKING TIME: 20 MINUTES

| |
|---|
| 3 sheets (1½ boxes) frozen puff pastry |
| 1 egg beaten with 1 teaspoon water |
| 3 cans (7 ounces each) solid white tuna, drained |
| 1 can (3 ounces) water chestnuts, drained and coarsely chopped |
| ⅓ cup chopped scallions |
| 3 sweet gherkins, chopped |

| |
|---|
| 1 teaspoon onion powder |
| ½ teaspoon celery salt |
| ½–⅔ cup mayonnaise |

Preheat oven to 400°F. Thaw puff pastry for 20–30 minutes. Unfold and cut each sheet into 4 equal squares. Cut each pastry square into a scallop-shaped shell. (You can use a real scallop baking shell for the pattern). Place shells on an ungreased baking sheet, brush pastry with egg wash, and score with a knife to resemble the lines of a scallop shell. Bake for 15 to 20 minutes, or until puffed and golden brown. Cool completely.

Combine tuna, water chestnuts, scallions, gherkins, onion powder, and celery salt in a mixing bowl. Blend in enough mayonnaise to "bind" the sandwich filling. Chill until ready to serve. Just before serving, split shells open with a sharp knife and fill with tuna salad.

## PIRATE SHIP PIZZAS

Grinder (hero) rolls, brimming with pizza filling, are turned into pirate ships with mozzarella sails.

PREPARATION TIME: 10 MINUTES
BAKING TIME: 25 MINUTES

| |
|---|
| 6 hero or hard rolls, about 6–7 inches long |
| 1 tablespoon olive oil |
| 1 tablespoon butter |
| 1 clove garlic, crushed |

| ½ pound fresh mushrooms, sliced |
| 1 large onion, sliced |
| 1 large green pepper, chopped |
| 1 can (8 ounces) pizza sauce |
| 2 tablespoons tomato paste |
| ½ teaspoon crushed oregano |
| ½ teaspoon dried basil leaves |
| 2 tablespoons grated Parmesan cheese |
| 1 package (8 ounces) sliced pepperoni |
| ⅓ cup sliced ripe olives |
| 1 cup grated mozzarella cheese, plus 12 slices mozzarella |
| 12 carrot curls (thin, lengthwise slices of carrot which have been soaked in ice water) |
| 12 rigid plastic straws, swizzle sticks, or bamboo skewers (with care) |

Preheat oven to 350°F. Slice rolls in half lengthwise. Hollow out a slight depression in each half to create a boat shape.

Heat oil and butter in a pan and sauté garlic, mushrooms, onion, and green pepper until tender. Stir in pizza sauce, tomato paste, oregano, basil, and Parmesan cheese. Set aside. (This sauce can be prepared in advance and refrigerated, or even frozen.)

Toast rolls in hot oven for 15 minutes to crisp the crusts. Fill rolls with pizza sauce and place on a baking sheet. Top with pepperoni, olives, and grated mozzarella.

Bake at 400°F for 10 minutes, or until the cheese is bubbling and melted.

Meanwhile, prepare sails by skewering a slice of mozzarella cheese with a plastic straw and sticking a carrot flag on the end. Just before serving, insert sails into pizza boats.

Note: Allow pizza to cool slightly, so that sails won't be melted by the heat.

# FROZEN FRUIT CARIBBEAN

What first appear to be chilled melon slices actually are frosty wedges of this cantaloupe and honeydew sorbet. Serve as a refreshing garnish with lunch or as the "ice cream" counterpart to cake.

PREPARATION TIME: 25 MINUTES
FREEZING TIME: ABOUT 12 HOURS
TOTAL

| 2 ripe cantaloupes |
| 1 large (or 2 small) ripe honeydew melons |
| ¼ cup lime juice |
| ½ cup honey |
| ½ cup confectioners sugar |

Slice melons in half. Scoop out seeds and discard. Gently scoop out all the fruit from the cantaloupes and place in a bowl; scoop out all the fruit from the honeydew and place in another bowl. Reserve shells by wrapping in plastic wrap and keeping chilled in the refrigerator.

Put cantaloupe and half the lime juice, honey, and confectioners sugar in the bowl of a food processor and puree. Pour into a shallow pan or into ice cube trays. Repeat the process with the honeydew and the remaining lime juice, honey, and confectioners sugar. Freeze trays until melon is firm, about 2 hours.

Remove cantaloupe from freezer. Break up into cubes or pieces and crush in food processor. Spoon back into tray and return to freezer for at least 2 hours. Repeat with honeydew.

After a couple of hours, the sorbets will be the right consistency to stuff into the melon shells. Scoop cantaloupe sorbet back into cantaloupe shells, pressing it against the shells with the back of a spoon. The idea is to form the original shape of the melon, leaving a hollow indention in the center. Cover with plastic wrap and return to freezer. Repeat process with honeydew, and freeze until very firm—at least 8 hours. Just before serving, slice into wedges with a sharp knife.

Note: These sorbets can be prepared as much as two weeks in advance and kept tightly wrapped in the freezer.

## JOLLY ROGER CAKE

Beneath the billowing white sails and the black Jolly Roger flag is this tropical banana cake.

PREPARATION TIME: 2 HOURS
BAKING TIME: 35 MINUTES

| |
|---|
| 1 cup butter, softened |
| 1 cup sugar |
| 2 eggs |
| 1 cup mashed ripe bananas |
| 1¾ cups flour |
| ½ teaspoon salt |
| ⅔ teaspoon baking soda |
| ⅓ cup buttermilk |
| 1 teaspoon vanilla extract |
| 1 cup chopped candied pineapple |
| Buttercream Frosting (recipe follows) |
| Sails (instructions follow) |
| Jolly Roger Flag (instructions follow) |
| Bamboo or wooden skewers, toothpicks |

Preheat oven to 350°F. Line two 9-inch layer pans with baking parchment or buttered aluminum foil.

Cream the butter and sugar until very light and fluffy. Beat in eggs, one at a time, and add the mashed bananas. In a separate bowl, combine flour, salt, and baking powder and then blend dry mixture into butter-egg mixture. Add buttermilk and vanilla. Beat 1 minute and then fold in pineapple. Pour batter into prepared pans and bake for 25 to 35 minutes, or until a cake tester inserted in the center comes out clean. Cool cakes completely and remove from pans.

Peel parchment paper or foil from the backs of cakes.

To assemble the cake, place 1 layer on a flat cakeboard or large plate. Cut the other layer into 2 semicircles. Sandwich together with a little chocolate frosting. Cut a slice from the bottom so that the ship will have a flat base. Cut a semicircle out of the middle and taper the edges of the bow and stern (fig. 7a). Anchor boat in the center of round layer with a little blue frosting. Frost boat with chocolate frosting. Pipe rows of "boards" with a pastry bag filled with chocolate frosting to create a hull effect. (You can also achieve this by making groove-marks with a toothpick.) It may be necessary to secure the boat in place with concealed toothpicks or skewers.

Use a pastry bag, fitted with a fine writing tip, to pipe double chocolate frosting portholes and also the trim around the deck. Insert mainmast in the center with the foremast in front and the mizzenmast in back. Insert toothpicks around bow and stern, and loop with string for a rail (fig. 7b). Attach a wooden skewer at the bow and stern of the ship and run a rigging line, over the top of the sails, from one end of the ship to the other. Loop string in place around the tops of sails.

Use a metal spatula to frost blue icing over the base layer of cake. Make cresting waves that break against the hull of the ship. Top waves with peaks of white frosting for "white caps" or sea foam.

Note: This cake may be baked,

then frozen and frosted at your convenience, or the entire ship may be assembled ahead of time and frozen.

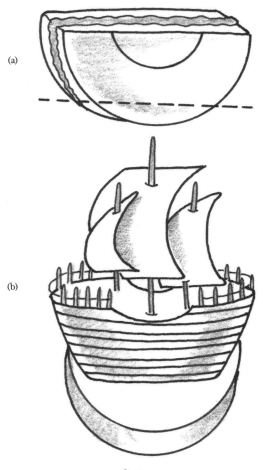

fig. 7

# BUTTERCREAM FROSTING

| |
|---|
| 1 cup butter, softened |
| ½ cup milk |
| 2 tablespoons vanilla extract |
| 2 pounds confectioners sugar |

Cream butter until light and fluffy. Add milk, vanilla, and

half the confectioners sugar. Beat until smooth. Beat in remaining sugar. Reserve ¼ cup for white frosting.

For blue frosting, tint ¼ of remaining frosting (after reserving white frosting) to a blue or blue-green for ocean water.

For chocolate frosting, beat ⅓ cup of cocoa with 2 tablespoons softened butter. Blend into the remaining frosting (after reserving white and blue frosting).

For the double chocolate frosting, take ½ cup of chocolate frosting and blend in 2 tablespoons of cocoa to make a darker shade of brown. (This is used for the portholes and trim.)

## SAILS

Fold a 9 x 12-inch sheet of white construction paper in half to 6 x 9 inches. Cut along the crease. Cut one section of paper in half along the diagonal. The square paper will be the mainsail and the 2 right triangles will become the lateen sails. The wooden skewers used for masts should be at least 10 inches long. Stick sails onto skewers at bottoms and tops, billowing or bending the centers. The mizzenmast and foremast should always be positioned lower into the cake than the mainsail.

## JOLLY ROGER FLAG

Cut out a 1 x 2-inch square of black construction paper. With a small brush, paint on a skull and crossbones with white acrylic or tempera paint. Tape to the top of the mainmast.

## CROCODILE COOKIES

Joe Froggers were a famous cookie that originated in Marblehead, Massachusetts. When sea travel was in its heyday, this spicy molasses cookie soon spread to every port from Boston to Barbados. The addition of crocodiles makes this version appropriate for a "Pirates' Plunder," complete with Captain Hook and the gang.

PREPARATION TIME: 30 MINUTES
BAKING TIME: 12 MINUTES

| ¼ cup shortening or margarine |
| --- |
| 2 tablespoons butter, softened |
| ¾ cup brown sugar |
| ¾ cup molasses |
| ⅓ cup water |
| 3 cups flour |
| 1 teaspoon salt |
| ¾ teaspoon baking soda |
| 1½ teaspoons ground ginger |
| ½ teaspoon ground cloves |
| ½ teaspoon ground nutmeg |
| ¼ teaspoon ground allspice |
| 2 tablespoons sugar |
| Crocodile Frosting (recipe follows) |

Cream together shortening, butter, and brown sugar until fluffy. Beat in molasses and water. Blend in remaining dry ingredients (except granulated

sugar) to form a smooth dough. Chill dough for several hours or overnight.

Preheat oven to 375°F. Roll dough out on a floured board until ¼ inch thick. Cut into 3-inch circles and place on a greased baking sheet. Re-roll and cut scraps. Sprinkle cookies with granulated sugar. Bake for 10–12 minutes, or until golden. Allow cookies to stand on cookie sheet for 5–7 minutes before removing to cooling rack. (This prevents cookies from breaking when lifted with a spatula.) When cookies are completely cool, decorate with a crocodile on top of each.

## CROCODILE FROSTING

| |
|---|
| ¼ cup butter, softened |
| 2 tablespoons milk |
| 1 teaspoon vanilla extract |
| 2 cups confectioners sugar |
| Green food coloring |
| Chocolate mini-chips |

Cream butter until soft and fluffy. Beat in milk, vanilla, and confectioners sugar to make a smooth frosting. Tint with enough green food coloring to make the right shade of "crocodile." Fill a pastry bag fitted with a star tip (about a #21 in size). Pipe a ruffled "caterpillar" shape onto each cookie, tapering at both ends. One end will be the head, the other the tail.

Change pastry bag nozzle to a fine round writing tip. Pipe 2 large round dots for eyes and 2 smaller dots for nostrils. Pipe legs on the body and insert chocolate chips on eyes for pupils (fig. 8).

fig. 8

## GINGER BEER

Next to "demon rum," ginger beer was one of the most popular drinks among pirates. This "soft" version is as simple as opening a bottle of soda. Half fill your mugs or cups with ginger ale. Finish them off with a foamy head of root beer. A wooden barrel filled with ice makes a perfect party prop, as well as a place to chill bottles.

# HOUSE HAUNTING

**H**alloween is when gremlins, goblins, and ghouls make their annual venture out into the night, along with strange creatures called "trick-or-treaters." An alternative to after-dark trick or treating is to entertain inside your own haunted house.

## MENU

SCARECROW SALADS

SLEEPY HOLLOW STEW

BROOMSTICKS

FROZEN JACK-O'-LANTERNS

GLOWING HOBGOBLIN CAKE

WITCHES' BREW

**FEATURES:** Halloween Costumes, Flying Bats

**GAMES:** Séance, Poltergeist, Headless Horseman

**INVITATIONS:** "A Psychic Message"

## INVITATIONS

In a psychic message, a transference of thought takes place from one mind to another. In this case, the spiritual messenger is a tissue-paper ghost with the invitation wadded up in its head!

12 INVITATIONS
PREPARATION TIME: 30 MINUTES

| |
| --- |
| 6 sheets (20 x 30 inches each) white tissue paper |
| Typing paper for photocopying |
| ¼-inch-wide ribbon or curling ribbon (black and orange) |
| 12 white paper tags or cards (1 x 2 inches each) |
| Black felt-tip marker |
| Scissors, hole punch |

Cut tissue paper (all thicknesses at once) into twenty-four 10 x 10-inch squares (4 squares a sheet). Type

*Flying Saucer Sandwiches (recipe pages 103-104), from Space Station Stopover*

*Frozen Jack-o'-Lanterns (recipe page 147)*

or write the invitation according to the model and make 12 photocopies.

Now for the fun part—crumple up your invitations into tight wads of paper! Lay 2 squares of tissue paper on top of each other as shown and place a wad in the middle (fig. 1a). Gather paper around wad to form a head. Cut ribbon into 8-inch lengths. Write on cards: UNTIE ME!, punch a whole in the corner (if there isn't already one on tags), and thread one orange and one black strand of ribbon through hole. Tie ribbons together around neck of ghost. Draw on a face with black felt-tip marker (fig. 1b).

Note: These can be mailed in legal-sized envelopes; however, they're a little lumpy.

## MODEL

*THIS IS A PSYCHIC MESSAGE*

*A SPIRIT SEEKS YOUR PRESENCE AT A SÉANCE*

*MATERIALIZE AT THE HAUNTED HOUSE*

*ON*

*[your address, date, and time]*

*CONTACT THE "MEDIUM"*

*[your phone number]*

*TELL 'EM [your child's name]*

*SENT YOU*

fig. 1

## DECORATIONS

"Haunting" the average house needn't take more than a couple of hours. Begin by stringing "cobwebs" with tape and twine in the corners of the ceiling. You can even add a few spiders made out of wadded-up black tissue paper and twisted pipe cleaners (fig. 2a,b). Hang "ghouloons" from the ceiling. Cut a hole in the center of a large sheet of lightweight cloth or tissue. String balloon through hole and tie at the base to form a neck. Decorate with a face. Make "tombstone slipcovers" to fit over the backs of chairs by sandwiching 2 sheets of poster board together for each chair. Each tombstone has the inscription: HERE LIES [child's name], serving as a place marker.

This is one party where costumes go without saying. It's very unusual when a child doesn't arrive as anything other than him- or herself.

## INSTANT INVOLVEMENT

Any child who has ever made a paper airplane will be challenged by creating the most aerodynamic bat in the belfry. As soon as the kids arrive, pass out black construction paper and blunt scissors. Let them custom-design their own version of a vampire by folding and cutting wings. This project will soon evolve into a flight test, as the prototypes will inevitably be tossed around.

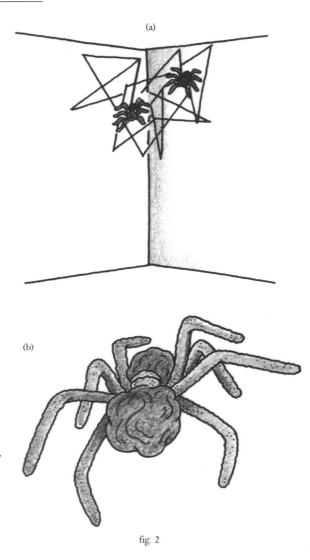

(a)

(b)

fig. 2

## GAMES

### SÉANCE

Children gather around the table or in a circle on the floor in another room. The lights are dimmed and the name of each child is printed on a piece of paper and placed in a Crystal Ball (a glass bowl). The role of Medium

(the one who contacts the spirits) is passed along by taking turns in a counterclockwise rotation around the circle. The Medium begins by drawing a name from the Crystal Ball. The child whose name was drawn becomes the Spirit. The Spirit draws another name from the Crystal Ball (this person will become the Victim) and keeps it a secret.

The Spirit goes into the next room, or the Other Side. Everyone holds hands and closes their eyes while the Medium makes contact with the Spirit. The Spirit begins moaning and groaning ad lib, and the Medium begins asking questions about the victim. When the Medium finally asks "Who are you trying to haunt?" and the answer comes out, the Victim "dies of fright." His or her head may rest on the table or floor, or go limp in the chair (melodramatic deaths are not uncommon). The Victim remains like this throughout the game, and they are "passed over" as a potential Medium. If, however, their name is drawn as a Spirit by a Medium, they may become one. If their name is drawn as a Victim again by a Spirit, then they, too, are released to go to the Other Side (in which case a new Victim's name is drawn). The object of the séance is that, eventually, all except one player will end up on the Other Side.

## POLTERGEIST

All of the children gather at the table or in a circle on the floor in another room.

They either cover their eyes with blindfolds, or keep them closed with their heads down on the table.

To start the game off, you or another parent quietly taps 3 children on the head. These children are taken out of the room, and each one is given an object: keys to jingle, a chain to rattle, and a hollow shoebox to knock on. The poltergeists wander about the room making their noises, until all 3 have tapped a different child on the head. If the children can then guess which poltergeist tapped them, they can trade places with that poltergeist. The game continues on like this with no real winners or losers. Basically, everyone wants to be a poltergeist as often as possible.

## HEADLESS HORSEMAN

A volunteer is selected to start off as the Headless Horseman. He or she wears a black cape pulled over his or her head. The Headless Horseman stands in the center of a circle of children and is given a "pillow pumpkin" to carry in one arm. (Any throw pillow can be used, even decorated to look like a jack-o'-lantern by taping a paper face on the pillow.) As the children walk in a circle around the Headless Horseman, the Headless Horseman throws the pillow out in any direction. Whoever the pillow strikes becomes Ichabod Crane, and must leave the circle. The last

child left in the circle is the winner, or becomes the next Headless Horseman in another round.

## RECIPES

### SCARECROW SALADS

Cold corn on the cob? Why not. It's not really very different from trying to eat it hot and dripping with butter. These corn cob salads are marinated in a vinaigrette dressing, and served like a scarecrow. The arms and legs even make convenient "handles" for easy eating.

PREPARATION TIME: 30 MINUTES
MARINATING TIME: 24 HOURS

| |
|---|
| 12 small ears of corn |
| Scarecrow Dressing (recipe follows) |
| 48 scallions |
| 12 leafy lettuce leaves (like salad bowl or romaine) |
| Sliced ripe olives |
| 12 pimiento strips |

Remove husks from corn (unless you're using frozen corn on the cob, in which case follow package directions) and place in a large kettle. Cover with boiling water and return to a second boil. Reduce heat, cover, and simmer 12 to 14 minutes. Remove corn from kettle and cool completely.

Place corn in a casserole or covered baking dish and marinate in dressing 24 hours, rearranging corn cobs a few times so they'll all absorb dressing equally.

Meanwhile, cut off roots of scallions and most of the top; they should be about 4 inches long. Cut lengthwise gashes in the top end about halfway down and soak in ice water, until scallions spread open, 2 to 3 hours.

Place corn cobs on lettuce leaves. Insert toothpicks into scallions (at the base) and stick into corn cobs for arms and legs. Decorate faces with sliced olive eyes and pimiento mouths (fig. 3).

fig. 3

# SCARECROW DRESSING

| |
|---|
| 1½ cups salad oil |
| ½ cup red wine vinegar |
| 2 tablespoons sugar |
| ½ teaspoon onion salt |
| 1 teaspoon dry mustard |
| 1 thick onion slice |
| 1 clove garlic, crushed |

Put all of the ingredients in blender and blend until smooth.

## SLEEPY HOLLOW STEW

The *Legend of Sleepy Hollow* is a literary classic that comes to life on Halloween night. Tales of Ichabod Crane, Brom Bones, and the Headless Horseman still send chills up the spine—especially the part when Ichabod crosses the covered bridge. The Headless Horseman throws his head at Ichabod, which turns out to be only a pumpkin. Tarrytown was a Dutch settlement, and Dutch food was a constant theme running through Washington Irving's story. This hearty beef stew, with caraway and spaetzle, is not unlike one that Ichabod would have eaten. It's even served in a "pumpkin head."

PREPARATION TIME: 30 MINUTES
COOKING TIME: 1 HOUR

| |
|---|
| 2 pounds lean chuck steak, cubed |
| 1 cup chopped onion |
| 1 cup coarsely chopped celery |
| ½ cup butter |
| 8 cups of water |
| 3 tablespoons beef base (BV or Bovril) |
| 1 can (16 ounces) stewed tomatoes |
| 1 teaspoon onion powder |
| 1 teaspoon black pepper |
| 2 teaspoons caraway seeds |
| ¼ cup flour |
| 1 cup sliced, cooked carrots |
| 1 cup cooked fresh green beans or 1 package (10 ounces) frozen green beans, cooked |
| 1½ cups cooked spaetzle (see note 1 below) |
| Pumpkin Head (instructions follow) |

Sauté chuck steak, onions, and celery in ¼ cup of the butter until meat is browned. Add water, beef base, tomatoes, onion powder, pepper, and caraway seeds. Bring to a boil, then cover and simmer for 1 hour. Melt remaining butter in a small saucepan and blend in flour to make a "paste." Stir into stew, blending with a spoon until the broth is thickened and smooth. Stir in carrots, beans, and spaetzle. Pour stew into "pumpkin head" and bring to the table; ladle stew out of pumpkin into bowls or large mugs.

Notes:1. Spaetzle is available in the imported section of most grocery stores, or substitute Pennsylvania Dutch egg noodles. 2. This stew may be prepared in advance and frozen.

## PUMPKIN HEAD

| 1 large, fresh pumpkin (no cracks, leaks, or soft spots) |
| --- |
| 1 potato |
| 2 radishes |
| 1 carrot |
| 1 turnip |
| Toothpicks |

Cut a lid out of the top of the pumpkin and scoop out seeds and pulp. Estimate thickness of shell; you may want to break your toothpicks into shorter lengths, so they won't completely penetrate it. Split potato in half lengthwise and stick into sides of pumpkin for ears. Stick radishes into the front for eyes, and a carrot for a nose. Slice turnip and cut into teeth. Stick teeth across face to look like a mouth.

## BROOMSTICKS

These long, crunchy breadsticks look like witches' broomsticks Your child will love pulling and stretching the dough, and it takes only one rising.

PREPARATION TIME: 40 MINUTES
RISING TIME: 45 MINUTES
BAKING TIME: 15 TO 20 MINUTES

| ½ cup warm water |
| --- |
| ½ cup warm milk |
| 2 tablespoons butter, softened |
| 1 teaspoon sugar |

| 1 teaspoon salt |
| --- |
| 1 active dry yeast (rapid-rise) |
| 2½ to 3 cups flour |
| 1 egg white, beaten with 1 tablespoon water |
| 2 tablespoons poppy seeds (optional) |

Stir water, milk, and butter together in a large mixing bowl. Add sugar and salt, then sprinkle on the yeast. Let stand for about a minute, then stir to dissolve. Add 1 cup of flour and beat until smooth. Add 1½ cups more flour, or enough to make a soft, manageable dough. Turn out on a lightly floured surface and knead for 1 minute; let rest for 10 minutes.

Resume kneading until dough is smooth and elastic, adding remaining flour as necessary. Place in oiled bowl and cover with plastic wrap. Let rise until doubled in bulk, about 45 minutes.

Preheat oven to 375°F. Grease 2 baking sheets.

Punch dough down. Knead briefly, then divide into 24 pieces. Roll each piece between your hands or back and forth on a board until you have a 9-inch pencil shape. Slash one end with 4 gashes about 2 inches deep. Give the end a "twist" and spread gashes slightly to resemble broom straws. Place broomsticks on prepared baking sheets. Brush with egg white and sprinkle "handles" with poppy seeds, if desired. Bake 15 to 20 minutes, or until lightly browned. Let cool.

Note: This is a good do-ahead recipe, but since these breadsticks can become very dry, wrap and freeze them if they are not to be eaten within 24 hours.

## FROZEN JACK-O'-LANTERNS

In this simple dessert, an orange becomes a pumpkin shell that is carved into a jack-o'-lantern. Peering from within is a deep, dark scoop of chocolate ice cream.

PREPARATION TIME: 30 MINUTES
FREEZING TIME: AT LEAST 3
    HOURS

| |
|---|
| 12 navel oranges |
| ½ gallon dark chocolate or fudge ice cream |
| 12 whole cinnamon sticks |

Cut off tops of oranges. Gently hollow out pulp (reserve for another use), leaving a thick shell; hollow pulp out of cut-off tops, too. Cut jack-o'-lantern faces into each orange. Pack scoops of ice cream into shells (avoid letting ice cream ooze out through eyes or mouth). Cut a hole in top of each orange. Set tops back on, over ice cream, and insert a cinnamon-stick stem through the hole (fig. 4). Place in freezer for at least 3 hours, or until serving time (photo opposite page 141).

fig. 4

## GLOWING HOBGOBLIN CAKE

Dim the lights—this cake is the climax of Halloween night! Glowing eyes bring this hobgoblin back to life, and watch how your own ghouls gobble it up.

PREPARATION TIME: 1 HOUR
BAKING TIME: 35 TO 40 MINUTES

| |
|---|
| 2 cups flour |
| 2 cups sugar |
| ¾ cup sour cream |
| ¼ cup butter, softened |
| 1 cup water |
| 1¼ teaspoons baking soda |
| 1 teaspoon salt |

| |
|---|
| ½ teaspoon baking powder |
| 1 teaspoon vanilla extract |
| 2 eggs |
| 4 ounces unsweetened chocolate, melted and cooled |
| Sour Cream-Chocolate Frosting (recipe follows) |
| Creamy White Frosting (recipe follows) |
| 2 eggshell halves |
| 2 sugar cubes |
| 2 teaspoons lemon extract |
| Piece of heavy cardboard (15 x 30 inches) |
| Gold or silver foil |

Preheat oven to 350°F. Line a 9 x 13-inch baking pan with baking parchment or aluminum foil.

Beat flour, sugar, sour cream, shortening, water, baking soda, salt, baking powder, vanilla, eggs, and chocolate in a large bowl on medium speed just until blended (about 30 seconds). Increase speed to high; beat, scraping bowl occasionally, 3 minutes. Pour batter into prepared pan and bake for 35 to 40 minutes, or until a toothpick inserted in center comes out clean. Cool cake completely.

Invert cooled cake on a rack or sheet and peel paper or foil away from bottom. Cut cake as shown in diagram (fig. 5a). Cover a 15 x 30-

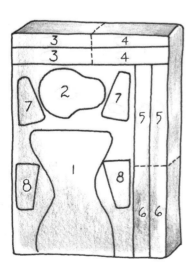

(a)

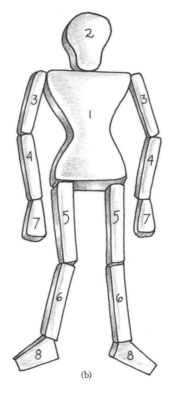

(b)

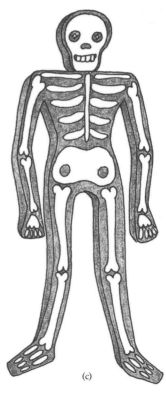

(c)

fig. 5

inch cardboard with foil and arrange cake on it as shown (fig. 5b).

Gently frost cake with sour cream-chocolate frosting, being careful not to break cake up. (It will be easier to apply frosting to arms and legs with a pastry bag, then spread with a spatula.) Fit a pastry bag with a large round writing tip. Fill with creamy white frosting. Pipe a "skeleton" as shown, giving the effect of bones; build up the skull with several thick rows of white icing (fig. 5c).

Just before serving, place eggshell halves where eye sockets are. Put a sugar cube in each eggshell and saturate with lemon extract. Light with a match.

## SOUR CREAM–CHOCOLATE FROSTING

| ½ to ¾ cup sour cream |
| --- |
| ½ cup butter, softened |
| 4 ounces unsweetened chocolate, melted and cooled |
| 2 teaspoons vanilla extract |
| 5½ to 6 cups confectioners sugar |

Beat together ½ cup sour cream, butter, chocolate, and vanilla. Stir in confectioners sugar and beat just until frosting is of spreading consistency. If necessary, stir in additional sour cream.

## CREAMY WHITE FROSTING

| 3 cups confectioners sugar |
| --- |
| ⅓ cup butter, softened |

| 2 teaspoons vanilla extract |
| --- |
| 2 to 4 tablespoons milk |

Beat all ingredients on medium speed until smooth and of spreading consistency. If necessary, stir in additional milk.

## WITCHES' BREW

"Boil, bubble, toil and trouble." You can recreate a caldron of steaming "witches' brew" by serving this cinnamon-orange cocoa from a deep, black cast-iron Dutch oven or kettle.

PREPARATION TIME: 12 MINUTES

| ½ cup unsweetened cocoa powder |
| --- |
| ½ cup sugar |
| 1 tablespoon ground cinnamon |
| 1 cup hot water |
| 1 can (6 ounces) orange juice concentrate, thawed |
| 2 quarts milk |
| 1 pint orange sherbet |

Combine cocoa, sugar, and cinnamon in a very large saucepan or kettle. Stir in hot water and simmer, stirring, over low heat for 2 minutes. Blend in orange juice and milk. Warm over low heat but do not boil. If desired, pour into a cast-iron Dutch oven and bring to the table. Ladle servings into mugs or cups and top with miniature scoops of orange sherbet.

# KNIGHTS AROUND THE TABLE

**L**ong ago, in the Land of Logres, there lived a king named Arthur, in a kingdom called Camelot. One day he summoned the noblest of knights and ladies fair to come to the castle for feasting and festivities.

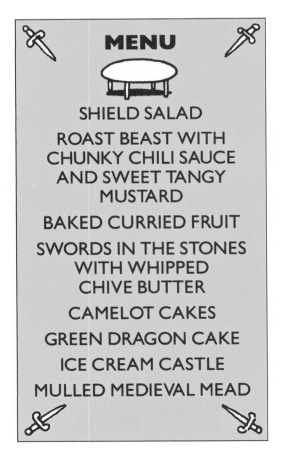

## MENU

SHIELD SALAD

ROAST BEAST WITH CHUNKY CHILI SAUCE AND SWEET TANGY MUSTARD

BAKED CURRIED FRUIT

SWORDS IN THE STONES WITH WHIPPED CHIVE BUTTER

CAMELOT CAKES

GREEN DRAGON CAKE

ICE CREAM CASTLE

MULLED MEDIEVAL MEAD

**FEATURES:** Coronets, Barbettes

**GAMES:** In Search of the Golden Grail, Banana Joust, Excaliber

**INVITATIONS:** Shield of Chivalry

## INVITATIONS

A knight's shield was his most prized possession, as well as his means of protection. Even the stylized motifs served a practical purpose. Underneath all that armor, it was pretty hard to tell one knight from the next. The crest emblazoned across the front was often the only identifying symbol they had. Ribbons and "ramping" (rearing) lions and leopards, crosses, crowns, and castles are some of the characters frequently on shields. In a way, a knight's shield can be likened to a snowflake—no two are exactly

alike. So why not personalize each invitation with a uniquely different design? You can assign a special shield to each knight (or lady) invited to the Round Table. Your child will also find this a very creative project because the possibilities are almost endless.

12 SHIELD CARDS
PREPARATION TIME: 1 HOUR

| |
|---|
| 6 sheets (9 x 12 inches each), assorted colors construction paper |
| Acrylic or tempera paints (red, white, blue, yellow) |
| Small- and medium- tipped brushes |
| Black felt-tip or opaque marker |
| 12 envelopes to fit a 4½ x 6-inch card |
| Scissors, ruler |

Each sheet of paper will make 2 cards. Split each sheet (with a ruler and scissors or a paper cutter) into a 4½ x 12-inch sheet. Fold in half, with the crease at the top, into two 4½ x 6-inch cards. Trim the open ends of each card together to form tapering point of a shield (fig. 1a). (It is much easier, and the results will be more uniform, if you use a pattern.) Decorate each shield as desired with paint (fig. 1b). Use the felt-tip marker to write the following message inside:

COME TO CAMELOT

NOBLE KNIGHTS AND

LADIES FAIR

for

FEASTING AND

FESTIVITIES

at

THE GREAT ROUND TABLE

[time, day, year—
given in the 500s A.D.]

at

[your address]
IN THE LAND OF LOGRES

R.S.V.P.

[or REGRETS ONLY]

[your phone number]

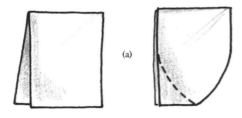

(a)

fig. 1

Be sure envelopes fit shields properly before sealing them, and include your child's *name* on the return address, so your guests will know whom the invitation is from.

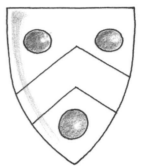

(b)

fig. 1

## DECORATIONS/HATS

Even the most modest room can be transformed into the great hall of Camelot Castle. All it takes is a little imagination on your part, as well as the children's. Begin by decorating the walls with actual-size cardboard shields. The designs on these should correspond to each invitation you've sent. When the guests arrive, they can immediately identify his or her shield hanging in a position of prominence (see page 152).

Large flags were also hung from the walls and ceilings of a castle. You can cut such flags from a wide roll of white freezer or wrapping paper, and decorate them in a style similar to that of the shields. If you or your child feel really ambitious, attempt making a tapestry. Simply illustrate a medieval scene on a 5- or 6-foot length of paper cut from a roll. You can fill in the color with a cross-hatch effect, giving the picture the appearance of a weaving. Foil-covered cardboard swords also add a dramatic touch. Hang them on the wall in a criss-cross fashion.

Of course, you should have a Round Table. Legend has it that the table was a gift to Camelot from King Leodegrance, Lady Guinevere's father. The idea was that all knights would be equal when seated in a circle. However, you may not have a round table that's large enough—you may not have a round table at all! Table-top extenders are available at most party rentals. These are large, round boards you can sit on top of a smaller (even square) table. You could also use 2 or 3 smaller round tables, such as card tables. If none of these options is available to you, forget about it! Simply regard it as some minor detail you'll have to overlook. (The kids' imaginations will take over where you leave off.)

## CORONETS

A coronet is a crownlike hat worn by nobles below the rank of sovereign. Lords and knights wore this less elaborate version of the king's head gear when they were not in armor. Any jewels or precious stones were usually modest in comparison to the royal crown.

PREPARATION TIME: 45 MINUTES

| |
|---|
| 1 posterboard (any color), 20 x 30 inches |
| Gold or silver foil or foil wrapping paper |
| 4 sheets, (20 x 30 inches each), crêpe paper (red, royal blue, or purple) |
| Large red, green, or blue sequins (as rubies, emeralds, and sapphires) |
| Scissors, stapler, glue |

Cut posterboard into twelve 1⅝ x 30-inch strips. Cover strips with foil or foil paper (paper will require glue or tape to secure it in place). Use your child's head as a model to adjust bands for proper fit. Staple bands into rings, overlapping excess ends. Cut each sheet of crêpe paper into three 12-inch circles. (This is easier if you use a pattern like a 12-inch cake pan or pot lid.) Tuck the edges of the circles into the bands and staple in place, forming caps (fig. 2a). Decorate the bands by gluing on sequin "jewels" (fig. 2b).

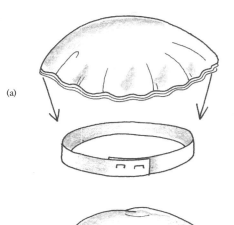

(a)

(b)

fig. 2

## BARBETTES

Ladies of the medieval court wore tall, pointed conical hats. In fact, imagine an ice cream cone trimmed with ermine, jewels, and a sheer silk veil.

PREPARATION TIME: 45 MINUTES

6 sheets of 20 x 30-inch posterboard (any color)

12 sheets of 20 x 30-inch colored tissue paper or twelve 1-yard lengths of netting or gauze

First-aid cotton on a roll or white flannel or fur cloth

Large red, green, or blue sequins (rubies, emeralds, or sapphires)

Stapler, scissors, tape, glue

Cut each sheet of posterboard into a 20-inch circle. Split circles into semicircles. Shape each semicircle into a cone and staple in place along the seam. Make a tiny hole at the point of each hat by cutting off about ¼-inch of the tip. Gather a sheet of tissue or netting at one end and push into hole. Pull into hat about 1 inch and tape in place from the inside. Trim hats around the base by gluing on strips of "ermine" (cotton, flannel, or fur cloth) and gluing sequins onto the strips (fig. 3).

Note: Because of the awkward balance of these hats, you may want to attach elastic bands to secure them in place.

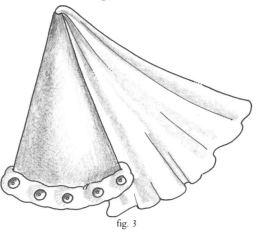

fig. 3

These instructions are for making 12 coronets and 12 barbettes. You probably won't need that many of either type, depending on the mix of boys and girls at the party. Remember, too, that some girls insist on being "one of the boys" and may want to wear a coronet.

## INSTANT INVOLVEMENT

A fanfare can bridge that awkward stretch of time between the first and last arrival, and it also gives each guest a special feeling of importance. Each child's grand entrance is greeted with royal regalia and the tantara of trumpets. As more children arrive, the larger and more impressive the ceremony becomes. At least 2 children must be present for the protocol to begin. There should be one "harbinger" and several "heralders" (the more the merrier). The ceremony commences when a guest comes through the door. The harbinger reads from his or her scroll in a booming voice the name of the child: "Announcing Sir Jonathan of Stewart" or "Announcing Lady Leslie of Warren." (The last name essentially becomes their place of origin.) The heralders bring their horns to their mouths and give a trumpeting fanfare in honor of the guest. As soon as the new arrival has made an entrance, he or she is given a horn and a hat and then joins the line of heralders. This pageant continues until every child is present and accounted for. By the time the last guest has arrived, the routine has grown into a ritual of pompous proportions, with as many as 10 heralders (for a party of twelve). Obviously, early arrivals may feel a little cheated out of all the glory and attention, so let them enter again! Some kids get so caught up in this ritual that it's hard to make them stop.

Heralding horns are easy to construct out of paper tubes (from wrapping paper, paper towels, or rolls of foil) and plastic cups and foil and crêpe-paper streamers. Children are pretty good at imitating anything that makes a noise, including trumpets. However, you can borrow a sound effects record from your local library. Because these are designed for school plays and other dramatic endeavors, they frequently have a whole section of "fanfare." Playing this record over and over again is bound to cause a riot of laughter and really help break the ice. The following instructions for heralding horns will make a dozen, since everyone will probably have to have one.

PREPARATION TIME: 45 MINUTES

| |
|---|
| 12 paper tubes, the longer the better (wrapping paper or aluminum foil tubes work well) |
| 12 funnel-shaped plastic cups (the kind that snap into coffee mug holders) |
| Gold or silver foil |

Crêpe-paper streamers (red, royal blue, or purple)

Tape, stapler

Make a hole in each cup by cutting out the bottom. Tape a cup to one end of each tube (fig. 4). This forms the "bell" of the horn. Cover cup and tube with a long strip of foil. The foil should be 12 inches wide and long enough to completely wrap around the horn, tucking in 1 inch at the mouthpiece and entirely covering the inside of the bell or cup. Mold foil tightly against the contours of the tube and cup.

Heralding horns usually had some kind of flag or streamers hanging from them. You can just staple a long strip of crêpe-paper streamer around the base of the bell, cutting a V-shaped notch at the end of the streamer.

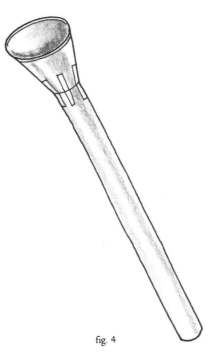

fig. 4

## GAMES

## IN SEARCH OF THE GOLDEN GRAIL

The quest for the Holy Grail was an underlying theme throughout the legend of King Arthur. It was a mission for only the purest and most noble of knights—all others would fail. These same qualities also fit Merlin's prophetic description of the knight who would eventually fill the special seat, Siege Perilous, at the Round Table. (We know from the story that this turns out to be Sir Gallahad.) You can transform either a metal goblet or a bowl into the Golden Grail. Some gold foil will do the trick; simply mold it around the goblet. The Holy Grail was supposedly so radiant that it was covered with a cloth of white samite (silk) to shield it from the view of mere mortals. You can achieve the same effect by draping your Grail with a white handkerchief. Now the Grail must be hidden in some "brilliant" place, either indoors or outside (season and weather permitting).

Arthurian lore presents many of life's problems in puzzling riddles; so does this game. Write up as many clues as you have players. They should not be obvious; on the contrary, they should be very obscure. "The sun always shines brightest in the shade," would indicate that the Grail is hidden underneath a lamp. "Seek out the serpent who swallowed the sea,"

*Ice Cream Castle (recipe pages 165-166)*

*Green Dragon Cake (recipe pages 163-165)*

means that the Grail is lying in the coil of the garden hose. To further confuse the issue, only one clue is correct! One clue will lead a knight to the Grail; the others will lead the rest of the knights on a wild goose chase. And that's where the fun really begins, because no one knows which one is right.

Merlin (either you or anyone who elects to take on this job) scrambles up the little pieces of paper and puts them into a magic hat. The knights and ladies each draw from the hat and try to solve their riddle. Each player investigates their intuition to see if he or she is on the right track. For example, if the Grail isn't in the garden hose, is it because it never was or because the clue was misinterpreted? Eventually, everyone begins searching everywhere until the Grail appears. In fact, the finder may not have been the recipient of the "right" riddle. This doesn't matter. As the legend goes, destiny determines who will take their rightful place in the Siege Perilous.

## BANANA JOUST

The joust was usually conducted as a sporting event, rather than a duel to the death. Lances used in such a contest were blunt, intended to knock the opposing weapon from the challenger's hand. When it comes to a harmless weapon, what could be more blunt than a banana? It certainly won't encourage

excessive acts of aggression. For armor, a helmet will suffice. The easiest way to make one is by covering a football helmet with silver aluminum foil. Staple a cardboard strip (for a handle) on the back of 2 cardboard shields. All in all, you'll need 2 helmets, 2 shields, and about 2 dozen bananas for lances.

A tournament begins with the first match. Two knights (ladies may don a helmet and play, too) square-off against each other on opposite sides of the yard or room. (Note: As an indoor sport, this can get messy, so select a recreation room.) The knights hold their lances (bananas) outstretched in their right hands, and their shields in their left hands. A lady of the court drops her handkerchief to signal the start. The knights charge toward each other at a galloping gate (the right foot always leads the left). At the moment of confrontation, each player tries to either break the opponent's banana or knock it from his or her hand in passing. If both knights miss each other, they must turn around and charge each other again. The victorious knight is one who still has most of the banana intact, while the opponent's banana may have suffered greater casualties. The winner is declared champion, and now must come up against a new challenger in the next match.

Squires rush in with replacement bananas and clear the field of any peels or slippery debris. Any knight who physically strikes an

opposing knight with his banana has fouled and loses the match by default. The tournament continues until everyone has a chance to challenge the champion. The player who remains champion throughout the most matches is declared Grand Champion by the King. (An amusing prize for the winner of the Banana Joust is a gift certificate for a banana split at your local ice cream parlor made out to the "Top Banana.")

## EXCALIBUR

"My lord King," said Merlin, "I see that you are determined to do battle with the Sable Knight. Therefore I shall not try to prevent you but shall do all in my power to try and help. Now, I must tell you that in a certain part of this forest is a place called the Forest of Adventure, and close to it is an enchanted land. In this land there is an enchanted lake, and in the center of this lake has been seen, rising straight out of the water, a woman's arm covered with brocaded white silk called samite. The hand of this arm holds high in the air a sword of great size and beauty called Excalibur.

"Now it seems that many knights have seen this sword and have tried to take it, but no man has yet been able to touch it. Either he drowns in the lake, or the sword disappears as he draws near. I can show you the way to the Lake of Enchantment, and you may see the wonderful sword with your own eyes; and if you are able to reach it, then you will indeed have a sword for always and one most fitting for a king and a king's battles."*

---

*From *King Arthur and the Knights of the Round Table* by Estelle B. Schnider. Random House, 1954.

To play the game "Excalibur," you will first need to make a sword of cardboard and foil, similar to the ones shown as wall decorations (see page 153). Next, you'll need an enchanted lake. This can be a circle that is anywhere from 10–15 feet in diameter, depending on whether you're playing indoors or out. It's important that the perimeter of the lake is clearly marked with chalk, string, or some other means. You'll need a Merlin, a Lady of the Lake, and an "arm" to hold up Excalibur, jobs which are quickly filled by volunteers. The child who plays the "arm" sits in the center of the circle, wrapped in a white sheet. The sheet should completely cover his or her body and head, with exception of the arm that holds Excalibur up high in the air. The Lady of the Lake stands along the bank, waiting to give directions to the knights.

To make this game a little more challenging, each knight is given a sealed envelope with a message inside, and the knight must be blindfolded before entering the enchanted lake. (The envelopes all contain blank pieces of paper, except for one, which says KING ARTHUR.) Merlin spins the first knight around in a circle 3 times (to disorient) and releases the knight to the mercy of the Lady of the Lake. She (or he if it's an all-boy party) directs the knight with instructions of "wet" or "dry," indicating whether or not the knight is inside or outside of the lake. When and if the knight finally stumbles upon Excalibur, he or she hands the envelope to the "arm." The "arm" takes the envelope with the left hand and pulls it under the sheet to open it in secrecy. If the message is a blank piece of paper, the "arm" pulls Excalibur under the sheet and the Lady of the Lake announces that the knight has "drowned." If the message says KING ARTHUR, then the "arm" hands Excalibur to the knight. The game can be played over and over, long after the KING ARTHUR shows up. In fact, if it happens at the beginning, simply reshuffle the envelopes and pass them out all over again. Many children may want to take turns playing Merlin, Lady of the Lake, and the "arm."

## RECIPES

## SHIELD SALAD

Crunchy bean salads are garnished with shields of cheese.

PREPARATION TIME: 20 MINUTES
MARINATING TIME: OVERNIGHT

| 1 pound fresh green beans |
| 1 pound yellow wax beans |
| 1 tablespoon red wine vinegar |
| 2 tablespoons lemon juice |
| ¾ cup salad oil |
| ½ teaspoon dry mustard |
| 1 large sweet gherkin |
| ½ teaspoon onion salt |
| 1 red onion, sliced thin |

| 12 lettuce cups or romaine leaves |
| Salad Shields (recipe follows) |

Wash beans and trim ends. Bring 3 quarts of salted water to a rolling boil. Drop beans (1 pound at a time) in water and boil 5 minutes. Immerse beans in a bowl of cold water to stop cooking. Cool or chill beans completely.

Prepare vinaigrette by placing vinegar, lemon juice, oil, mustard, gherkin, and onion salt in a blender and blending until smooth. Layer beans in a bowl with sliced onion and pour vinaigrette over beans. Marinate for a day or two (at least overnight). Just before serving, arrange beans and onions on individual lettuce cups and garnish each with a shield.

## SALAD SHIELDS

| 1 package (8 ounces) sliced Swiss cheese (no *holes*) |
| 1 jar pimientos |

Using the patterns provided on page 152, cut shields from cheese. This is easier if you just stack 8 slices together at a time (you'll get 16 shields). If you're not doing this just before serving, wrap shields (stacked) together, tightly with plastic wrap. Just before serving set a shield on top of each bean salad. Cut narrow strips of pimiento and arrange in a cross or diagonal pattern to form an emblem on each shield.

Note: Don't place pimientos on cheese too far in advance or the pimiento will "bleed" or stain the cheese.

## ROAST BEAST

Serving a boar's head on a large platter is an old English tradition dating back to the Middle Ages. It was quite a ceremony, calling for lots of fanfare and festivity. Today the idea of roasting a boar is totally impractical and probably unappetizing to you, but your kids will agree that this facsimile is fantastically fun!

PREPARATION TIME: 40 MINUTES
BAKING TIME: 1½ HOURS

| 4 eggs, lightly beaten |
| --- |
| 6 cups whole wheat or bran cereal |
| 1½ cups milk |
| 1 tablespoon Worcestershire sauce |
| 1 tablespoon onion powder |

| 1 teaspoon garlic powder |
| --- |
| 2 teaspoons celery salt |
| 2 teaspoons poultry seasoning |
| 3 pounds ground cooked ham |
| 3 pounds ground veal or pork |
| 2 long, curved, "knobby" carrots (that look like boar's tusks) |
| 2 jumbo pimiento-stuffed olives |
| 1 spiced or picked apple with stem |
| 1 baking potato |
| Sprigs of fresh parsley |
| Chunky Chili Sauce (recipe follows) |
| Sweet Tangy Mustard (recipe follows) |

Preheat oven to 375°F. Combine eggs, cereal, milk, and seasonings in a large mixing bowl. Mix until cereal is completely moistened and seasonings are thoroughly

fig. 5

combined. Mix in ground ham and veal or pork until well blended. Line a large roasting pan with foil. Shape this meat loaf mixture into a boar's head; it's a lot like working with modeling clay. Use the apple to help prop open the jaws of the mouth, shaping a snout. With your thumb make 2 indentations in the nose for nostrils. The carrots become tusks when set into each side of the jowls or cheeks. Use stuffed olives for eyes. Cut away sides of potato, with skin attached, for ears. Place on each side of the head (fig. 5). You may want to brush the ears and tusks with a little melted butter to prevent them from drying out while baking. Bake for approximately 1½ hours, although it could take slightly longer if you shaped a particularly thick head.

Allow the head to cool slightly before carefully removing to serving tray. (This is much easier if you place it, foil and all, right on the platter and gently tear the foil, slipping it away from underneath. Use a broad, flat spatula to help free meat from foil.) At this point, the boar's head can be wrapped in foil, refrigerated, and reheated before serving. Garnish the platter with plenty of parsley, and serve with Chunky Chili Sauce and Sweet Tangy Mustard.

## CHUNKY CHILI SAUCE

| 1 bottle (12 ounces) chili sauce |
| 1 jar (10 ounces) pineapple preserves |
| 2 teaspoons Worcestershire sauce |

Combine chili sauce, pineapple preserves, and Worcestershire sauce in a saucepan and bring to a boil. Cool to room temperature before serving.

## SWEET TANGY MUSTARD

| ½ cup spicy brown mustard |
| 1 cup brown sugar |
| 1 teaspoon dry mustard |
| ¼ cup lemon juice |
| ¼ cup apple juice or cider |
| 3 eggs, beaten |
| ¼ cup butter, melted |

Combine mustard, brown sugar, dry mustard, lemon and apple juices, eggs, and butter in a saucepan. Beat well with a wire whisk and place over a low heat. Beat constantly until mixture begins to thicken (don't allow eggs to "scramble"). Serve chilled or at room temperature.

Note: Some children are more inclined to eat yellow as opposed to brown mustard. If this sounds like your group of kids, substitute yellow for brown mustard and then use granulated for the brown sugar in the recipe.

## BAKED CURRIED FRUIT

In medieval times spices were as precious as gold, and with good reason. They had come from faraway parts of the world. Food preservation also left much to

be desired, and meat frequently had to be masked with pungent sauces. Sweet and savory condiments were appropriately seasoned to disguise many "less than delicate" dishes.

PREPARATION TIME: 15 MINUTES
BAKING TIME: 1 HOUR

| 4 cups sliced apples, unpared |
| --- |
| 4 cups sliced pears, unpared |
| 4 cups sliced pitted red or purple plums, unpared |
| 2 tablespoons lemon juice |
| 1 teaspoon grated lemon peel |
| 2 teaspoons grated orange peel |
| 1 cup chopped walnuts |
| ½ cup firmly packed brown sugar |
| ½ cup sugar |
| ⅓ cup flour |
| 1½ teaspoons ground cinnamon |
| 1½ teaspoons curry powder |
| ½ teaspoon ground nutmeg |
| ¼ teaspoon mace |
| ⅓ cup butter, melted |

Preheat oven to 425°F. Combine apples, pears, and plums in a large mixing bowl. Sprinkle with lemon juice, lemon peel, and orange peel. Add walnuts and toss. In a small bowl, combine sugars, flour, and spices. Toss with fruit until well coated. Pour melted butter over fruit and toss again. Spoon fruit into a 4-quart casserole and cover with foil.

Bake for 30 minutes. Remove foil and continue baking 30 minutes longer, or until fruits are tender and the juices begin to thicken slightly. (This could take slightly more or less time, depending on the depth of your dish.) Cool slightly, then serve. This dish can be prepared ahead of time, baked, and reheated, or bake for the first time about an hour and 15 minutes before you plan to serve it.

## SWORDS IN THE STONES

As Arthurian legend goes, "Whoso shall pull the sword out of the stone is King of England by right." This prophesy was made by Merlin the Magician and fulfilled by young Arthur, stepson of Uther Pendragon. Now, every knight at your party can try their hand at this noble feat, while they eat.

PREPARATION TIME: 15 MINUTES
BAKING TIME: 1 HOUR

| 12 medium-sized baking potatoes |
| --- |
| 12 plastic knives |
| 12 strips, (4 x 12 inches each), foil (*not* heavy-duty) |
| Whipped Chive Butter (recipe follows) |

Bake potatoes at 370°F for 1 hour. Meanwhile, make each sword as follows: Place a plastic knife lengthwise along the edge of each foil strip. Fold knife up tightly into foil. Pinch foil to conform to the contour of the knife and flatten

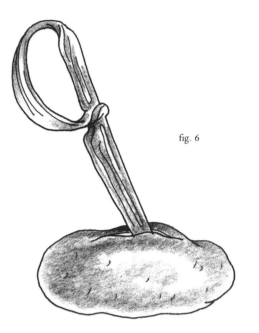

fig. 6

## CAMELOT CAKES

Made with oats and currants, these could also be called "medieval muffins."

PREPARATION TIME: 8 MINUTES
BAKING TIME: 25 MINUTES

| |
|---|
| 1 egg |
| 1 cup buttermilk |
| ½ cup dark brown sugar |
| ⅓ cup butter, melted |
| 1 cup quick-cooking rolled oats |
| 1 cup flour |
| 1 teaspoon baking powder |
| ½ teaspoon baking soda |
| ½ teaspoon salt |
| ½ cup dried currants |

Preheat oven to 400°F. Grease the bottom and sides of a 12-muffin cup pan. (Each cup should be 2¾ inches in diameter.) Beat egg. Stir in buttermilk, brown sugar, and butter. Add dry ingredients and currants and mix with a fork *just* until flour is moistened (batter should be lumpy). Fill muffin cups ⅔s full. Bake for 20–25 minutes or until light brown. Immediately remove from pans. If wrapped while fresh in plastic wrap, muffins may be frozen, then reheated in foil.

excess foil at the top. Fold foil end over to form a handle for the sword, tucking the end around the knife. Insert each sword into a hot baked potato and serve with a crock of Whipped Chive Butter (fig. 6). Children can use their swords for spreading after they've pulled them out of the "stones."

## WHIPPED CHIVE BUTTER

| |
|---|
| 1 cup butter, softened |
| ½ cup sour cream |
| 2 tablespoons chopped chives |
| ½ teaspoon onion salt |

Whip butter until light and fluffy. Beat in sour cream, chives, and onion salt. Spoon into a crock and chill. Bring to room temperature before serving.

## GREEN DRAGON CAKE

A day in the life of your average knight would seem incomplete without encountering at least one dragon. The Green Dragons were the most common of the fire-breathing species, highly prized as a royal delicacy. Perhaps it was the moist texture, creamy cheese frosting, or chocolate scales that made this a dish fit for a king.

PREPARATION TIME: 1 HOUR
BAKING TIME: 40 MINUTES
CHILLING TIME: 1 HOUR FOR
   SCALES

| |
|---|
| ⅓ cup boiling water |
| 2 cups finely chopped zucchini |
| 1 cup flour |
| 1¼ cups sugar |
| ½ cup oil |
| 1¼ teaspoons baking soda |
| ½ teaspoon salt |
| 1 teaspoon ground cinnamon |
| 1 teaspoon ground cloves |
| 1 teaspoon ground nutmeg |
| 1 teaspoon vanilla extract |
| 3 eggs |
| 1 cup chopped walnuts |
| Creamy Cheese Frosting (recipe follows) |
| Chocolate Scales (recipe follows) |
| Marshmallow |
| Red licorice twist |

Preheat oven to 350°F. Line two 9-inch round cake pans with baking parchment or aluminum foil.

Pour boiling water over zucchini in a large mixing bowl. Add next 11 ingredients and beat at medium speed for about 3 minutes. Pour batter into prepared pans and bake for 35–40 minutes, or until a toothpick inserted in the center comes out clean. Cool cakes completely. Turn cakes out of pans and peel away parchment paper or foil.

Cut cakes as shown in diagram (fig. 7a) and arrange on a foil-covered 18 x 36-inch cardboard (fig.7b). Prepare frosting and frost cake, completely coating it. Fill a pastry bag fitted with a leaf tip with remaining frosting. Pipe scales on the body of the dragon, beginning at the neck and working toward the tail. Insert chocolate scales down the back and tail. Slice marshmallow in half and insert in position for eye (use a piece from chocolate scales for pupil). Split licorice twist at one end and insert the other end in the mouth (fig. 7c; see also photo opposite page 157).

## CREAMY CHEESE FROSTING

| |
|---|
| 1 cup butter, softened |
| ½ package (8 ounces) cream cheese, softened |
| 2 pounds confectioners sugar |
| ¼–⅓ cup lemon juice |
| Green food coloring |

Beat butter and cream cheese until soft and fluffy. Beat in sugar and enough lemon juice to make a smooth, spreading consistency. Tint frosting to the desired shade of green with food coloring.

(a)

(b)

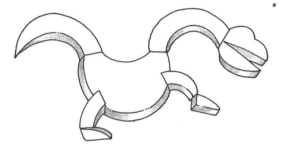

(c)

fig. 7

# ICE CREAM CASTLE

Ice cream castles—that stuff which dreams are made of! As in every fantasy, this can be created in any flavor your child desires. It can be a realistic, stone-colored chocolate or mocha chip or a fairytale pink peppermint or pale green pistachio ice cream.

PREPARATION TIME: 25–30 MINUTES
CHILLING TIME: SEVERAL HOURS
  TOTAL

| |
|---|
| 2 half-gallon cartons of ice cream (rectangular boxes, approximately 6¾ x 4¾ x 3½ inches and about ½ pint additional ice cream for towers |
| 3 Hershey's special dark chocolate bars (8 ounces each) |
| 1 whip or string black licorice |
| Chocolate-Covered Cones (recipe follows) |

Cover a sturdy 12 x 14-inch piece of cardboard with foil. (It's important to keep the ice cream castle very cold at all times to prevent melting. You may have to place it back in the freezer a couple of times while working on it. The important thing is to always work quickly with ice cream.) Carefully unwrap ice cream so that you have 2 solid blocks. Center one block on the foil, so that it stands 4¾ inches high. Slice the second block into two 6⅜ x 2⅜ x 4¾-inch bricklike blocks. Stand blocks on end, one on each side of the main block. Use toothpicks to secure ice cream in

place. With a sharp knife, separate 2 of the chocolate bars into individual squares (there are 16 in each bar). Cut the remaining bar into two 2 by 3-square segments and six 2-square segments. Press windows and door into ice cream and line the top edges of the castle with chocolate squares to form "battlements" (fig. 8). At this point, the castle may need to make a trip back to the freezer.

Make 2 large scoops of ice cream from the additional half pint, and press on top of each tower. Top scoops with chocolate-covered cones. Use any leftover melted chocolate from cones to attach licorice strings and drawbridge to door (see photo opposite page 156. If desired, you can make paper flags on toothpicks, and insert into the tops of cones. Keep frozen solid until serving time.

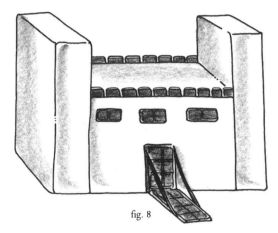

fig. 8

# CHOCOLATE-COVERED CONES

| 2 ounces semisweet chocolate |
| --- |
| 1 tablespoon vegetable shortening |
| 2 sugar cones |

Heat chocolate and shortening over low heat, stirring until melted and smooth. Spread evenly over the surface of the sugar cones, using a metal spatula. Invert cones on a sheet of foil or waxed paper and place in the refrigerator until the chocolate coating sets.

# MULLED MEDIEVAL MEAD

Warm spiced cider drinks were the most popular beverage during the Middle Ages. However, if you're having this party in warm weather, you can also serve it chilled.

PREPARATION TIME: 5 MINUTES
HEATING TIME: 10 MINUTES

| 1 cup brown sugar |
| --- |
| 1 teaspoon ground allspice |
| 3 sticks cinnamon |
| ¼ teaspoon salt |
| 1 teaspoon whole cloves |
| ½ teaspoon ground nutmeg |
| 3 quarts apple cider |

Mix brown sugar, spices, and cider in a very large kettle or saucepan and simmer 10 minutes. Strain through cheesecloth into a second saucepan and reheat before serving. This can also be served chilled from a pitcher.

# CHRISTMAS COOKIE FACTORY

**C**hildren love to get involved with cooking, from the first bite of batter to the last lick of frosting. At Christmastime, Santa's bake shop goes into full swing. He calls in all of the helpers he can get hold of to COME TO THE COOKIE FACTORY and help fill the orders.

## MENU

*Production Line*

**COLOSSAL COOKIE TREES**

**CHOCOLATE-CHIP COOKIE WREATH**

**EDIBLE ORNAMENTS**

**TOY SHOP SUGAR COOKIES**

**DOUGH DOLLS**

*Other Refreshments*

**IGLOO CAKE**

**FROSTY SNOWMEN**

**MILK MIX-IN BAR**

**FEATURE:** Reindeer Antlers

**INVITATIONS:** Gingerbread Boys

## INVITATIONS

An invitation to a Christmas Cookie Factory can be hand delivered on the real thing. However, if you plan to send them through the mail, gingerbread boys can also be cut out of construction paper or poster board. Use cookie patterns to cut gingerbread boys out of brown poster board. Decorate with white paint or opaque marker instead of icing. Attach tags in the same manner as you would with real cookies, only punch holes in the top with a paper punch.

12 GINGERBREAD INVITATIONS
PREPARATION TIME: ¼ HOURS

CHILLING TIME (FOR DOUGH):
 4 HOURS
BAKING TIME: 7 TO 10 MINUTES

| |
| --- |
| 3½ cups flour |
| 1 teaspoon baking soda |
| ¼ teaspoon salt |
| 1½ teaspoons ground ginger |
| 1 teaspoon ground cloves |
| ½ cup butter, softened |
| ¾ cup brown sugar, firmly packed |
| 1 egg |
| ¾ cup light molasses |
| Royal Icing (see page 75) |
| Christmas Tags (instructions follow) |

Combine flour, baking soda, salt, ginger, and cloves in a small bowl. Beat butter, sugar, and egg in a large mixing bowl until light and fluffy. Beat in molasses until well blended. Mix in flour to form a soft dough. Divide dough into 4 parts, wrap in plastic, and chill at least 4 hours.

Preheat oven to 375°F. Line 2 or more baking sheets with foil or baking parchment.

Roll out dough ¼ inch thick on a lightly floured surface, working with one part at a time and chilling scraps before rerolling. Use pattern to cut at least 12 gingerbread boys; you'll probably be able to cut more. Place gingerbread boys on prepared baking sheets. Pierce a hole in the top of each with a plastic straw. Bake 7 to 10 minutes, or until lightly browned. Let cool on the foil or paper. When cookies are firm, peel off. Fit a pastry bag with a small, round writing nozzle; fill with Royal Icing. Outline cookies with icing; pipe on faces. Write name of each child the cookies are to be given to across front. Make tags and string ribbons through holes in gingerbread boys, tying in a bow (fig. 1).

## CHRISTMAS TAGS

Use commercial folded-over gift tags or make your own out of 3 x 5-inch construction paper, folded in half. Punch a hole in the corner for stringing with ribbon. On the inside, write:

COME TO THE COOKIE
FACTORY
SANTA'S BAKE SHOP
[your address]
NORTH POLE
RESERVE YOUR ORDER NOW
[your phone number]

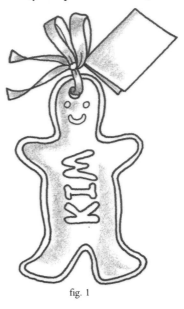

fig. 1

## DECORATIONS/HATS

Turn your house into Santa's Bake Shop by adding touches of the North Pole. Wrap chairs, table legs, posts (everything you can think of) with red and white crêpe paper streamers to resemble candy canes. Hang paper doilies from the ceiling for snowflakes. Christmas ball balloons are made by hanging round pink balloons from ribbon loops, like ornaments; first decorate with red or green magic markers (fig. 2a). Of course, Christmas lights and greenery always add to the atmosphere. Make cardboard signs: the first can be an arrow at the end of your street pointing to your house, TO THE NORTH POLE; the second can be over your doorway, SANTA'S BAKE SHOP (fig. 2b); The final sign ends up in the party room, COOKIE FACTORY. You can even tape an old-fashioned oven, which has been painted on paper, against the wall (fig. 2c).

(b)

(a)

fig. 2

(c)

## ANTLER HATS

Dasher, Dancer, Prancer, Vixen, Comet, Cupid, Donner, Blitzen—and even Rudolph—have to keep busy the other 364 days of the year. When they aren't pulling Santa's sleigh, they like to help out in any way they can—especially when it involves eating cookies! These antler hats are simple to make out of poster board. For a touch of realism, you can give them a light touch of spray flocking.

PREPARATION TIME: 1 HOUR

| |
| --- |
| 3 sheets (20 x 30 inches each) of lightweight brown poster board |
| Spray flocking (optional) |
| Scissors, stapler |

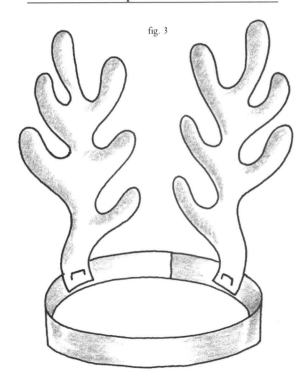

fig. 3

Cut twelve 2 x 20-inch strips from one sheet of poster board. Using your child's head as a form, staple ends together to form headbands, overlapping by about ½ inch. Draw 6 pairs of antlers on each of the remaining 2 sheets of poster board (you should have 12 pairs) and cut out (see pattern, page 184). Staple antlers to headbands in pairs, one antler on each side (fig. 3). If desired, give antlers a very light spray of flocking just around the edges.

## INSTANT INVOLVEMENT AND GAMES

The advantage to this type of party is that it can entertain the children from start to finish without a great deal of structure. The activities actually become the refreshments. If some kids enjoy one project more than another, they can stay with it the whole time. Others may just enjoy eating, and there's more than enough to occupy their mouths. Children can get started as soon as they receive their antlers. A nice closing activity is to provide a Packaging Department to enable them to take home their goodies as a gift (probably to themselves). Pass around white paper shopping bags, with crayons and ribbon to decorate them. Have colored tissue paper on hand so the children can individually wrap more fragile creations.

# COLOSSAL COOKIE TREE

Imagine a mountain of everyone's favorite cookie—chocolate chip. They're piled into a pyramid and held together with melted chocolate. Add candied fruit and pecan pine cones and the creation becomes a Christmas tree. Depending on the age group, they can help you build up the tree or you can do it ahead of time and they can help "tear it down." The most fun is in the decorating and the eating.

You should *double* this recipe by making it in 2 batches. (It's easier to handle the dough that way.) No 2 trees will take exactly the same amount of cookies because they just sort of "grow like Topsy." That's why it's best to have more than enough. Any leftover cookies can be used to make a cookie wreath (see page 173). However, if the kids help you actually build the tree at the party, be prepared to have most of the construction materials consumed. In this case, you may want to reserve some cookies just for making a wreath.

TREE (15 INCHES TALL)
PREPARATION TIME: VARIES
   ACCORDING TO THE NUMBER OF
   HELPERS

| |
|---|
| 4½ cups flour |
| 2 teaspoons baking soda |
| 2 teaspoons salt |
| 2 cups butter, softened |
| ¾ cup granulated sugar |
| ¾ cup brown sugar, firmly packed |
| 2 teaspoons vanilla extract |
| 4 eggs |
| 2 packages (12 ounces each) semisweet chocolate chips |
| 1 cup chopped nuts |
| Chocolate "Cement" (recipe follows) |
| Pecan Pine Cones (recipe follows) |
| Candied fruit (red and green cherries, glazed pineapple, and glazed apricots) |
| 9- or 10-inch round cake board or flat plate |

Preheat oven to 375°F.

Combine flour, baking soda, and salt in medium-size bowl. In large bowl, beat butter, sugar, brown sugar, and vanilla extract until smooth and light. Beat in eggs, one at a time. Stir in flour, chocolate chips, and nuts. Drop by heaping teaspoonfuls onto ungreased baking sheets and bake for 8 to 10 minutes. (No one ever seems to have enough baking sheets, and waiting for cookies to come out of the oven before you can wash the sheets and drop more is time consuming. Try dropping cookies on sheets of aluminum foil or baking parchment. When you're ready, you simply slide the baking sheet under the foil. This also makes cleaning up a breeze.) Cool cookies completely on racks while you make the second batch.

To assemble tree, set a 9- or 10-inch round cake board (or flat plate) on a square of foil (this is to catch the drips). Spread a little of the chocolate cement on bottoms of enough cookies to cover board.

(a)

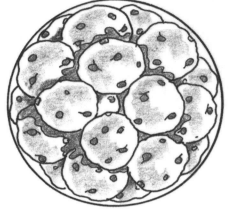

(b)

fig. 4

Stick cookies to board. Continue stacking cookies in this manner, sandwiching them together with the chocolate (fig. 4a). Each tier will gradually taper in diameter until the pile is as high as you want to go, ending with one final cookie on top (15 inches is a good height) (fig. 4b). At this point, the chocolate holding the cookies together should be allowed to set. Any extra chocolate cement should be kept warm, or remelted before applying decorations. (You may want to preassemble the tree up to this point and let the kids decorate and eat it at the party.)

To decorate, drizzle sides of tree with more chocolate cement. Place bowls of candied fruit around and let children add their touch of trimmings. Give each child a pecan pine cone to put in a special place. After everyone's had sufficient time to admire their work, let them start tearing tree down, taking it apart cookie by cookie until they've had their fill.

## CHOCOLATE "CEMENT"

| |
|---|
| 2 packages (12 ounces each) semisweet chocolate chips |
| ⅔ cup butter |
| ⅓ cup light corn syrup |

Put all the ingredients in top of a double boiler over (not in) very hot, barely simmering water. (Do not allow any moisture to get into the chocolate.) Stir until smooth and melted.

Note: If you're also making
Chocolate-Chip Cookie Wreath (recipe
follows), you might need to make a
little extra chocolate "cement."
This recipe can also be cut in half,
using one 12-ounce bag of chocolate
chips, ⅓ cup butter, and about 3
tablespoons of corn syrup.

## PECAN PINE CONES

| 1 can (3 ounces) pecan halves |
| --- |
| ⅓ cup Chocolate "Cement" (see preceding recipe), cooled slightly |

Begin making pine cones by
sandwiching 2 pecan halves together
with chocolate. Use more chocolate
to stick 3 pecans around the
cluster. Overlap 3 more pecans
over these (fig. 5). It will take 8
pecan halves for each pine cone.

fig. 5

# CHOCOLATE-CHIP COOKIE WREATH

Leftover chocolate-chip
cookies can be used to make
a Christmas wreath. It only
takes about 2 dozen cookies for a
9- to 10-inch wreath. A plaid bow
really adds a beautiful touch.

PREPARATION TIME: 15 MINUTES

| 2 dozen chocolate-chip cookies |
| --- |
| 1 cup Chocolate "Cement" (see recipe, page 172) |
| Red and green candied cherries, glazed pineapple, dried apricots, and Pecan Pine Cones (see preceding recipe) |
| 9- or 10-inch round cake board or flat plate |

Spread some chocolate "cement"
on backs of 8 cookies and arrange in
a circle on a 9- to 10-inch cake
board or plate. Overlap with a
second row of 8 cookies, "glued"
together with more chocolate (fig.
6a). Finish off with another row of
8 cookies, overlapping second row.

(a)

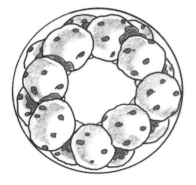

fig. 6

Drizzle with remaining chocolate and decorate with fruit and pine cones (fig. 6b; see also photo opposite page 13).

(b)

fig. 6

## EDIBLE ORNAMENTS

Each child gets a "box" of edible ornaments to decorate and bring home. These bonbon cookies look like Christmas tree balls and have a surprise in the center. Use sections of styrofoam egg cartons for ornament boxes.

PREPARATION TIME: 20 MINUTES
BAKING TIME: 12 TO 14 MINUTES

| |
|---|
| 1 cup butter |
| 1½ cups confectioners sugar |
| 2 tablespoons vanilla extract |
| 3 cups flour |
| 2 to 4 tablespoons heavy cream |
| ¼ teaspoon salt |
| Red and green food coloring |
| 2 dozen chocolate kisses, unwrapped |
| 2 dozen maraschino cherries |

| |
|---|
| Ornamental Icing (recipe follows) |
| Chocolate jimmies, colored sugar, crushed peppermints, confetti sprinkles, gold or silver dragées |
| 3 styrofoam egg cartons |
| Cellophane |
| Ribbon |

Preheat oven to 350°F.

Cream butter, sugar, and vanilla together until fluffy. Blend in flour, salt, and just enough cream to hold dough together. Divide dough in half. Tint one half red (or pink) and the other half green. Mold a tablespoon of red dough around each chocolate kiss. Mold a tablespoon of green dough around each cherry. Roll cookies between palms of your hands to make smooth, round balls.

Place balls 1 inch apart on ungreased baking sheet. Bake for 12 to 14 minutes, or just until cookies are set. (Cookies *must not* brown.) Let cool completely.

Cut lids off egg cartons, and cut bottoms into sections of 4 egg cups. Place 2 red and 2 green ornaments in each section and pass out to children. Set out bowls of icing and decorations. Children dip balls in the icing color of their choice and sprinkle with the desired topping. Ornaments are placed back in egg cartons and allowed to dry. Before bringing home, cartons are covered with cellophane and tied with ribbon.

# ORNAMENTAL ICING

| |
|---|
| 2 cups confectioners sugar |
| ⅓ cup heavy cream |
| 2 teaspoons vanilla extract |
| Red and green food coloring |

Blend sugar, cream, and vanilla extract. Divide frosting into 2 parts; tint red and green.

## TOY SHOP SUGAR COOKIES

Santa's helpers are set to work, busily painting toys. Tin soldiers, trucks, puppy dogs, and airplanes are given a fresh coat of shiny egg yolk paint.

PREPARATION TIME: 35 MINUTES
CHILLING TIME (FOR DOUGH):
  1 HOUR
BAKING TIME: 10 TO 12 MINUTES

| |
|---|
| ¾ cup butter |
| ⅓ cup shortening |
| 1½ cups sugar |
| 3 eggs |
| 1 teaspoon lemon extract |
| 3¾ cups flour |
| 2 teaspoons baking powder |
| 1 teaspoon salt |
| Egg Yolk Paint (recipe follows) |

Beat butter, shortening, and sugar together until light and fluffy. Beat in eggs, one at a time, and lemon extract. Blend in flour and baking powder to make a soft dough. Chill at least 1 hour.

Preheat oven to 400°F.

Roll dough out ¼ inch thick on a lightly floured surface and cut with assorted animal- and toy-shaped cookie cutters. Place on ungreased baking sheets and bake for about 5 to 6 minutes (cookies should be set, but not color). Cool cookies completely on a rack.

Pass cookies around on a tray for children to choose their favorite shapes. Fill 3 or 4 plastic watercolor paint pans (available at art and craft shops) with egg yolk paint and provide a separate brush for each color. After the children paint the cookies, allow them to dry.

Note: You can speed up the drying time by setting cookies in a warm (200°F) oven for about 3 minutes.

## EGG YOLK PAINT

Put egg yolks (at least 1 for each color) in separate custard cups. Tint each yolk a different color with food coloring: red, green, blue, yellow, orange, and brown.

## DOUGH DOLLS

This easy-to-make-and-mold fondant will remind you of modeling clay, or a sort of "mock marzipan." Children shape the candy dough into dolls with chocolate-chip eyes, licorice lips, and coconut hair. The dolls will dry to the touch after a few hours—if the kids can keep them out of their mouths for that long!

PREPARATION TIME: 15 MINUTES

fig. 7

| 1⅓ cups light corn syrup |
| 1 cup butter, softened |
| 4 teaspoons desired flavoring (vanilla, almond, or peppermint extract) |
| 4 pounds confectioners sugar |
| Red, blue, and yellow food coloring |
| 2 cups shredded coconut |
| 3 tablespoons unsweetened cocoa powder |
| Miniature chocolate chips, red licorice laces or whips, red hot candies, gold or silver dragées |

Use a very large mixing bowl to beat together butter, corn syrup, flavoring, and 2 cups of the sugar until smooth. Work in remaining sugar, 2 cups at a time, until smooth and blended. Divide dough into 4 equal parts. Leave one white and tint one pink, one blue, and one yellow. (Color can be worked in evenly by kneading dough with your hands.) Wrap each dough separately in plastic wrap; it must not dry out. (If you prepare it in advance and refrigerate it, bring to room temperature (still tightly wrapped, for 24 hours before using.)

Make coconut "hair" by shaking 1 cup of the shredded coconut in a jar with 2 drops each of red and yellow food color, and the remaining 1 cup of shredded coconut in another jar with the cocoa.

Divide each color of dough up into enough balls so that children can easily reach whatever color they want to use from where they're sitting. Divide decorations into small dishes or nut cups and place around the table. Put the orange and brown coconut "hair" in shallow bowls, so that doll heads can be easily dipped in.

Start by giving a "demo" doll-making lesson. This will get the kids off on the right track. Shape a ball of white dough into a head and give it a face with chocolate chip eyes and a licorice smile (cut off a ½-inch piece of licorice lace). Dip the head into coconut for hair, pressing in whatever starts to fall out. Use different colors to make the body—perhaps a blue coat and yellow pants. Add hands and shoes. Decorate with silver, gold, chocolate-chip, or red-hot buttons (fig. 7). Of course the rest is really up to a child's imagination. You'll probably see a lot of cars and airplanes along with snakes and blobs.

# IGLOO CAKE

Santa lives at the North Pole, where there are several igloos in the neighborhood. This one happens to be right across the street, so he turns it into a bake shop during the Christmas rush. Unlike ordinary igloos (made out of ice and snow) this one was probably built by an architect from Candyland. The walls are soft and creamy, and the inside tastes like an Eskimo pie.

PREPARATION TIME: 50 MINUTES
BAKING TIME: 1 HOUR 5 MINUTES
TO 1 HOUR 15 MINUTES

| |
|---|
| 2¼ cups flour |
| 1⅔ cups sugar |
| ⅔ cup shortening |
| 1¼ cups milk |
| 3½ teaspoons baking powder |
| 1 teaspoon salt |
| 5 egg whites |
| 1 teaspoon peppermint extract |
| Green food coloring (optional) |
| ¾ cup finely diced Andes mint candies |
| Igloo Icing (recipe follows) |
| 1 round chocolate wafer |
| 1 candy cane |
| 1 small construction paper flag |

Preheat oven to 350°F. Grease and flour a 1½-quart round-bottomed casserole and line 2 muffin cups with paper liners.

Beat flour, sugar, shortening, milk, baking powder, and salt in a large bowl on medium speed until blended (about 30 seconds). Increase speed to high, beat, scraping bowl occasionally, for 2 minutes. Add egg whites and peppermint extract. Beat on high speed for 2 more minutes. If desired, tint batter green with a few drops of food coloring. Fold in diced mint candies. Fill prepared muffin cups two-thirds full and pour rest of batter into casserole. Bake cupcakes 20 to 25 minutes and casserole 1 hour 5 minutes to 1 hour 15 minutes (or until toothpick inserted in center comes out clean). Cool cupcakes completely and peel away papers. Cool casserole 10 minutes, then invert onto a rack; remove dish, and cool completely.

Place cooled large cake, dome side up, on a large plate or tray. Sandwich cupcakes together with a little frosting and place in front of large cake to form an entrance to igloo (fig. 8a). Completely cover with frosting, smoothing with spatula. Use a toothpick to make grooves for blocks of snow and place chocolate wafer on entrance for a door. (If desired, you can write something like PLEASE KNOCK LOUD with white icing on the chocolate door. Santa's helpers make a lot of noise and have a hard time hearing visitors.

Tape a small construction paper flag around the top of a candy cane and write SANTA'S BAKE SHOP on it. Stand candy cane signpost up alongside entrance (fig. 8b).

(a)

fig. 8

(b) SANTA'S BAKE SHOP

Please Knock Loud!

Note: This cake freezes nicely and may be prepared in advance. Defrost the night before the party.

## IGLOO ICING

| 1 pound confectioners sugar |
| --- |
| ½ cup butter, softened (or part butter, part shortening for whiter icing) |
| 1 teaspoon vanilla or peppermint extract |
| 1 to 2 tablespoons milk |

Beat sugar, butter, and flavoring together until blended. Beat in enough milk to make a smooth, creamy frosting, adding more if necessary.

## FROSTY SNOWMEN

Coconut ice cream snowballs are a childhood favorite, especially during the Christmas season. By stacking 3 together and topping off with a hat, you have Frosty the Snowman (he's a natural guest at a North Pole party).

PREPARATION TIME: 15 TO 20 MINUTES

| 2 quarts vanilla or coconut ice cream |
| --- |
| 2 cups shredded coconut |
| Miniature chocolate chips |
| 12 chocolate mint patties |
| 12 chocolate mint (or any flavor) bonbon candies (see note) |
| Toothpicks |

For these you'll need to have 3 ice cream scoops: a large, medium, and small. For the smallest scoop, you can try using the large end of a melon baller. If you don't have a medium scoop, try scooping the center balls smaller than the ones you scooped for the base.

Scoop 12 large balls of ice cream (about ⅓ cup), place on wax paper, and return to freezer. Scoop 12 medium-size balls (about ¼ cup) and place them in the freezer, too. Scoop 12 small balls (2 to 3 tablespoons) and place in freezer. Pour coconut into a shallow pan or pie plate. Remove large balls from freezer, roll in coconut, and return to freezer. (The idea is to always keep frozen whatever ice cream you're not working with.) Repeat with medium and small balls. Stack balls into twelve, 3-tiered snowmen, starting with the largest ball at the bottom and ending with the smallest ball for the head. Press balls gently together so they will stick. Press chocolate chips into ice cream to form a face and buttons, just like ones made out of coal. Place a bonbon on top of a mint patty, securing with toothpick, to form a hat (fig. 9a). Make 12 of these and insert into the tops of snowmen's heads (fig. 9b). Place snowmen back in the freezer until ready to serve.

Note: The bonbons should be round and of a smaller diameter than the mint patties, so as to form the crown and brim of a hat.

(a)

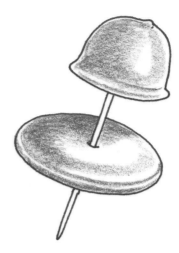

(b)

fig. 9

## MILK MIX-IN BAR

Cookies and milk are a classic combination. To make this wholesome but uneventful beverage a little more exciting, serve it as a Mix-in Bar. Put out a large pitcher of milk with dishes or jars of ice cream toppings: strawberry, pineapple, chocolate syrup, crème de menthe syrup, and crushed peppermint candies (these can be practically powdered in a food processor or blender). Use 2 large glass tumblers (one should be bigger than the other) or a glass tumbler and a stainless-steel cocktail shaker. Each child can create their own favorite flavor. Pour a glass of milk into the smaller tumbler and let the child add anything they like. Invert the larger tumbler or cocktail shaker over the glass so it fits tightly. Turn upside down, and holding the two together, shake vigorously until milk and topping are smoothly blended and foamy. Pour from the large tumbler into the child's own cup or glass. Now you're ready to take the next order.

# PATTERNS

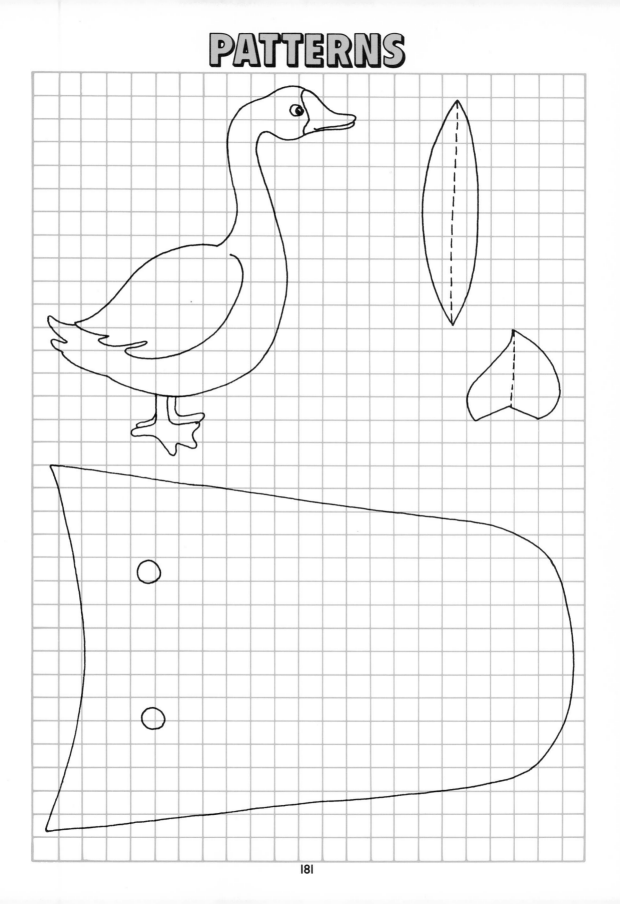

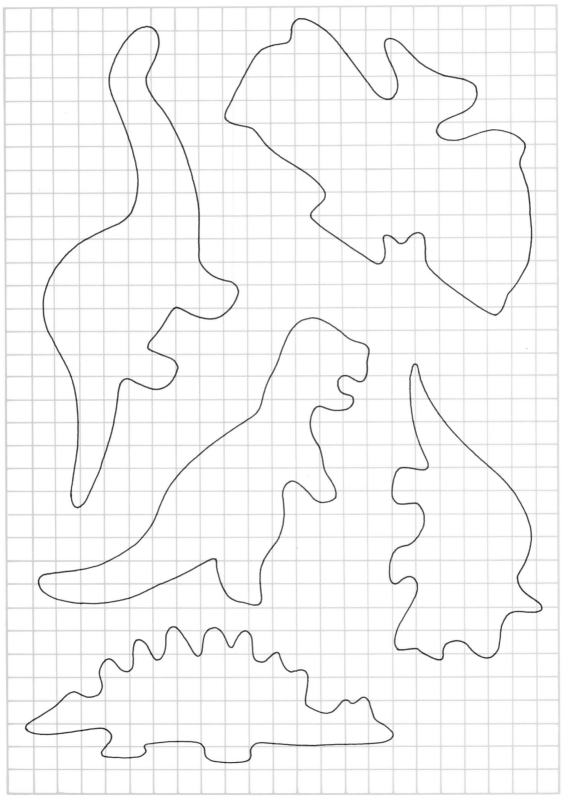

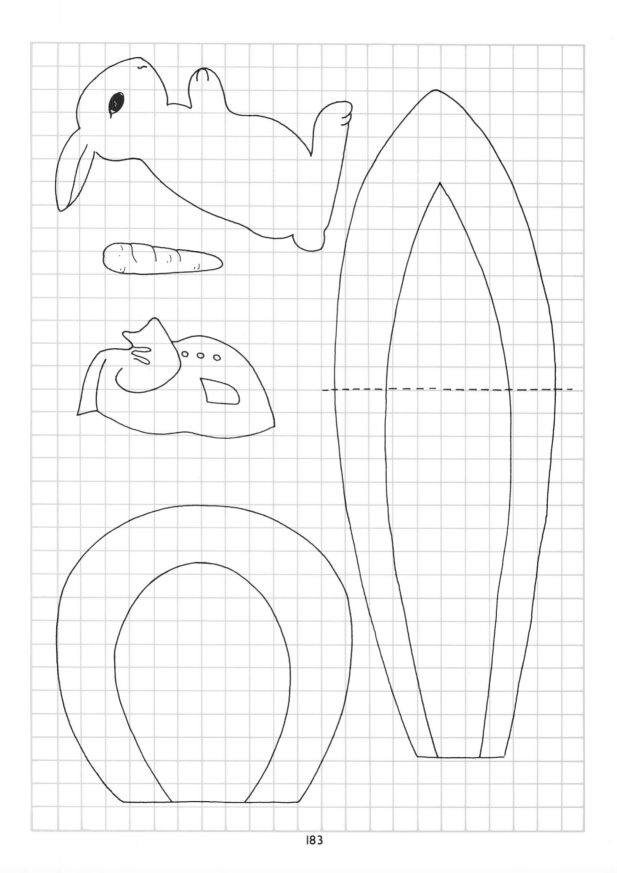

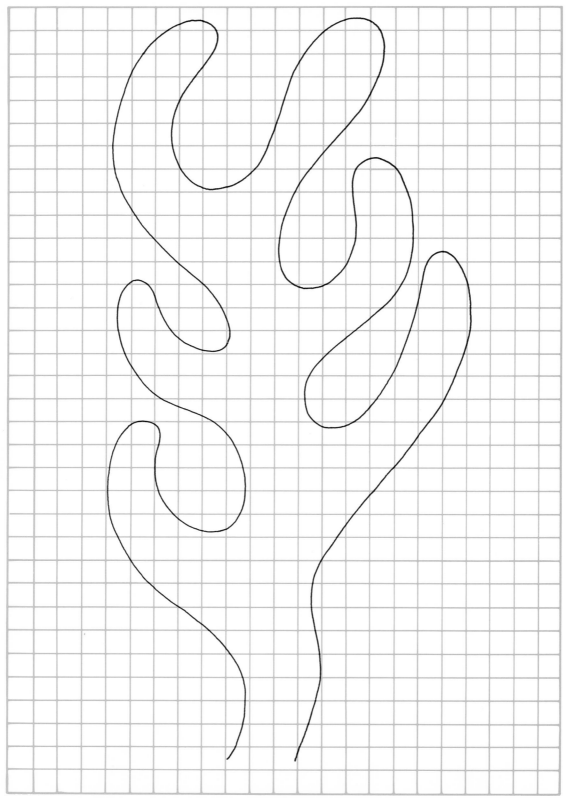

# RECIPE INDEX

# CONVERSION TABLES

## SOLID MEASURES

For cooks measuring items by weight, here are approximate equivalents, in both Imperial and metric. So as to avoid awkward measurements, some conversions are not exact.

|  | U.S. CUSTOMARY | METRIC | IMPERIAL |
|---|---|---|---|
| Butter | 1 cup | 225 g | 8 oz |
|  | ½ cup | 115 g | 4 oz |
|  | ¼ cup | 60 g | 2 oz |
|  | 1 Tbsp | 15 g | ½ oz |
| Cheese (grated) | 1 cup | 115 g | 4 oz |
| Fruit (chopped fresh) | 1 cup | 225 g | 8 oz |
| Herbs (chopped fresh) | ¼ cup | 7 g | ¼ oz |
| Meats/Chicken (chopped, cooked) | 1 cup | 175 g | 6 oz |
| Mushrooms (chopped, fresh) | 1 cup | 70 g | 2½ oz |
| Nuts (chopped) | 1 cup | 115 g | 4 oz |
| Raisins (and other dried chopped fruits) | 1 cup | 175 g | 6 oz |
| Rice (uncooked) | 1 cup | 225 g | 8 oz |
| (cooked) | 3 cups | 225 g | 8 oz |
| Vegetables (chopped, raw) | 1 cup | 115 g | 4 oz |

## LIQUID MEASURES

The Imperial pint is larger than the U.S. pint; therefore, note the following when measuring liquid ingredients.

| U.S. | IMPERIAL |
|---|---|
| 1 cup = 8 fluid ounces | 1 cup = 10 fluid ounces |
| ½ cup = 4 fluid ounces | ½ cup = 5 fluid ounces |
| 1 tablespoon = ¾ fluid ounce | 1 tablespoon = 1 fluid ounce |

| U.S. MEASURE | METRIC APPROXIMATE | IMPERIAL APPROXIMATE |
|---|---|---|
| 1 quart (4 cups) | 950 mL | 1½ pints + 4 Tbsp |
| 1 pint (2 cups) | 450 mL | ¾ pint |
| 1 cup | 236 mL | ¼ pint + 6 Tbsp |
| 1 Tbsp | 15 mL | 1+ Tbsp |
| 1 tsp | 5mL | 1 tsp |

## DRY MEASURES

Outside the United States, the following items are measured by weight. Use the following table, but bear in mind that measurements will vary, depending on the variety of flour and moisture. Cup measurements are loosely packed; flour is measured directly from package (presifted).

|  | U.S. CUSTOMARY | METRIC | IMPERIAL |
|---|---|---|---|
| Flour (all-purpose) | 1 cup | 150 g | 5 oz |
| Cornmeal | 1 cup | 175 g | 6 oz |
| Sugar (granulated) | 1 cup | 190 g | 6½ oz |
| (confectioners) | 1 cup | 80 g | 2⅔ oz |
| (brown) | 1 cup | 160 g | 5⅓ oz |

## OVEN TEMPERATURES

| Fahrenheit | 225 | 300 | 350 | 400 | 450 |
|---|---|---|---|---|---|
| Celsius | 110 | 150 | 180 | 200 | 230 |
| Gas Mark | ¼ | 2 | 4 | 6 | 8 |

# THE AUTHOR

At age 10, Alison Boteler wandered back into the kitchen of her favorite restaurant in the hope that the chef would divulge a few secrets. By 12, she was on her way to being a food critic, and by the time she was 19, Alison was considered a "culinary whiz kid," with her own radio talk show, "Alison's Restaurant." Her guests ranged from mentors like Julia Child and Craig Claiborne to the "Great Pumpkin."

Alison's creations have showed up at many star-studded parties, where Brooke Shields and Andy Warhol have munched on her Baby Burritos and Big Apple pizzas. Peter Allen commissioned Alison to sculpt an enormous chocolate piano for each of his Radio City Music Hall concerts. She's made novelty cakes for David Letterman, Jane Pauley, and Dick Ebersol of "Saturday Night Live." Alison has also created "edible architecture" for the "Today Show," including an extravagant gingerbread house and small-scale versions of Big Ben, Noah's Ark, and the Disneyland castle.

This book represents the best of Alison's ideas—creative but simple projects that will help you make your child's party an original and memorable occasion.

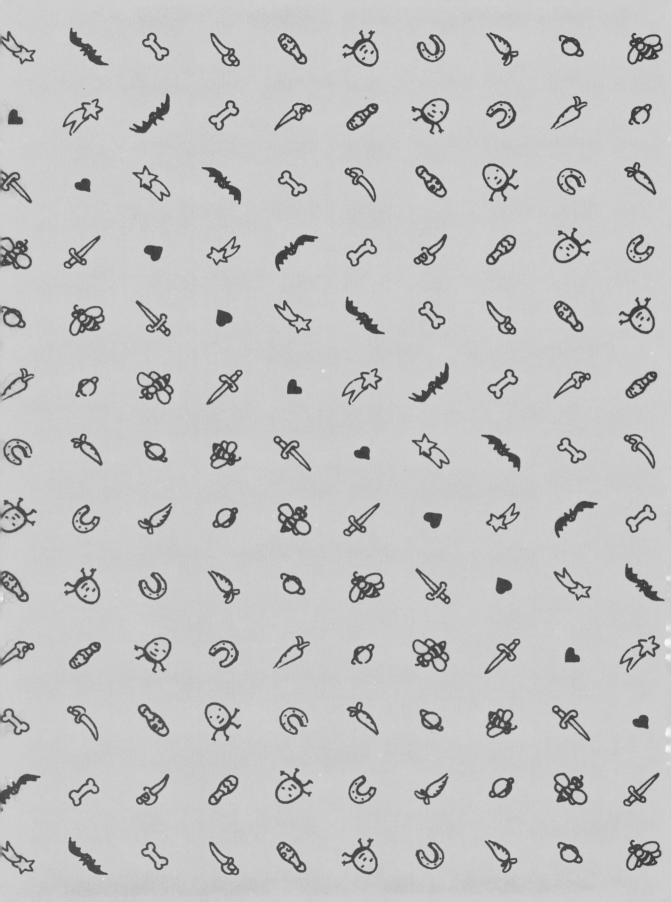